DAUGHTERS OF THE TRADE

THE EARLY MODERN AMERICAS

Peter C. Mancall, Series Editor

Volumes in the series explore neglected
aspects of early modern history in the western
hemisphere. Interdisciplinary in character, and
with a special emphasis on the Atlantic World
from 1450 to 1850, the series is published in
partnership with the USC-Huntington Early
Modern Studies Institute.

DAUGHTERS

of the

TRADE

Atlantic Slavers
and Interracial Marriage
on the Gold Coast

PERNILLE IPSEN

PENN

UNIVERSITY OF PENNSYLVANIA PRESS

PHILADELPHIA

Publication of this volume was assisted by a grant from the
USC-Huntington Early Modern Studies Institute.

Published by
University of Pennsylvania Press
Philadelphia, Pennsylvania 19104-4112
www.upenn.edu/pennpress

Printed in the United States of America on acid-free paper
1 3 5 7 9 10 8 6 4 2

Library of Congress Cataloging-in-Publication Data
A catalogue record for this book is available from
the Library of Congress.
ISBN 978-0-8122-4673-5

For Steve

When the White's Negress has borne him a couple of Mulatto children he cares as much for her and his children as a man does who has his true wife and children in Europe. Some among the Europeans do not wish to leave their family on the Coast even if they know they could live better in Europe.

Ludewig Ferdinand Rømer, 1760

The one I have to thank this time for my poor, wretched life, besides God, is my Mulatinde [Mulatresse]. I can never repay her for her many sleepless nights, her concern for me night and day.

Wulff Joseph Wulff, 1839

CONTENTS

═══

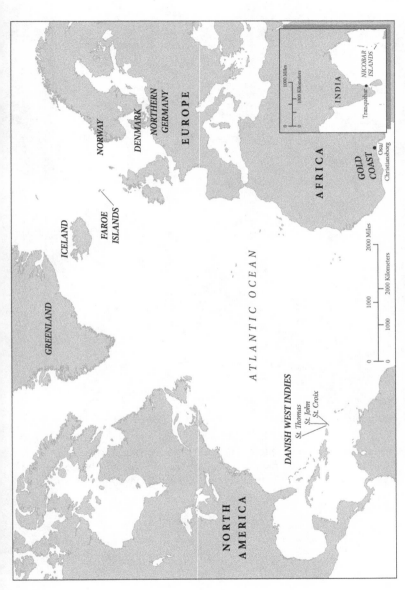

Map 1. The Gold Coast and the Danish Conglomerate State in the Atlantic World

From 1680 to 1814 the conglomerate state under the king of Denmark consisted of duchies and colonies in present-day Norway, Iceland, the Faroe Islands, Greenland, the Virgin Islands (St. Croix, St. John, and St. Thomas), and a part of northern Germany, besides the kingdom of Denmark. Outside this territory the Danish king had trading posts in India (Tranquebar and the Nicobar Islands) and on the Gold Coast. In the eighteenth century Christiansborg by Osu, in present-day Accra, the capital of Ghana, served as headquarters for the Danish slave trade on the Gold Coast.

Map 2. The Gold Coast

In the seventeenth and eighteenth centuries a number of European slave-trading forts were established on the Gold Coast. In the same period towns along the coast grew and developed. Note the proximity of the three Ga coastal towns Osu, Soko, and Aprag.

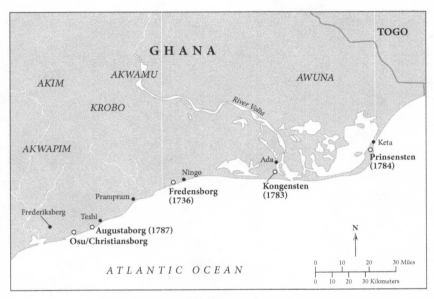

Map 3. Expanding the Danish Presence on the Gold Coast

The Atlantic slave trade—and the Danish part of it—expanded over the course of the eighteenth century, and new Danish trading factories were established east of Osu to secure a more permanent hold on a larger part of the trade. The Danes thus had a broader range of contact and influence in a larger area of the coast. The new factories were primarily for slave trading, but they also served as protection for local African trading partners and their families in case of attacks from other African groups. The growing trade also led to an expansion of both Osu and Christiansborg.

Severine's Ancestors

Severine Brock was born and raised in Osu, a small town on the Gold Coast. Her first language was Ga, yet it was not surprising when, in 1842, she married Edward Carstensen, the last governor of the Danish Fort Christiansborg. Women in her family had been marrying Danish men for generations. Already by 1800, when Severine's grandmother married merchant H. C. Truelsen and lived with him in a European-style stone house with storage rooms and cobblestones, it had become a familiar choice for Ga women of a certain status to marry European men. The practice of interracial marriage on the Gold Coast began shortly after Europeans started trading in the area in the seventeenth century and continued in Osu for generations after the official Danish slave trade was abolished in 1803. The practice was called "cassare" or "calisare"—for setting up house—and both the word and the practice were inherited from earlier Portuguese traders in West Africa. When Severine married Edward, she was only about sixteen years old, but she could draw on many generations of experience with Danish language and culture, and on a hybrid Ga-Danish culture with deep historical roots in Osu as well as in the larger world of the Atlantic slave trade.[1]

This book is the story of the century and a half that preceded Severine Brock's marriage to Edward Carstensen; of six generations of Ga families in Accra marrying their daughters to Danish men at Christiansborg. The story begins in the early eighteenth century, when Christiansborg became the headquarters for the Danish slave trade in West Africa, continues over the course of the century, and ends in 1850, when the fort was sold to the British. It traces the changing power dynamics of the Atlantic world. It shows how the increasing strength of the European colonial system shaped individual lives and families of West African and European slave traders, and how the spatial organization and the material culture of these families shifted in a

European direction. The first generations of Ga women who married Danish men continued to live in compounds in Osu with their mothers, sisters, other female relatives, and children, but toward the end of the century some Ga-Danish women lived with their Danish husbands in European-style stone houses, with European clothes, furniture, and cooking pots, and had children with European names, whom they sent to church and school at the Danish fort. Over the course of the Atlantic slave trade, the cultural frontier shifted toward the expectations and practices of the European husbands.[2]

Stories like those of Severine and the other women in her family are part of a larger history of the racialization of social difference that took place in West Africa during the era of the slave trade. In the first generation of Euro-African marriages in Osu, neither Ga nor Danes attached very distinct meanings to racial difference. For this early generation, social status and position in their shared world was determined primarily by class and gender; race, though present as a relatively flexible category, remained an indeterminate marker of social hierarchy. As the slave trade evolved over the eighteenth century, however, race gained importance as a social marker. At Christiansborg the Danes distinguished between Euro-Africans[3] and other Africans, and consequently Euro-African families gained different access to the trade and the fort because of their mixed heritage. The Danes hired Euro-Africans into higher positions than other Africans, accepted Euro-African children and adults into the Christian congregation, and supported Euro-African children—and to some extent their mothers—from a special "mulatto chest."[4] Over generations, intermarrying with Europeans opened a special position for Euro-Africans in an increasingly stratified social hierarchy, which was defined by race as well as class and gender.

The local history of interracial marriage in Osu was a particularly intense expression of a process that happened throughout the eighteenth-century Atlantic world. Marriages and less formal relationships across lines of ethnicity and skin color played a central role in the production of racial difference throughout the early modern world, but nowhere were negotiations over social difference more critical than in the trade in human beings, which was both enabled by and contributed to a hierarchy of racial difference. For both African and European slave traders it was crucial to uphold clear lines between people who were for sale and people who were not, and definitions of difference between slave and free were therefore at the center of negotiations in the trade. The process of attaching meaning to racial difference took place in response to this need to distinguish slave from free, and the families at the center of

Daughters of the Trade lived in and with these negotiations over social differ-ence. The production of race happened in many different areas of the early modern Atlantic world: slave ships and plantation colonies were important local contexts, but so were slave-trading posts. Negotiations of social difference were always situational and always local, and the Atlantic slave trade on the Gold Coast offers a particularly clear example of how slavery and blackness be-came linked, and, more broadly, how the meaning of racial difference changed from its early modern to its more rigid and biological modern version.[5]

Entangled as they were in both the local history of the slave-trading towns in West Africa and the larger history of the European colonial system, the cassare marriages in Osu functioned as loaded transfer points of power. Not only were the marriages produced by the cultural encounters between Europeans and Africans in the Atlantic world; they simultaneously partici-pated in the production of a new hybrid culture, new meanings, new people, and new practices. Both daily practices and Atlantic structures of meaning shaped the production of this culture, as people negotiated Atlantic power relations in their daily lives, and their daily practices and meanings in turn helped shape larger Atlantic structures. The diplomatic and intimate negotia-tions in and around cassare marriages brought the local and the Atlantic into a powerful encounter.[6]

Understanding the racialization of difference that took place in Osu re-quires tracing the process over the course of more than a century. If we en-tered the history through any particular family, at any given point in time, it would often be unclear who was influencing whom, whose culture was being mapped onto whose. Throughout the decades, for example, Danish men car-ried amulets under their shirts, given to them by their lovers and wives, just as often as Ga women carried the ornamental keys their Danish lovers had or-dered from Europe. Neither Africans nor Europeans fully adopted or con-verted to each other's culture. Even when Ga women settled with Danish men in stone houses such as the one that Severine and her sisters grew up in, what they did in those houses probably more closely resembled Ga practices than Danish ones. Yet, by the time Severine Brock and Edward Carstensen were married in 1842, racialized distinctions between Severine and other Africans in Osu had become embodied culture, part of a complex hierarchy of race that defined many aspects of life throughout the nineteenth-century world.

Edward Carstensen's cassare marriage to Severine Brock was not his fam-ily's first contact with the Atlantic world. Like Severine, Edward (Figure 1)

Figure 1. Edward James Arnold Carstensen (1815–98). Royal Library, Copenhagen (Kort- og billedsamlingen).

was following in the footsteps of his forebears—generations of Danish men who had taken employment in overseas trading posts and colonies—when he arrived in Osu in the nineteenth century. Though nobody in eighteenth-century Osu or Copenhagen operated with a concept of an Atlantic world, connections across the Atlantic—economic and cultural ties forged by trade and colonies, agents, companies, and individuals—could be as strong and important as those made over land. It was not uncommon for Europeans or Africans in Osu to have connections to Copenhagen, the Danish West Indies, London, or Amsterdam, as well as to the world beyond the Akwapim mountains or the forested kingdom of Asante.[7]

Edward also had a more personal family legacy that seasoned him well to be a European man in Africa. He had spent his childhood in Algiers, where his father was consul general, and in his application to serve as an assistant at Christiansborg he highlighted his early years to explain why he was "more protected against the climate than most others."[8] Indeed, it was not only from his father's side that he had picked up a desire to travel: his maternal grandfather had also served as consul general in Algiers, which was where his parents met, and his maternal grandmother was born in the Danish West Indies. The overseas administration was an obvious career choice for Edward, though going to Africa was not his first choice. If he had been a more patient student and not ended up with a mediocre result on his law exam, he could have gone directly to a more desirable post in Iceland or the West Indies; perhaps he could even have stayed in the administration in Denmark. As it was, he went to Africa. His friends ridiculed him for taking such an unimpressive position, but at least chances of a promotion in Africa were very good, if one made it through a term.[9]

When Edward arrived in Africa he was twenty-six years old and ready for a romantic relationship. He had already been in love several times back in Copenhagen and—like many contemporary young European men—was searching for romance as portrayed by Goethe in *Die Leiden des jungen Werther*. As he wrote of his years as a law student in Copenhagen, "I was introduced to le beau monde, I was in love, and ready to be in love over and over again."[10] He was not accustomed to seeking "distraction" from prostitutes, and when he settled at the fort he found it unbearable to think of living for years "without a womanly heart near me." Instead he was looking for a woman who could make a home for him on the coast.

Conveniently, Edward was introduced to the practice of cassare in his very first days in Osu. While he was waiting to get his own room at the fort, he stayed with a fellow assistant, Wulff Joseph Wulff, and Wulff's Euro-African cassare wife, Sara Malm. He also met Euro-African women partnering with Europeans all over Osu, as well as in the nearby Dutch and English trading posts in Accra, Cape Coast, and Elmina. Not surprisingly, Edward seems to have known what his options were when he met Severine. When one of the other Danes at Christiansborg made fun of his haste to cassare her, Edward replied, "When Severine and I are married you will be coming to me to smoke a cigar in a circle that can vaguely resemble a home."[11]

Edward Carstensen and Severine Brock met at a party in Osu. After dinner there was dancing, and the festivities lasted until two in the morning. The following day, Edward noted in his diary that Severine had been the only girl worth paying attention to, and apparently Edward was not the only man who felt that way: the newly instated interim governor Bernhard Johan Christian Wilkens, who had arrived in Africa at the same time as Edward Carstensen, was also quick to inquire about her. Carstensen wrote:

> June 5. . . . I only saw one girl worth paying attention to; Severine Brock; she left during Laterna Magica, when the gentlemen would not leave her alone; she was a true exception to the rule. And this girl only 14 years old, but almost full-grown and very beautiful, caught many eyes. W[ilkens] let the mother [Caroline Truelsen] be asked how much she wanted for her daughters virginity! I soon found out about this the next day and it led to an amusing conversation at the table. Everything happened in jest, but seriousness was looming in the background. I said that if the mother agreed to a deal about the daughter's virginity, then I would immediately cassare the girl.[12]

Though Edward did not explicitly reveal which "rule" he was referring to, he indirectly revealed its substance. To him, Severine was exceptional because she was young and innocent. When he declared that he would cassare Severine, Governor Wilkens teased him and asked if he would also defend all other virgins on the coast, to which Edward replied that, in his opinion, Wilkens could buy all the virginities he could get a hold of from the dancers at the party, adding in parenthesis "(they would be cheap)," but that Severine Brock was too young and too innocent to corrupt. By this suggestion—that Severine's innocence made her an exception—Edward implied that the rule was promiscuity, corruption, and guilt. He implied that the men at Christiansborg assumed African women in Osu were *not* innocent, that they were not worth marrying, and that their virginities were cheaply bought.

By the time Edward and Severine met, this belief that African women were inferior not only to European men, but also to European women, had been circulating in the Atlantic world for centuries. It had been strengthened by the European colonial plantation system and the institution of racial slavery, and by generations of European men who had come to the Gold Coast specifically to buy and sell Africans. Even though Edward considered Severine an exception, the rule still lingered: living with her would only "resemble" a home. Perhaps it was also this rule of racial difference that made Edward stand back from his proposal to Severine and place less emphasis on Severine's opinion than on her mother's. At least he did not mention having asked Severine what she wanted. Instead he described the "trading deal"—as he called it—with Severine's mother as an exotic event, strange, foreign, perhaps even amusing. Presumably, this was not the way he would have described courting a Danish woman in the upper-class social circles of Copenhagen to which he belonged. He may have thought of Severine as an exception to the rule of corruption, but he did not place her in a position equivalent to that of a European woman.

Severine Brock and Edward Carstensen's marriage belongs to the last chapter of a history in which generations of families on the Gold Coast married their daughters to European traders stationed in Africa and formed cross-cultural alliances in a complicated and competitive world of trade in human lives. During the slave trade these cassare marriages were central in establishing the cross-cultural connections that made trade possible. In that regard the slave trade was no different than any other intercultural trading encounters in the early modern world. Whether Europeans were trading fur in North America, textiles in India, or gold and slaves in Africa, they gained access to local trading networks by marrying into local families. Such trading marriages became important social and political networks in the history of early modern European trade and colonial expansion. Indeed, both during and after the Atlantic slave trade, Euro-African families often did much more than "resemble homes" for Danish and other European men stationed on the Gold Coast: those families were key elements of the regional and global economies, essential means by which Europeans gained access to the knowledge and networks that underwrote the trade.[13]

When European men settled on the Gold Coast to work as assistants and soldiers at the slave-trading headquarters of Christiansborg, they needed all the help they could get adjusting to new circumstances; marrying into an African family could be crucial. Survival—physical and mental—was not just about overcoming malaria and other tropical diseases; it also involved a complicated transition to very different physical, cultural, and political terrain. In Edward's case, there is no question that living with Severine made him feel more at home in Africa, but his was a familiar story: for a century and a half before that, Danish and other northern European men at Christiansborg had settled in Africa through the help of African women. As Danish slave trader and travel-account writer Ludewig Rømer put it in 1760, even a "wanton" European would not starve to death if he had a wife: "It is possible for her to obtain food for her husband from her parents or friends, and to take care, when her husband receives his salary, that they are repaid, although not very much, and at a lower price than a foreigner could purchase the food."[14]

For African families in Osu, as in other parts of West Africa, cassare marriages functioned as a key economic and social institution that allowed Ga and Akan families to "integrate" culturally inexperienced European men. The cassare marriages were an official recognition of a relationship, allowing Ga and Akan families to ensure that the children would belong to the African family. As in so many other societies, trade alliances followed lines of kinship and family on the Gold Coast, and when European traders settled on the coast, they were integrated as kin. The cassare practice—like most encounters between Europeans and Africans in the early modern period in West Africa—was therefore developed in and shaped by the needs and dynamics of intercultural trade, and only indirectly affected by the colonial power structures of the Atlantic world. The slave-trading posts in the Gold Coast were not colonial societies; none of the European trading posts in West Africa were.[15]

Concurrently the dynamics of interracial marriage in Osu and other West African slave-trading towns also differed quite a lot from those in plantation colonies of the period. In European colonies, interracial marriage was a threat to European control and was therefore prohibited and policed—particularly in plantation colonies based on racial slavery, where interracial marriage was directly subversive to strict societal order. In many colonies interracial relationships were unofficial, at best tolerated, and directly embedded in the colonial power hierarchy. If and when a European trading post developed into a colony, interracial marriages were often one of the first forms of interracial contact to be forbidden. Where European colonization led to social regulation, the space for interracial marriage diminished accordingly. How long into the nineteenth century the early modern practice of interracial marriage continued as an official institution therefore depended on the efficiency and extent of European colonization. None of the interracial marriage institutions in trading posts continued into the twentieth century.[16]

The cassare practice lasted at least three centuries on the Gold Coast, assuming different forms in different locales. Portuguese traders were the first Europeans to marry into West African families in the late fifteenth and early sixteenth centuries. When the English, Dutch, and Danish traders settled on the Gold Coast in the seventeenth century they adopted the Portuguese words along with the practice itself. In the Danish case, cassare persisted throughout the entire period of Danish trade on the coast: there are references to Danish men cassaring African women as early as the 1680s in Fetu, at the first Danish headquarters, Frederiksborg. By the 1780s fort surgeon and travel writer Paul Isert claimed that finding an African woman to cassare was often the first thing a man thought of when he got to the coast.[17] Cassare was just as common between Akan and Fante women and European employees at the Dutch and English trading posts in Accra, Cape Coast, and Elmina.[18]

Interracial marriages on the Gold Coast resembled Luso-African marriages in other parts of West Africa in much more than name. As in the Luso-African cases women on the Gold Coast not only helped their European husbands survive and resettle in Africa; they also helped them as translators, cultural ambassadors, and trading partners. The wealthiest of these women owned slaves, European-style houses and furniture, and gold and silver, and they had both power and influence in the coastal communities. They frequently married several European men in succession, and when their husbands died or left Africa they inherited property and slaves. Their children had European names but were brought up by African families, and from early on a pattern formed wherein it was primarily Euro-African women who married European traders.[19]

One factor that varied in different parts of West Africa was whether European traders were cassared to daughters of free African women or enslaved African women. In Osu, it was customary to cassare free Ga women, whereas in other trading posts in West Africa, and on the Gold Coast, it was as common, if not more so, for European men to cassare enslaved women. In his work on Euro-African marriages in Senegambia, historian George Brooks has found that there was a difference between how "stratified and patrilineal" societies north of the Gambia River and the "acephalous and matrilineal" societies south of the Gambia approached marriages to European traders. While the former groups mostly married daughters of enslaved women to the traders, the latter also married daughters of free women to European traders.[20] This pattern does not quite correlate with the Ga case, since the Ga were patrilineal and, at least to some extent, already socially stratified by the seventeenth century, when the European traders settled in Osu. It should not be surprising, however, that the pattern of Euro-African marriage was different in Osu, given that the Ga in the precolonial period were extraordinarily interested in and willing to integrate foreigners and foreign cultures into their own.[21]

By the nineteenth century, when Severine and Edward were married, this practice had been perfected, and women like Severine, her mother, her sisters, and her grandmother had attained the knowledge they needed to make ideal marriage partners for a Danish man stationed in Africa. After centuries of trading with Europeans, Euro-African women in Osu had extensive knowledge of Danish and other European cultures and languages. Many of them had attended the church school at the Danish fort, where Severine's oldest sister, Nicoline, was employed as a teacher in the 1830s. They cooked in European pots; owned European furniture, linen, silverware, and plates; stored goods for European traders; fed them; and lent them money and material goods.[22]

The hybrid Euro-African culture that Severine embodied had developed in a context of commodity exchange that was indirectly and powerfully shaped by the colonial Atlantic world. Euro-Africans in Osu did not wear European clothing and other markers because they were required to by law, as in the eighteenth-century Danish West Indies. Nevertheless their choices to do so were shaped by the colonial system: Euro-Africans in Osu employed markers of European culture to signal connections to the European trade and to distinguish themselves from other Africans in Osu. When they decided how to equip their households, what to name their children, how to dress them, and which languages and religions to teach them, they not only produced new generations of people but also adopted and reproduced a system of cultural identifications. The slave-trading families of Africans and Europeans created their own mixed and hybrid culture, which was specifically adapted to their position in the slave trade, on the Gold Coast, and in the Atlantic world.[23]

Cultural transformations similar to that which Severine's ancestors experienced have often been described as a process of "creolization," but there are important differences between the experience of Severine's ancestors and generational Euro-African cultural transformations in other areas of the Atlantic world. Unlike creolization in the Americas during the early modern period, for example, cultural transformation in West Africa was thoroughly embedded in African society—institutionally, culturally, and religiously. In other words, though the cultural mixing of European and indigenous elements happened in both West Africa and the Americas, the power structures that guided this mixing were not as directly colonial in West Africa as they were in plantation societies on the other side of the Atlantic. Christian Euro-Africans at Christiansborg did not have to hide that they were mixing their newly adopted religion with Ga and Akan religious practices. They might dismay the Danish chaplain, who at times levied double fines for Christian Euro-Africans who visited the Ga priest, but the administration at Christiansborg employed Ga religious oaths when forming alliances or partnerships with their Ga neighbors and did not seek to maintain strict or exclusionary borders between Christianity and African religions. If anything, the trading encounter in Osu was more marked by Europeans adopting African practices than the other way around.[24]

Even the cassare practice, Portuguese as it sounds, was itself mostly an African institution. Official recognition of the unions between African women and European men allowed African families to fully integrate children born to the couple, which was particularly important if and when the European man left or died. Like other people living on the West African coast, the Ga in Osu were important facilitators in adopting both the long-distance trade and the cassare practice. The production of a hybrid Euro-African culture in Osu should be seen in the light of this flexibility: when Euro-Africans distinguished themselves from others in Osu by way of European markers of material culture and religion they were not adopting European identities or becoming European in any sense of the word. Their position was always a hybrid, and it was the hybrid nature of the position that made it powerful: the successful Euro-African traders in this history did not inhabit a space in between two cultures but rather were fully grounded in both.

Over time this Euro-African hybrid culture also became an embodied identity. The well-studied Luso-African examples from Cape Verde and Senegambia suggest that members of similar West African Euro-African cultures shared a sense of distinct identity as early as the seventeenth and eighteenth centuries, but Gold Coast historians have not argued that such distinct Euro-African identities were present until the nineteenth century. And even historians writing about the nineteenth century have been careful to stress the fluidity of Euro-African identities on the Gold Coast. Likewise, Euro-African families in Osu employed European names and material culture to present themselves as Euro-African to both Europeans and Africans, but this does not mean that they were no longer culturally African. This self-presentation was a key feature of their hybrid culture but, like all cultures, this hybrid was loosely bounded and only relationally coherent. [25]

Despite the essential role they played in the Atlantic slave trade, the families at the center of this story have not previously been central to its historiography. Not only has West Africa most often appeared as an opening chapter in Atlantic histories—as an exporter of peoples and cultures whose stories unfolded elsewhere—but most of the Africans who appear in Atlantic historiography have been enslaved Africans sold to Europeans. A few have been Africans escaping from slavery in the Americas, or traveling in the Atlantic world, and an even smaller number have been male African traders on the West African coast. Given the complicated story presented by slave traders and their families, it is perhaps not surprising that they have been absent from the literature.[26]

The moral horror of the Atlantic slave trade has for a long time caused historians to steer away from the more human dimensions of the trade, and to err in the direction of what Marcus Rediker has called a "violence of abstraction" that has plagued the study of the slave trade.[27] In recent years historians writing about the Atlantic slave trade have added more human agents to the history, focusing on African as well as European slaves, sailors, captains, planters, and travelers. Historians have brought intimate, personal, and politically important human connections across the Atlantic to life in biographies following, for example, two African princes, a West Indian missionary, and an African healer traveling around the Atlantic. Other historians have focused on specific social worlds created in and adapted to the slave trade and shown how this large colonial Atlantic world shaped the lives of everyone involved in the trade, in Africa and America, as well as in Europe. By placing human connections in the center of the story this new literature has created a much more complex and vivid history of the Atlantic world.[28]

Likewise, the European and African slave traders at the center of this story complicate and open the history of the Atlantic world. Not only were these men and women centrally placed in the history of how people in both Europe and Africa invested in and gained from the colonial Atlantic system, but their history also reveals much about the uneasy connections between intimacy, human reproduction, and the production of racial prejudice. They remind us that not only enslaved people, but also slave traders—both European and African—were real humans with full lives and families. They show us that agency can lead in many directions. As we get closer to the people who lived in the Atlantic colonial system, they no longer appear simply as captives or captors but become full human beings with all their capability for survival, greed, and complicated kindness toward some and not others.[29]

The women at the center of *Daughters of the Trade* belonged to the group of people who benefited—at least in an economic sense—from the slave trade, but they also lived with the risks, terror, and violence produced by the trade in human beings. Protecting oneself or one's family from the trade was far from easy. On a local level they were, in other words, responding to both opportunities and threats of a world they were helping to create.[30] But on an Atlantic or global level they were simultaneously contributing to a system of European trade and colonialism based on racial slavery that potentially threatened every African. Severine Brock's ancestors had benefited from the Atlantic slave trade, but they had also helped strengthen the racial discourse that Edward Carstensen and his contemporaries brought with them to Osu. Indeed, Severine and Edward's marriage took place at the historical juncture between this time-honored cassare tradition of trading alliances and a racial discourse that deemed interracial marriage inappropriate or outright wrong.

With roots in an early modern interracial trading practice that was changing alongside an increasingly racialized colonial discourse, Severine Brock and Edward Carstensen's marriage represents a much broader Atlantic history of how interracial marriages—once central to European trading enterprises—came to be discredited, policed, and forbidden in the nineteenth-century colonial Atlantic world. With each generation of Atlantic slave trading, the racialization of slavery made it increasingly clear that even the wealthiest and most powerful Euro-Africans were nonetheless Africans, and that their skin color alone made them questionable marriage partners. This was why Edward made Severine an exception to the rule. In 1842 it was far from certain that Severine was an appropriate marriage partner for Edward. In fact, an increasingly rigid discourse of racial prejudice argued otherwise. Racial difference meant that in spite of their Danish names, Severine and her

Euro-African family and cultural peers were not Danes. They were European enough to be more familiar to Edward than other Africans and yet African enough that they would not be creating a "real" family for European men. While Severine was different enough from other African women in Osu that Edward would allow himself to fall in love with her, their life together would only "vaguely resemble a home."

This curious phrasing is part of a pattern in Edward's diary, which rarely mentions Severine. Despite his expressions of being in love with Severine, he paid very little attention to her in his diary, and the few places she does appear suggest that he was rather ambivalent about his love for her—as if he was also not quite sure that it was appropriate. On the day of his wedding, for example, he wrote a detached account, placing himself at a safe distance from the event. Early in the day he sent Severine's mother the "cassare-costume" (bridewealth) consisting of pipes, tobacco, and spirits to distribute among family and friends to announce the connection; to Severine he sent a trunk filled with silk clothes, scarves, stockings, and shoes. Then he had lunch with a friend, and at three o'clock he sent his valet to the "the bride's house" to call the bride. This was repeated three times until "the bride" (he mentions Severine by name only once) went with Edward's valet, followed by a retinue composed of "the Mulatresses of the town." After a little while "the bride" went home for a few hours, but she returned later in the evening with a smaller following of "Mulatresses," who left her with Edward. They spent the night together, but in the morning she returned to her mother's house. This was repeated for seven more nights, and after the eighth night she remained with Edward in his room at the fort.[31]

Edward's account of his wedding took on a personal tone only when he described how the neighboring English governor played practical jokes on him—like leaving a drunk rooster in the hall in front of Edward's bedroom— on the first of the eight wedding nights. Otherwise, it seems as if Edward, rather than describing his own wedding, was taking notes for a later ethnographic account. In general, there are very few references to his private life in his diary, but he did describe dinner parties and relationships with friends without making any reference to Severine. After the detached account of their wedding day he mentions her only a few times over the following year and a half. Months after the wedding, he noted that she gave him medicine when he was ill, but then in September 1843, when Severine died, Edward reported her sudden illness and death in a strange little parenthesis:

(Sept. 22nd in the evening I was at Richter's; I came home at 9 and found Severine well and already in bed. In the night at 2 o'clock she got cramps. The 23rd at 5 o'clock she died. This is more than I can bear or express. At 6 o'clock I took my hat and left for the plantation. I let Lutterodt see to the funeral.)[32]

If he was as struck by grief as the quote suggests, it is perhaps understandable that he would miss her funeral. Yet the parentheses imply something further: that Edward, unable to cope with his grief, was seeking to bracket, contain, and suppress his response to her death. More broadly, it may have been not only her death that he needed to conceal, but their whole life together. He was not the first or the last to have one family in Osu and another in Copenhagen and to have to deal with the dilemmas that this entailed. Though the world of Osu and the world of Copenhagen had become heavily and directly entangled during the Atlantic slave trade, these two worlds were also incompatible; they were not easily intermingled.

After Severine died, Edward described in his diary how he no longer felt at home on the coast, how he felt isolated and began orienting himself toward Copenhagen again. He described his alienation from other Europeans on the coast, men who had been there longer, had made it their home, and no longer felt tied to people anywhere else: "Their emotions are callous and fallen to the level of those of Negroes and Mulattoes. And I stand alone among beings that are completely strange to me."[33] Osu could apparently no longer resemble a home for Edward: once the exceptional Severine was gone, all Africans and European traders seemed the same.

Edward's ambivalence about his feelings for Severine and their life together should be seen in light of the pressures of nineteenth-century racial discourse, the cultural and social distance between Osu and Copenhagen, and the constant collision between the local world of Osu and the larger world of the Atlantic colonial system. On the Gold Coast, cassare marriages were a time-honored tradition; Severine belonged to a small elite of Euro-African traders who had intermarried with European men for centuries. In this local world, class and Europeanization had diminished (though hardly erased) the importance of race in encounters between Europeans and Africans. Edward's description of his meeting with Severine and how he fell in love with her was shaped by this local tradition, in which interracial marriage was not only possible, but common: nowhere did he suggest that Severine's color made her inappropriate as a marriage partner or as an object for romantic male love. In the broader Atlantic world, on the other hand, interracial marriages were increasingly vilified, racial difference was phrased in terms of biology, and differences between white and black overshadowed other social hierarchies.

The local tradition of interracial marriage on the Gold Coast and the production of racial difference had never actually been separate. Indeed the cassare marriages took place and were negotiated right where racial discourse and local practice of slave trading met. As Euro-African families claimed a powerful position in the racial and gender hierarchies of the Atlantic world they participated in attaching meaning to racial markers of difference. In doing so they pushed the meaning of racial difference in its modern direction. By the nineteenth century, these forces converged with currents in the broader Atlantic to forge the rigid biological understanding of race that caused Edward to press Severine to the margins of his story.

The juxtaposition of local practice and Atlantic discourse raises a significant question regarding the cassare system: what explains the convenient coincidence that in the nineteenth century when Danish men like Edward Carstensen could no longer see past racial difference, they could choose to settle with women whose cultural difference from other Africans allowed them to make them "exceptions"? The answer is that it was not a coincidence. Neither the Euro-African culture that Severine Brock embodied nor the racial prejudice that required that Edward make her an exception had arrived suddenly on the historical stage. They had developed together: the material culture—of clothes and cookware and daily practices—that marked Euro-African women as distinctive and the ideological structure of modern race that made the Danish men group all Africans together into one undifferentiated category to which there could be only individual exceptions. The practice of the Atlantic slave trade, the culture of Euro-African families like Severine's ancestors, and ideologies of racial difference came into being deeply entangled and interdependent.

They developed together, but over time they became incompatible. As racial hierarchies hardened in the Atlantic world in the nineteenth century, interracial marriage became a contradiction, and in 1842, as the Danes prepared to leave Africa, it is not surprising that this discrepancy between the local traditions in Osu and what race meant in the larger Atlantic world caused Edward to be ambivalent about his relationship with Severine. Perhaps it was not only private grief, then, but also this awareness of what racial difference meant that caused Edward to place Severine in that strange little parenthesis.

Earlier in the history of interracial marriage in Osu, she would not have been as easy to bracket off. During the slave trade, European men not only depended on African women to survive but also traded with them. African women were active members of the slave-trading community and therefore appear relatively often in the limited and often inaccessible sources from the eighteenth century; but in the richer sources for the nineteenth century, Severine's day, her presence does not increase proportionately. The cassare marriages had all but lost their practical purpose, interracial marriage was being policed and argued against in Europe and in America, and Edward Carstensen all but erased Severine's presence. If only she had written her own version of the story. This book is not her story, but it draws us closer to it—and to her and her ancestors—than we have been before.

CHAPTER 1

Setting Up

In 1700, the village of Osu amounted to fewer than a hundred family compounds spread out along rows of trees and broad paths that led down to the beach and the Danish fort. The clay and thatched dwellings consisted of smaller huts arrayed around interior courtyards, with long roofs that extended over the street; during the heat of the day people sat beneath them on clay benches, watching the comings and goings in the village. In the morning and again in the evening, Ga women carried their goods and foodstuffs to and from their stalls in the market square, from which they sold fresh, dried, salted, and cooked fish; palm wine; kenkey, fufu, or other prepared meals; and cloth and beads. Almost all the sellers in the market were women. They were renowned for their skill and industry as traders, and people came from near and far to the market. Some buyers were villagers or people from nearby towns on the coast. Others were farmers from farther inland, bringing baskets of oranges, limes, bananas, sweet potatoes and yams, millet, maize, rice, pepper, chickens, eggs, bread, and other foodstuffs, which they exchanged for fish or European products that could be found only on the coast. A final small group of buyers were white men from the Danish fort down on the beach.[1]

Perhaps Koko Osu and her friends watched when Frantz Boye arrived in Osu in February 1700. It was only a short walk from their compounds to the beach, where fishermen's canoes rested and where Europeans would land after months of sailing. European ships did not come in often, so it was a big event when they did. Koko would have known about Europeans. Her father, Tette Osu, was a powerful man; the Europeans called him *caboceer*,[2] and he made a living trading with them. Maybe Koko and her friends sat on the warm cliffs and watched as the men stepped out of the canoes and onto the beach for the first time. Perhaps they compared notes and made bets about which among the new arrivals would survive the longest in Africa. Far from all Europeans made it. Some stayed only until the next ship left the coast, many got sick, and some died.[3]

Koko was *cassaret* to Frantz not many years after that. Tette Osu had probably concluded that Frantz would be a good trading ally, which he was, but the marriage was at least as important for the Dane. Over the next decades he did extremely well in Africa. Surviving on the coast was itself an achievement that could mean rapid advancement, but marrying into one of the most powerful trading families in Osu also helped. After a few years Frantz was promoted to assistant and sent on expeditions on behalf of the Danish West India and Guinea Company, carrying messages and presents to the king of Akwamu. Within six years he was appointed chief assistant at the fort, and by the time he was appointed governor in 1711 he was well acquainted with several African languages, as well as the Portuguese lingua franca of the coast. By that time Koko and Frantz had one child together, who was followed by another, a son who bore the very Danish name David Frandtsøn. He, like their marriage, was born of the trade.[4]

                              *   *   *

In the first generation of cassare marriage in Osu, Ga women and Danish men were much more foreign to each other than Severine and Edward were a century and a half later. Both Koko's parents were African, and it is highly unlikely that she wore European clothes, or owned European goods and furniture. Both Koko and Frantz came from families of traders; Frantz had grown up in Copenhagen (København, meaning "merchants' harbor"), which had been a trading center since the Middle Ages. They even had a culture of smoked and salted fish in common. Yet to recognize their similarities, they would both have to look beyond vast cultural differences. At least one of them had to adjust to the other's culture, and since they were in Osu and since Europeans were fully dependent on their African trading partners in the early eighteenth century, it was mostly Frantz who adjusted. Even more important, Danish men relied on African women not only to succeed in trade, but also—humblingly and immediately—to survive.

The cassare marriages largely happened on initiative of the Ga, who were interested in and accustomed to integrating "foreign" African (primarily Akan) and European traders into their kinship groups. They made trading and political connections with Europeans by marrying their daughters to them, and both the gendered settlement patterns and division of labor in the Ga community, as well as the practice of adopting children of absent or deceased fathers, made the integration of foreign men easy. The men at Christiansborg, in turn, depended on relationships with an African kinship group: the process of overcoming cultural displacement when settling in Africa was not going to happen at the fort, but in Osu; and having a steady relationship with a Ga woman was crucially important in this process. Finally, the cassare marriages have an important story to tell about the familial, generational production of racial difference in the slave trade, which we will turn to in the last section of the chapter.

Osu, like Christiansborg on the beach nearby, grew up with the trade. The village—or town, as it would soon become—was one of a number of Ga villages along a twenty-mile stretch of the eastern Gold Coast that had been settled in the seventeenth century, after the Ga kingdom of Ayawaso was conquered and destroyed by the Akwamu. Besides farming and fishing, the Ga, from the earliest years, made their living as intermediaries in trade between Europeans and politically powerful groups of Akan-speaking peoples further inland (such as the Asante, Akwamu, and Akyem). Until the late seventeenth or early eighteenth century, gold was the major export from the Gold Coast; in the eighteenth century, the Atlantic slave trade became the most important by far. Ga and other coastal traders brought European commodities inland and exchanged them for enslaved people, whom they brought with them back to the coast to sell to Europeans.[5]

People on the Gold Coast had been trading with European men at least since the late fifteenth century, when Portuguese traders had begun tapping into an already well-developed commercial economy in West Africa from the sea (Figure 2). When the Danish West India and Guinea Company arrived in the seventeenth century, Dutch, English, French, and Swedish companies were already competing in the West African trade, and the later-arriving northern European traders adopted many practices and patterns from their Portuguese predecessors. Portuguese at first functioned as a fully developed lingua franca in the trade between Europeans and Africans, and the practice lived on for centuries in the shape of Portuguese loan words and phrases—including, most important for this study: *cassare* for marriage (from *casar*, meaning "to marry"); *casse* or *kasse* for "house" (from the Portuguese *casa*); *caboceer* for "head" or "chief" (from the Portuguese *cabeceire*); and *neger* for Africans (from the Portuguese *negro*, meaning

Figure 2. "The market at Cabo Corsso," 1602. The population of Cape Coast grew from around one hundred inhabitants in 1555 to around three or four thousand in the early eighteenth century. The rest of the coast also saw a significant (though not quite as dramatic) increase in the urban-based, nonfarming population between 1550 and 1650. De Marees, *Pieter*, 62.

"black"; this term was adopted by Danes and other Europeans as a term for Africans).

Trade between Europeans and Africans was intense on the Gold Coast. During the seventeenth and eighteenth centuries, sixty European forts and lodges were established along the coast, and the political situation and power balance in the coastal region changed constantly. However, European traders who arrived in West Africa always had to accommodate to the African societies they encountered. Europeans who built forts or lodges on the coast did so with permission from local African rulers, who required tribute as a prerequisite for good trading relations. As Portuguese and all other European traders in West Africa understood, trading on the coast required close connections to both inland rulers and the coastal middlemen they supplied.[6]

Danes had been involved in long-distance trading for centuries, at least since the early Middle Ages—the Viking age, as that period is still referred to in Denmark—and Danish merchants had been interested in trading with Africa since early in the seventeenth century. They adopted the Portuguese word *Guinea* to describe the area from the Gambia River to Congo, along with the Portuguese practice of describing areas of the coast after the primary products traded there: the Pepper Coast, the Ivory Coast, the Gold Coast, and the Slave Coast. The first Danish company trading in West Africa was started in the 1650s, but the Danes did not gain a steady presence on the coast until the eighteenth century. The Danish administration on the Gold Coast was for the most part the responsibility of chartered Danish trading companies, regulated at the top level by charters (*octroyer*) issued by the Danish king. Responsibility for maintaining and manning the forts was a regular point of conflict over the centuries, though ultimately the king's administration often took on the obligation.[7]

Fort Christiansborg was built by Swedes in 1652 and taken over by Dutch traders in 1660, then by the Danish West India and Guinea Company in 1661. From 1679 to 1683 the fort was briefly in the hands of the Portuguese after being sold to a merchant for thirty-six pounds of gold. In 1685 the fort became the Danish headquarters on the coast, and during the eighteenth century the fort was by far the biggest of the Danish trading forts on the Gold Coast. In the early years the fort consisted of about half a dozen living and storage rooms that could not be defended against any attacks, but it became more substantial as the Danish slave trade expanded during the eighteenth century. From a tiny and unstable beginning, the Danish trading companies managed to gain a fragile, unenforceable monopoly on the trade eastward from Osu, as far as Keta and through a chain of nine subordinate forts and lodges (see Map 3). Between 1660 and 1806 Danish ships brought about eighty-five thousand enslaved Africans across the Atlantic.[8]

A few miles west of Osu both the English and the Dutch had smaller forts; their own headquarters were farther off, in Cape Coast and Elmina, respectively. Each of these European trading posts in the Accra area developed trading relations with one or more of the local Ga towns. During the eighteenth century these settlements were known as Osu (Danish Accra), Soko (English Accra), and Aprag (Dutch Accra) (see Map 2).[9] Since they were competitors in the slave trade, the nearby Europeans were both potential rivals and cultural peers for the Danes. During peacetime they paid social visits to the other forts, but they were often at odds with one another, which led to disagreements and sometimes even hostile confrontations. However, trade required successful dealings with African slave traders more than with other Europeans, and the cassare marriages became central to those trading alliances.[10]

The first key to understanding the context of the cassare marriages is that Danish and other European men had almost no direct support from European colonial or trading institutions in the early decades on the Gold Coast. Their forts in Africa were built with permission from African rulers, and they survived on the mercy of their African trading partners. Indeed, during the slave trade it was a common saying among Europeans on the Gold Coast that heaven was high and Europe far away. Late in the eighteenth century, Danish surgeon and travel writer Paul Isert used the expression to comment on the style of government at Christiansborg, where the governor was so far from his superior authorities that he could rule the trading post as a despot without fear of any retaliatory measures. Another Dane, chaplain H. C. Monrad, believed the saying suggested that it was easy to cheat and to trade in illegal and inhumane ways when trading so far away from home.[11] The saying echoes a feeling many European men must have had on the Gold Coast, that both familiar authorities and familiar ways had little relevance to their daily lives.

In the seventeenth century, the Danes' position on the Gold Coast had been even more precarious. In 1672, fifteen years after the Danes had first settled on the Gold Coast at the small fort of Frederiksborg, it was indeed difficult for the Danes to maintain contact with heaven, Europe, or any other superior authority. There were only eight Danish men left at Frederiksborg and three at Christiansborg when Governor von Groenestein described the situation in a letter to the Danish king Christian V: "Our situation here worsens day by day; and will worsen all the more if the Company cannot be got to send men here for the coming spring of 1673; for then we and HRM's [his Royal Majesty's] stations will be in great peril of being lost. . . . We cannot live here with empty hands under a barbaric nation that keeps neither faith nor promises; nor are we able, in an open station, to defend ourselves against them."[12] The governor continued that the Dutch and the English would be of no help if the Danes were attacked, since they would "like nothing better than to see us dispossessed."[13]

When Governor Prange arrived on the coast in 1681, the Danish establishments in Africa teetered on the edge of failure. Christiansborg had been sold, and Frederiksborg, following a series of deaths, had fallen under the control of first one and then another self-appointed "interim governor," who reportedly squandered all the company's wealth on "whores and other fri-volities."[14] The only Danish subjects remaining at the fort were two young Norwegians, one of whom offered an account of what had happened. After Governor Crull died, assistant Mathias Hansen had taken control of the fort with support from "the Negroes," to whom he had given so many gifts that they would "make him" general.[15] Hansen lasted five weeks as governor until another assistant, Pieter Valck, convinced "the Blacks" to shift their allegiance to him, and with the help of a hundred men he overwhelmed the fort. Pieter Valck thereafter sent Mathias Hansen to the Dutch at Elmina and ruled Frederiksborg in a "bestial" manner for four months until "we whites" (the two surviving Norwegians) asked the king of Fetu for help. The king then sent his men to the fort to seize Pieter Valck. According to Andreas Jacobsen, the king of Fetu at this point suggested that Jacobsen become general: "The King came into the fort and asked if I now wished to be general; otherwise he would appoint his son."[16]

Pieter Valck was still in Fetu when the new governor Magnus Prange arrived from Copenhagen, but it is unclear whether he was there as a captive or was staying voluntarily. In an undated and rather confused letter from Fetu, Valck wrote to Frederiksborg requesting to be allowed to stay with "the hea-then" but nevertheless added that he would like to come to the coast if only he had the opportunity, though he knew he would be arrested. He claimed that his reason for writing was to request that clothes be sent to Fetu, since he had no more than "a torn shirt and trousers" left, but he went on to ask for ink and paper, a small pot of brandy, and a little tobacco. Whatever Pieter Valck was doing in Fetu, it is interesting to note that the king of Fetu not only could decide who was going to be in charge at the Danish fort, but also had a say in how long they stayed in power.[17]

While assistant Pieter Valck was in Fetu, Governor Prange died. This left Frederiksborg in the hands of the German Johan Conrad Busch, who had started his career on the Gold Coast in 1673 as a cadet in the Dutch West Indian Company at Elmina. Hans Lykke, who was soon to become interim governor, reported to the West India and Guinea Company that Busch had been constantly drunk for eight days, had shot off about eight hundred pounds of powder for no reason, had given the company's best *pantje*[18] and gold away to whores and strangers, and had threatened to kill whoever approached him. Not only was the situation bad for the employees at the fort, but the king of Fetu was also upset about the governor's behavior and threatened to stop supplying the Danes with the millet[19] and water they needed to survive. Hans

Lykke ascribed some of Busch's misbehavior to his marriage to "a young Mulatto woman from de Mina," who the dissolute governor said was "to decide in all matters."[20]

This young woman, whose name was not recorded in the sources, had apparently benefited materially from her marriage to Busch, and there was nothing the Secret Council could do to stop her.[21] When Busch was arrested and dismissed from office, the Secret Council also arrested his wife to restore his debt to the company, but they had to let her go again soon after, when "the great caboceers" and the king of Fetu declared that since she was Busch's wife, everything he had given her rightfully belonged to her. Lykke tried to reason with the king's caboceers, asserting that the goods that Busch had given to his wife belonged to the company and had not been Busch's to give away, but he had to admit that the company could do nothing to get the goods back. As they would do many times in the following century, Danish traders opted not to press this inherently political issue further. They lacked the resources to exert real power on the coast, and by stressing their point they only risked harming the balance of trade.

The Danish slave traders strove to remain on good terms with their African trading partners throughout their time on the coast. In 1685, when the Danish West India and Guinea Company headquarters was moved from Frederiksborg in Fetu to Christiansborg in Osu, the coastal area was controlled by the king of Akwamu. The king of Akwamu, whose capital, Nyanawase, lay about twenty miles inland from Accra, let the Ga continue their daily trade with the Europeans but demanded that the Ga caboceers pay tribute to him. Whether the Danes cultivated ties with the king of Fetu at Frederiksborg, the king of Accra, or the king of Akwamu, they had to do so by sending gifts, maintaining good relations with the kings' caboceers, and behaving diplomatically. Local contacts were essential. As the Danish governor Anders Pedersen Wærøe put it in 1733: "it is impossible to expect any trade at a fort below [next to] which no Negroes live."[22]

Slave trading was an unpredictable and complicated business, requiring violence, warfare, or enslavement of prisoners. Despite periods of relative calm the Gold Coast was therefore a region in turmoil, suffering from the effects of direct warfare, rumors of war, conflicts between Akan states, conflicts within these states, and conflicts among or with European competitors in the slave trade. Most enslaved Africans sold during the slave trade on the Gold Coast were war captives or people who had been kidnapped by raiding parties from the northern (inland) parts of what is today Ghana. A smaller number of the people sold to European slave ships had lived as slaves on the coast prior to their sale, and an even smaller number came from free African families on the coast.[23]

Slaves captured in wars or kidnapped were sold at slave markets in the north and bought by middlemen who brought them to the European forts on the coast. European traders were dependent on the Ga, Akan, and Fante middlemen who brought European goods with them inland to exchange for slaves. To ensure that their African middlemen came back with slaves rather than running off with their goods, European traders adopted an African pawning system in which African middlemen would leave an item (gold, iron, or other valuable goods) or a person over whom they had authority (a family member or an enslaved person) as a pawn at the fort while they traveled inland to buy slaves. At Christiansborg the Danish administration kept long lists of pawned goods and persons whom African traders had left in Danish custody until they returned. For the European traders, human pawns had an almost immediate monetary value. If the pawn was not redeemed within a set time limit, the administration considered it their right to sell the pawns, which made the practice of human pawning more immediately threatening for African families participating in the Atlantic slave trade.[24]

At Christiansborg, enslaved people waited in the dungeons for a slave ship to arrive. It was both expensive and difficult to keep people healthy in the dark, unsanitary dungeons, and many became sick and died before the ships arrived. Over and over again, Danish governors noted the difficulties of planning the trade in human beings and complained to the company in Copenhagen, which, particularly in the early years, appears to have had little understanding of how the slave trade worked. In 1703 Governor Hartvig Meyer, for instance, complained to the administration in Copenhagen about their instructions to always have a shipload of slaves ready when a Danish ship arrived on the coast. The administration suggested that the Danish traders make trading deals ahead of time with traders in the area and bring the slaves as soon as the ship came in, to which Governor Meyer replied with some annoyance that trading on the Gold Coast was not like trading at home; the supply of slaves could not simply or consistently match the demand. It would be several decades before the Danes became efficient and profitable slave traders, and even then the slave trade was never an easy business.[25]

The Danes' dependence on their African trading partners—on the Ga in

Osu and on the inland Akan-speaking groups who supplied the slaves—is crucial to understanding the dynamics of the cassare institution on the Gold Coast. Europeans' reliance on trading connections led them to go much further in their acceptance of African conditions and practices than we—living in a postcolonial era—might expect. On numerous occasions, for example, Danes at Christiansborg abided by the social, spiritual, and religious rules of Osu. One such emblematic anecdote related by Ludewig Rømer is of what transpired when a newly arrived Danish assistant caught a bird that the people in Osu considered a sacred animal, or a "fetish,"[26] in the words of the Danes. The Danes wanted to take the bird back to Christiansborg and keep it in a cage, but the Ga priests complained so much that the Danes had to hand the bird over to them and in addition placate the offended sacred fowl with a bottle of brandy.[27] Similarly, when Johannes Rask in 1710 described how people in Osu considered snakes sacred, he emphasized that if any European "should be unlucky enough, either drunk or sober, to kill a snake, he would scarcely get away with his life if the Negroes should see it."[28] In such a case the administration at Christiansborg would probably not be of much help. They were not interested in working against the interests of their trading partners. They were in Africa to trade, not to colonize.

In this precolonial encounter during the slave trade, the cassare marriages were fundamentally important for the European men's survival and well-being. In Osu, Ga women nursed their Danish husbands through illness, managed their money, fed them, and made sure they got the best trading deals.[29] The local Danish traders at Christiansborg were quick to realize the importance of the marriages, and if the West India and Guinea Company in Copenhagen had outlawed the cassare marriages, they would probably have met a lot of resistance. As it was, the company made only one early attempt to completely prohibit sexual relations with African women, avoiding the issue of marriage specifically. The ban on all sexual relations with African women came in 1711 after Governor Frantz Boye wrote to the company in Copenhagen, asking how to deal with employees who were "mixing" with African women. Boye asked if the employees in Africa should be expected to follow the same rules as "other real Military officers" in Denmark.[30] Boye's immediate reason for posing the question was that some of the men who were sleeping with African women also wanted to attend church, which had concerned the chaplain at Christiansborg.

Boye's own opinion—as expressed to the company—was that it would be impossible to keep the men from having sex with women in Osu: to enforce a complete restriction he would have to keep the men inside the fort on their days off, which Boye found unthinkable. Boye, who was cassaret to Koko at this point, doubted that a single man would stay in the company's service if he was not allowed to sleep with African women. But despite Governor Boye's forecast, the company's first response was to ordain that any man found "mixing" with African women should be punished. The first time a man was caught he was to pay a fine of one month's salary, the second time two months', and the third time four months'. In 1717, the company restated the importance of punishing men who were caught with African women, to which the Secret Council replied—in a tone, which, considering that so many men at Christiansborg, before and after, themselves had relationships with African women, sounds rather mocking—that the administration would ensure that any man, regardless of rank, found with an African woman within or outside the fort would be punished: "we will not hereafter turn a blind eye, even less provide grounds for scandal by acting so ourselves."[31]

However, this ban on sexual relations with African women was never enforced at Christiansborg. To begin with, Governor Boye was probably not the most determined prosecutor of such a ban. Nor did the company in Copenhagen pay much attention to the ban's execution. Just how little interest the company showed in the issue is apparent in a case against the very same Governor Boye for private trading while in company employment. The case took place in 1717, the same year that the company restated its ban on interracial intimacy, but the detailed minutes from the case reveal no discussion of Boye's own relationships with African women. The first witnesses in the case were called by the Secret Council at Christiansborg, who must have been aware of Boye's marriage to Koko. The fact that Boye's relationships with African women were not used in the case against him suggests that, compared to private slave trading, having sex with or cassaring African women was not an important offense. At the very least, neither the governor nor the assistants in the council had any interest in throwing the first stone when they all lived in glass houses.[32]

As time passed, the administration at Christiansborg began to openly favor cassare marriages, and the company in Copenhagen made no more attempts to enforce its ban. The Secret Council did occasionally complain about cassare marriages to the company, for example when connections between men from Christiansborg and their African wives' families interfered with or worked against the company's trade. Yet overall the administration supported cassaring—not surprising since at any given time the governor and a high number of the members of the Secret Council were themselves cassaret to women from Osu.

The administration at Christiansborg supported the cassare marriages, but the institution was initiated and developed around preexisting African culture. Danes used *cassare* as a broad term for "an African marriage," not only a marriage between a European and an African, and there is no question that the cassare marriages, in ritual as well as practice, were more African than European. When Paul Isert described cassare weddings in 1788 he simply commented that the celebration was "no different from the one I described ... about the Blacks," and cassare negotiations and ceremonies in Osu do appear to have been very similar to other Ga marriages.[33] Comparing Edward Carstensen's description of his negotiation with Caroline Truelsen for Severine's hand with descriptions of Ga marriages, for example, shows many similarities in the number and nature of gifts, the calling of the bride, and the festivities following the wedding. A cassare nuptial agreement, like Ga and Akan marriages, consisted of a payment of bridewealth from the man to the woman's family; as in Ga marriages, the cassare engagement included a series of payments of cloth, money, and drinks; the distribution of drinks among the bride's relatives was the most important.

Cassare marriages, like Ga marriages in early modern times, as it does in the present day, involved three stages: a marriage payment (bridewealth), an engagement, and a wedding. Ga marriage was usually initiated by the parents (usually the father) of the groom, who received the bridewealth. This of course was not possible in the case of the marriages with Danish men, since their families were far away. In any case, when a family had accepted a match, the groom gave the bride's parents a first gift to show that he was serious, and the bridewealth thereafter consisted of a series of gifts from the husband to the bride's parents. If the engagement was broken off, the bride's family was expected to pay back the bridewealth. The last gifts were given at the wedding—the official handing-over of the bride. The wedding party usually ended with a visit to a Ga priest in Osu.[34]

Cassare marriages developed as a social institution on the coast because Ga and other African families had an interest in making connections with foreign traders and integrating them into their kinship groups. Indeed, the Ga in Osu seem to have been particularly interested in and accustomed to integrating foreigners, at least from the time the central Ga kingdom in Ayawaso fell to Akwamu in 1677. The Ga state fragmented into seven towns along the coast, each with a number of closely connected small farming villages inland; these smaller towns and villages integrated a large number of foreigners, European and African, as well as foreign words, people, and material goods without much hesitation. How deliberately the Ga were engaging in a practice of what we might call "ethnogenesis" is not clear, but their social organization made the integration of foreign traders easy.[35]

One aspect of Ga life that helped the integration of foreigners was the Ga's polygamous patrilineal clans. Women and men lived in different households, meaning that the cassare marriages did not entail setting up a new household. Often the female and male compounds were connected to the same courtyard, but men and women ate and usually slept separately. When and if a husband wanted to sleep with his wife—or one of his wives, if he had more than one—he would call for her to spend the night in his compound. Children were the primary connection between husband and wife, but food was another strong symbolic and practical connection. Women were expected to cook for their husbands, while husbands were expected to support their wives and children with fish, meat, and produce for their subsistence or for them to sell in the market.[36] Through most of the eighteenth century, when Ga women married Danish men, they did not move in with their husbands, who kept living at the Danish fort.

This gender-segregated living arrangement made it easier to integrate the foreign men. By comparison, in Denmark, as in most of Europe, integrating foreign men into important families would not have been nearly as simple, since inheritance, ownership, and rural production were organized around the conjugal couple living together. Not only was a heterosexual couple the center of the household in early modern Denmark, it was also the primary economic and legal unit as well as the primary location of production in both farming and industry. The primary source of wealth in Denmark was landownership, and keeping land within a family was one of the important functions of marriage. The eighteenth-century Ga social world, on the other hand, was structured around a different and broader conception of kinship. Kinship ties could be formed though blood, adoption, or marriage, and when people were married or adopted into a kinship group they, in theory at least, ceased to be foreigners. In West Africa the size of a kinship group and the number of slaves was a more immediate measure of wealth than landownership, which probably meant that Ga families were actively seeking to expand their families by integrating foreigners.[37]

Another factor making it easier for Ga families to let their daughters marry European men was that it was relatively simple for another of the women's male family members to assume paternal responsibility for the children if and when a European died or left Africa. Shortly after a child was born in precolonial Osu the parents would perform a naming ceremony, in which the father assumed his parental responsibility and both parents' kinship groups recognized the child. Many of the children at the fort school and on the lists of soldiers at Christiansborg carried their fathers' names, so presumably the Danish men had recognized their parentage. If, however, a biological father would or could not take responsibility for his child, then another man in the mother's family could do it, though until someone did so the child was considered illegitimate. Like all other children, Euro-African children lived in their mother's compound until puberty, and they were integrated into their Ga families. Indeed, according to the Danish chaplains at the fort, the Ga mothers had far too much influence on their Euro-African children.[38]

The gendered division of labor in Ga families also assisted in the integration of foreign men. Apart from trade, fishing was particularly important to people living in and around Osu; men were responsible for fishing, whereas women did the preserving, cooking, and trading. Trading fish and many other products meant that some women were economically quite independent from their husbands, which, in turn, meant that not only their families but they themselves had a direct and personal interest in the marriages to European traders. When Ga women married Danish men they helped them settle as traders on the coast; in many ways, the married couples appear to have been just as much trading partners as intimate partners. The marriages were, like most other marriages, both important economic and reproductive units.

The separation of men and women in traditional Ga families did not mean that they had equal status in society. When accepting the bridewealth, a woman's relatives recognized her husband's rights to her domestic, economic, and sexual services. A wife was expected to perform domestic duties for the husband, to help him in his economic activities, and to abstain from sexual relations with other men, whereas husbands did not have the same responsibilities toward their wives.[39] In a society where the struggle to control labor was more important to social organization than the right to own land, women's double roles as producers and reproducers made them especially important. Most slaves in West African society were women, and whether women were given to other men as slaves, pawns, or wives, they had an immediate material as well as a long-term productive and reproductive value. Yet, as in other African societies, the separate lives of women and men does seem to have given women significant economic autonomy from their husbands, allowing them to own property and trade independently from them.[40] African women could take advantage of this autonomy, as we will see in later chapters.

The cassare marriages were not only African in ritual and initiated by the Ga; they were also largely controlled by the Ga. The story of Auchue and her three successive husbands from Christiansborg suggest just how little control Danish men could have over their cassare marriages in the early decades of the eighteenth century. Auchue was born in Aprag (Dutch Accra) but moved to Osu when she was married to Governor Friderich Pahl at Christiansborg in 1725. When he died in 1727, she was cassaret to another Danish employee at Christiansborg, barber-surgeon Johan Rudolph Muxol, after permission both from her friends[41] (kin) and from the Danish chaplain Heigaard, who, according to Governor Andreas Wellemsen, blessed the union from the pulpit.[42] Muxol died not long after the wedding, and a third Danish man, Sergeant Franz Carl Minche, got permission from the Danish governor and Auchue's kin to cassare her.

Shortly after their wedding, Sergeant Minche complained to the Danish governor, claiming that Auchue would not stay with him in Osu, but had run off to be with her family in Aprag. Governor Wellemsen then called Minche and Auchue together and "urged both to live in concord, and not cause me any problems." After this, according to Wellemsen, "the Negress and the Sergeant agreed well with each other for a long time." Yet at a later point Sergeant Minche again complained about Auchue to the governor, this time after having heard rumors that she had been sleeping with other men. Governor Wellemsen urged Minche to investigate the accusation and promised that if Auchue was guilty, "Those who have been involved with her would pay for it after the custom of this country."[43]

To investigate the question of Auchue's guilt, Sergeant Minche had a "Negro from the countryside" perform a ceremony in the courtyard at Christiansborg, drinking *adom*[44] above Auchue's head, and he concluded that she was guilty of adultery. Her kin, who were present at the ceremony, protested the result and said that the Adom the man had brought was bad. The Danish governor then ordered that the man from the country "who had brought this Adom and drunk it over her head" should swear an oath to prove that the Adom was good and that he had "treated it and acted as he should." The man swore that the Adom had been good, after which Auchue was arrested and questioned, and she confessed to having had sex with five different African men for money while married to Sergeant Minche. Later, though, when these men were called in for questioning by the Secret Council, Auchue withdrew her confession, claimed to be innocent "of having had relations with anyone but the persons she had been calesaret [cassaret] to," and offered to "eat fetish" to prove her innocence.[45]

Even under Danish jurisdiction, Ga practices dominated. The Secret Council, headed by Governor Wellemsen, decided to order Adom once more, "since there is no other possibility of finding out the truth in this case." They received another Adom from Aprag, and, after the boys who brought it swore that it was good, "Adom was drunk here at the fort over the head of the said Negress, Auchue, after which the boy who drank vomited the water up and thus affirmed that the Negress was innocent." The council then resolved that Auchue would be fully divorced from Minche and free to cassare whomever she wanted after her kin had paid back half of the amount Sergeant Minche had spent on her bridewealth.[46] However, Wellemsen's efforts to end the case by a compromise were hampered when Auchue's kin neglected to pay the settled amount, apparently at first trying to buy Minche off with a bunch of old clothes that he had given Auchue while they were cassaret. It was not until further threats and diplomatic efforts had been made that the caboceers from Aprag paid Minche back half of the bridewealth, and Auchue was set free. Unlike Auchue, Sergeant Minche was not permitted to cassare again. In its resolution, the council did recognize that it was customary in Osu for a person who wanted to be divorced from a marriage partner to pay back the whole bridewealth (cassare-costume), but since the sergeant had accused Auchue without "certain proofs" she was to return only half of it. Or, as Governor Wellemsen explained it in his memorandum about the case, "all this I would forgive to keep friendship." In order to stabilize relations with Aprag, Wellemsen promised Auchue's kin that the sergeant would be content with the half.[47]

These developments must be understood in a larger intercultural context of power relations in the Ga coastal towns. In the late 1720s, the Ga towns were in the middle of a rebellion against the king of Akwamu, who had been in control of the area since 1680. Unlike the Dutch and the English fort administrations in Accra, the Danish governor Wellemsen was undecided about whether he would support Osu and the other Ga towns in their rebellion until very late in the 1720s. In November 1728—right around the time when Auchue was arrested for adultery at Christiansborg—Osu was the only neutral Ga town left, and people had begun fleeing the town for Aprag and Soko. But toward the end of the year, Governor Wellemsen settled the differences with the other towns and the administrations at the European forts and joined them in the rebellion.[48] Wellemsen's eagerness to settle the case with Auchue's kin, the caboceers in Aprag, was probably influenced by his concerns about the larger political environment on the coast.

Yet, more broadly, the story about Auchue's conflict with her Danish husband, and the Danish governor's involvement in their personal issues, also indicates the extent to which interactions between Europeans and Africans were taking place on African cultural terms in the eighteenth century. Sergeant Minche drew on African spiritual-legal practices to settle the question of his wife's adultery; indeed, the major proof in the case in the Secret Council was produced by drinking Adom. The Secret Council's resolution of the matrimonial conflict, in which Auchue was acquitted while Sergeant Minche was forbidden to remarry, also indicates the power relations on the coast. It would not have been in the Danish trading company's interest to maintain a highly principled position that adhered to Minche's paternal right to follow up on a suspicion about his wife's adultery. Since trading was the Danes' primary purpose on the coast and they had no means to implement any principles by force, the first priority in a case like this was to safeguard good trade relations.

Auchue's marriages to Danes were typical in a number of ways. They were all agreed on by her family, who became involved and supported her when her third cassaret husband accused her of adultery. The cassaring was also supported by the administration at Christiansborg, where the governor took responsibility for solving controversies between Auchue and Sergeant Minche, both when Minche first complained about Auchue and again when his accusations led to a larger case. The governor's involvement in the marital affair shows that the administration found the matter important; the involvement of Auchue's kin and the two caboceers in Aprag—who ended up paying back half of the bridewealth that Minche was due—suggests why the governor was interested in settling the case. Auchue's kin in Aprag were important players in the coastal communities, and it probably did not make the situation less urgent that Aprag, Osu, and their European trading partners were seeking to solve a larger diplomatic problem at the same time.

Auchue's cassare marriage to Minche was also typical in that her kin seem to have been specifically interested in her marrying a European man, at least after she had been married to Governor Pahl. When the governor died in 1727, a prince from Akwamu requested permission to marry Auchue, but her kin turned him down. Considering that Aprag was already in rebellion against the king of Akwamu at the time, Auchue's kin rejection of one of his princes is quite understandable, but, according to Governor Wellemsen's later account, their explanation was more general: since Auchue had already been married to a European man they would not give her to an African. They would, on the other hand, be interested in marrying her to another man from Christiansborg.[49] Now, it is easy to imagine that Auchue's first husband, Governor Pahl, was a good connection for her kin in Aprag. Trading with the Danes a few miles away was not a given for people living closer to the Dutch fort, and a direct connection to the Danish governor could surely be useful. However, her two subsequent husbands were not governors, which reflects the fact that some Ga families saw advantages in cassaring daughters even to men of lower rank at Christiansborg.

At least two other examples from the 1720s suggest that it was not uncommon for important families on the coast to let their daughters cassare lower-ranking employees at Christiansborg. Two Euro-African boys, Christian Protten and Friderich Pedersen Svane, who went to Denmark with the Danish chaplain Elias Svane in 1727, both had mothers who came from important families on the coast and fathers who served as soldiers at Christiansborg. Svane's mother was from a good family in Teshi, and his father was the soldier Henrik Petersen, who played no important role at Christiansborg. Christian Protten's mother was the daughter of the Ga king Ofori in Little Popo, and his father was also a Danish soldier, Jacob Protten, who is mentioned only a few times in the Danish sources on some pay lists and in a letter from 1722, where Governor Herrn mentioned that he was "given to drink."[50]

Both Christian Protten and Friderich Pedersen Svane were christened either while they were still on the coast or after arriving in Copenhagen. In Denmark they were educated in theology at the University of Copenhagen and lived at Regensen, a residence hall in the center of the city. They later both returned to Christiansborg and taught, at different times, at the fort school. When Christian returned to Osu after his stay in Copenhagen, his mother's brother, Assiambo (also known as Ashangmo), was in power, and Christian took up contact with his mother's family. After he left for Copenhagen at the age of twelve, he seems not, on the other hand, to have had any contact with his Danish father.[51]

Considering the important contacts that families like Svane's and Protten's could have established by marrying their daughters to men from other families on the coast, why would they choose to cassare them to common soldiers at Christiansborg? One possibility is that Svane and Protten's mothers were never officially cassaret to their biological fathers. We do not have a reference to a ceremony taking place. But, like Auchue's family, their families clearly accepted the union, which suggests that they were officially recognized at some point. If we then assume that their mothers' unions with soldiers from Christiansborg were at least to some extent recognized, then why? Perhaps it mattered that even soldiers at Christiansborg were better off than many Africans. Soldiers at Christiansborg had a small but steady income, and precolonial West African bridewealth was relatively inexpensive for European men.[52] As Chapter 2 will describe, a marriage to a European man at Christiansborg and the connections that followed also involved economic opportunities other than the initial bridewealth. Children of Ga-Danish couples were at least partially supported by a monetary fund called "the poor Mulatto children's fund" and from the 1720s had access to a school run by chaplains at the fort, which opened opportunities for future employment. Whether one's father was a governor or a soldier at Christiansborg, European heritage linked children and their Ga families to the fort, and this must have made the cassare marriages attractive. But, at least in the case of elite African trading families, the bridewealth's size and their future access to the fort cannot fully explain why they would prefer to marry their daughters to Europeans.

The unions make sense only when we think of them as alliances between kinship groups in the multiethnic coastal trade, where Christiansborg represented its own kinship group. The status of Protten's and Svane's biological fathers was simply less important than the opportunities offered by allying with the kinship group they belonged to. Across the eighteenth century Atlantic world, marriages were not so much individual arrangements as broader alliances between kinship groups. In West Africa, as well as in Denmark, marriage was always a contract between families and communities, and when Ga families married their daughters to Danish men at Christiansborg, they made a much broader alliance with the fort. The Danish men's families presumably had no say in the matter, and the women's families did not get connected to these families. Yet the men brought other connections with them to the cassare unions—to their employer, the company; to European ships and goods; and to other European traders.[53]

Exactly how interested families in Osu were in marrying their daughters to European traders is hard to say. Few sources speak as directly to the thoughts behind the cassare marriages as the ones citing Auchue's kin's considerations, and European travel writers certainly had a tendency to overemphasize the appeal of a marriage to a European man. In 1760 Ludewig Rømer, for example, suggested that a marriage contract between two Africans could be broken off if a European man wanted to cassare a married woman. Or, along the same lines earlier in the century, the Dutch Willem Bosman made boastful remarks about how even a king's daughters were easily available to European men—in his words, "very cheap"—on the Gold Coast.[54] Neither of the writers explained why African families were so interested in cassaring their daughters to European soldiers, but if in fact kings on the Gold Coast frequently married their daughters to low-ranking Europeans it seems likely that there would have been other reasons than that their daughters were "very cheap." In a difficult trade structured around larger kinship groups, lasting and trustworthy connections between Africans and Europeans were valuable to both sides.

While it begins to make sense that Ga families were interested in letting their daughters marry Danish men, another question is why the Danish men chose to pay the bridewealth and go through a cassare ceremony. The most important reason was probably that the Ga kinship groups expected them to do so. The men at Christiansborg could probably have made do with a steady relationship to a woman who would take responsibility for their well-being and help them both survive and trade, but to get this they had to agree to cassare. This idea, that they had to get married to get to have a long-term relationship with a woman, cannot have been foreign to them. In Denmark extramarital sexual relations could be severely punished, and though such relations were still not uncommon, the Danish men who came out to Africa must have been familiar with marriage as the only officially recognized venue for sexual relations. This, of course, does not mean that they were actually looking to get married in Africa, but when and if the Ga families insisted on a cassare ceremony they were presumably not surprised.[55]

Most of the men at Christiansborg were single when they arrived and were therefore—in the eyes of the Danes—legally free to marry. They were young. Most men who worked at the fort were in their early twenties. Some higher assistants or men who came out to Africa for the second or third time were more than thirty years old, while some soldiers were sent out right after their confirmation and had only just turned fourteen.[56] Among the married men, only a very small number brought their Danish wives with them. Unlike other northern European trading companies, the Danish West India and Guinea Company had no rules against European women following their men to West Africa.[57] But the company did not encourage their employees to bring their wives, and married men received the same wages as unmarried men. The few men who did bring their wives were therefore governors or chaplains, who could afford to support a European wife at Christiansborg.

A relationship with a Ga woman was likely an easy choice for most young men at Christiansborg. Even a rudimentary study of the social world of Christiansborg would suggest that Danish men stationed at the fort could have both personal and psychological reasons for wanting a long-term relationship with a woman who was well versed in local culture and language. Daily life at the fort was characterized by abysmal living conditions and high mortality. Many men died soon after their arrival in Africa; the mortality rate among Europeans in West Africa was extremely high, and almost everyone appears to have been sick at some point during his stay. Danes were used to a high mortality rate in Denmark in the eighteenth century, and yet they were acutely aware of the health risks of being stationed on the Gold Coast. One example of this constant awareness of the many deaths at Christiansborg is chaplain Johannes Rask's account. Rask meticulously recorded every death at the fort, which was part of his job as the chaplain, but he also commented on the many deaths, and when he got sick himself he noted, "However, then I began to feel weak and since we time and again heard of so many Europeans dying, I often thought completely seriously about [death]."[58]

Even for men in good health, though, being stationed in Africa was a trial. After six o'clock at night the company employees were to stay inside the close quarters of the fort until the morning. Before the expansion of the fort in the 1740s, Christiansborg consisted only of the governor's rooms, a chapel in the middle of the fort, and a few smaller rooms in which all assistants and soldiers lived. The company's idea was to have around twenty men at the fort at any given time: one governor, higher and lower assistants, a bookkeeper, a cooper, a barber-surgeon, some carpenters, a sergeant, a corporal, a few soldiers, and a chaplain. But it was seldom possible to keep up with the mortality rate and keep all positions filled.[59]

The men did not always stay inside the fort in the evenings or at night, but when they did they spent the evenings drinking, playing games, and quarreling. The books from the Secret Council, as well as letters from the chaplains at the fort, often refer to disagreements between employees; many of these took place while at least one of the parties was excessively drunk and out of control, and company records and travel accounts note that the drinking habits among the men at the fort caused them both social and work-related problems. Some men were dismissed from their positions when they failed to fulfill their responsibilities, while others became sick from drinking.[60]

According to Ludewig Rømer, the Danish assistants drank punch (brandy, water, limejuice, and sugar), much like their English contemporaries on the Gold Coast, while the poorer Danish soldiers and workmen drank straight brandy, schnapps, or pito (a beer brewed from millet). Rømer reported that Danes lacked the proper constitution for drinking punch and therefore could be hungover for up to a week after drinking it. He also noted how the men at Christiansborg pressured one another into drinking; if someone refused to drink he was considered "obstinate and an evil person," and apparently it was prestigious to get as drunk as one could, as quickly as possible. In the seventeenth century, Jean Barbot had also noticed the habitual drinking at Christiansborg and suggested that the Danes were more prone to sickness than other Europeans on the coast.[61]

The Danish men might have been accustomed to drinking excessively before they came to Africa; contemporary Danes and other Scandinavians did consume a great deal of alcohol. Drinking could also have been a response to the heat and the social environment at Christiansborg. Life at the fort must have strained even the most stable personalities. In 1786 Paul Isert tied the excessive drinking at Christiansborg to a lack of other social activities, and there is no question that it must have been an intensely stressful experience to live at the little fort, buying enslaved people and keeping them captured in the dungeons, before selling them to European slave ships.[62] In any case there is reason to suspect that the men who came out were less well adjusted even to their native environment than the average Danish male. The Gold Coast was on the very bottom of the hierarchy of Danish overseas possessions, and not a place to go if one had any other colonies to go to or, even better, a chance to stay in the state administration in Copenhagen.

Drinking probably did not help in a stressful foreign environment. In 1688, when Gunner Thomas Bentzen asked permission to cassare, he had already been "bound" to another African woman for three or four years. Bentzen insisted that he had to marry someone else because the woman he was with "consumed everything he had," and he would starve to death unless he could marry another woman. Governor Fensman concluded that he would once again turn a blind eye to what Bentzen did, since the man was usually drunk on brandy before seven o'clock in the morning and caused much trouble at Christiansborg. Bentzen's wedding was set for the same day. In the case of Gunner Bentzen, surviving on the coast was presumably closely connected to his marriage to a woman who could take care of him.[63]

Danish men's lives at Christiansborg, shaped by stress caused by boredom, drinking, and slave trading, were further troubled by malaria (or climate fever, as they called it), diarrhea, Guinea worms, other infections and tropical diseases, as well as the general constraints of living in a culture that was fundamentally foreign to them. Though they heard stories about Africa before they left Denmark or on board a ship on their way to the coast, the world they met was culturally vastly different from northern Europe. Settling in Africa was an act of cultural displacement that involved, as Isert dramatically put it, adjusting to "a land in which both our blood and our habits change."[64]

The conditions of living in a foreign culture, combined with the difficulties and fluctuations of the slave trade—long periods of inactivity punctuated by the brutality of the task of keeping people imprisoned in the dungeons—caused psychological reactions that the men would have to overcome to survive on the coast. Later, in 1760, Rømer described the men's reaction to encountering Africa: "When we first arrive in that land it is as if we have come to another world. . . . Everything is strange to us. We grieve, and wish that we were forced to seek our daily food at every man's door [begging in Denmark] rather than to have to come to such an uncomfortable land. The food does not taste good to us and we would rather starve than eat the food of the Blacks. The Blacks with whom we are to have close contact are surly and evil people who seek to cheat us or beg from us."[65] Rømer tied the Europeans' rejection of African food and mistrust of Africans in general to the fact that they had just arrived from Europe, and he drew a clear distinction between newly arrived Europeans and those who had been on the coast for a while. This differentiation indicates that the latter group had gone through a transition that made them more capable of living in Africa.[66]

After some time on the coast, the men's initial mistrust and confusion was replaced by an attachment to the new cultural context through friendships and intimate relations with members of the host culture. In this process the Danish men adopted characteristics and habits from the Ga and Akan people they were living among. They crossed over through the liminal space of cultural transition and reestablished themselves in Africa. Rømer described this transition to life on the coast in detail. The first year after the men arrived was a trial to overcome, after which the men were integrated into coastal society, began to like the food, and made friendships with members of the host culture. "If he lives longer [than the first year] he learns to speak a little Negro-Portuguese.[67] He then becomes acquainted with a Black in the town, who becomes his friend and gives him advice for his benefit," Rømer related and continued: "Yet we have almost no examples of them managing on their own, earning something, and returning to Europe. They wish to have one of the daughters of the country, or keep a black mistress."[68]

One important difference between newly arrived men's anxious and unsettled life on the coast and the life that the men who stayed longer could achieve was, according to Rømer, interpersonal relations with people in Osu, and specifically intimate relations with African women. Further on in Rømer's account it becomes apparent that it was not so much a mistress as a wife the men were looking for, and when a man had stayed with this wife for a while, he "cares as much for her and his children as a man does who has his true wife and children in Europe. Some among the Europeans do not wish to leave their family on the Coast even if they know they could live better in Europe." Cassaring with a woman in Africa had made them less homesick and, as Rømer phrased it, "not as desperate to leave the country as before."[69] Just as Edward Carstensen (mentioned in the Introduction) felt at home at Christiansborg only while Severine was alive and distanced himself from both Africans and Europeans on the coast after her death, many other Danish men remained culturally displaced until they entered into a relationship with a woman in Osu.

This is not to suggest that the initial period of resettling in Africa only provoked disabling reactions. There also seems to have been a strong sense of liberation from European cultural restraints, particularly for men who stayed only shorter periods on the coast. Sailors, temporary workers, and other short-term visitors often shaped the social world in Osu by their lack of understanding of and association with coastal life and by spending their spare time roaming about Osu, drinking and having sex with women in town. Letters home and travel accounts describe the great merriment and parties at the forts, while court books from the Secret Council recorded when the rowdy behavior led to conflicts, and the priests reported to the bishops in Copenhagen about "ungodly" social life at the fort.[70] Yet it is equally important not to overemphasize the liberating aspects of cultural displacement for Danish men living in Osu. For men who stayed longer than a few months on the coast, the psychological instabilities and anxieties caused by cultural displacement were barriers that they needed to overcome in order to resettle in Africa for the long term.

For the men at Christiansborg resettling on the coast was not a simple act of arriving, but a mental and practical process of accepting food, language, and friendship. We should not, however, overstate the extent to which the Danish men were integrated in Ga families in this early part of the century. The separation of the sexes in Ga families made it easy for them to accept Danish men into their kinship groups without fully integrating them. Though marrying a Ga woman was a tremendous help for survival, resettling, and trade relationships, the Danish men kept living at the fort; they did not move into their wives' family's male compound, and they would have been obviously foreign in the African community. They were therefore not so much assimilated into the Ga community, as they were allowed by the Ga to resettle in Osu and have their presence accepted.[71]

The cassare marriages were therefore about much more than access to sex with African women. Sexual encounters without cassare marriage also took place. There are, for instance, cases of Danish men having sexual relations with enslaved women working at the fort or imprisoned in the dungeon, which show up in the sources only because the sexual encounters led to a pregnancy or a child for whom a chaplain felt responsible. In 1708, for example, chaplain Anders Winter requested permission to christen a drummer, Jan de Wit, who was a son of a fort slave and a Danish employee. In 1727 interim governor Wellemsen wrote to former governor Hendrick von Suhm, now on St. Thomas, that he, on behalf of Suhm, had freed a fort slave named Massa, "because on 20th September she gave birth to a fine Mulatto boy who has been baptized and called Hendrick Andreas Christian." Both Suhm's interest in the freeing of the woman named Massa and the fact that her child was given his first name, Hendrick, suggest that it was the former governor's son.[72]

A few sources also suggest that the men at Christiansborg used their superior positions as jail keepers to sexually abuse enslaved people imprisoned in the dungeons. In one case, the abuse of a slave woman was mentioned in a broader claim against Governor Wærøe for misusing his office while governor in the 1730s, where Governor Schielderup implied that Wærøe had been involved in selling enslaved women specifically for sexual abuse. In a later case Governor Jessen was accused of keeping a woman with him in his room at the fort for a few days and then selling her to a European slave ship. This incident surfaced in the company archive only because the woman Jessen had sold was actually free, which led to an outcry from the woman's family. If Jessen had bought an already enslaved woman instead, there would have been no reason for Danes at Christiansborg to record it. Danish men probably had sex with enslaved women more often than the company archives suggest. Yet, because sexual relations with women enslaved at the fort did not interfere with trade or relations to people in Osu, there was no reason to mention them in the sources, whereas the cassare marriages with free African women, so central to trade relations, come up more often.[73]

However, cassare marriages may even have been about more than survival and trade. The exchanges of amulets between Ga and Danish lovers, for instance, hints at the otherwise inaccessible emotional side of the relationships. Danish men ordered "beautifully worked" keys from Europe to give to their lovers in Osu, which in the West African context had both religious and emotional significance. Keys and locks were understood as objects of empowerment, and particularly padlocks with keys as evidence of desires made firm. Inserting pegs or keys in holes or locks had spiritual significance of enclosure and protection, empowering the wearer of the keys. Likewise, Ludewig Rømer described how some of the men at Christiansborg wore amulets under their clothes—occasionally seen by roommates—that they had been asked to wear by "their mistresses," which were "supposed to be good for this or that." Perhaps their wives and lovers were giving them amulets to protect them from contracting diseases. In any case, combined with the references to how much European men loved their African wives and children and how strongly they felt connected to their new home in Africa, such exchanges of keys and amulets to wear might be indicative of real attachments between husbands and wives in an otherwise very practical arrangement.[74]

Emotions aside, the cassare marriages were undeniably practical, and since both Ga and Danes had interests in the marriages, the cassare institution could function as a central cultural meeting point. Ga, Akan, Danes, and other Europeans and Africans knew and accepted marriage as a social institution. They also all seem to have accepted marriage as a "system of exchange," since marriages entailed a transfer of goods and/or services. But apart from the direct payments involved in entering a marriage contract, the union had broader economic functions as the primary institution for wealth and property distribution between generations and as the basis for the division of labor between the sexes. Moreover, West African trade was organized through conjugal relationships, which meant that connections formed between wives and husbands in trading families were just as much trading partnerships as family ties.[75]

Interracial marriage institutions like the cassare marriages that developed on the Gold Coast and in other parts of West Africa were common throughout the early modern world, wherever Europeans traded. Marriage was an important procreative, sexual, emotional, and economic social institution that could be recognized across cultural differences on the middle ground that trading demanded. They officially recognized rights and duties for the married couple, determined the status of the offspring born to the couple, and tied groups of people together in larger alliances, whether the contracts were negotiated between kinship groups, patriarchs, families, or individuals. Not surprisingly, the institution therefore played an important part in the history of European expansion.[76]

European traders in many parts of the world discovered that settling with a woman from the local trading population could be of great importance in forging cross-cultural diplomatic and political connections. In recognition of the threat that such connections could pose to colonial control, interracial marriage was often one of the first social practices to be banned when an area was colonized by Europeans. In the French plans to turn the fur-trading enterprise in Louisiana into an agricultural colony in the early eighteenth century, for example, the idea was to supply the French farmers with European women to avoid "country marriages," which, according to the French authorities, kept the men from settling down and therefore prevented the establishment of a stable and self-sufficient colony. Likewise, when English colonization reached western Canada it was followed by European women, missionaries, and agriculture, and within a few decades interracial marriage was regarded as immoral and, with time, became illegal.[77]

In India, interracial relationships were allowed and to some extent encouraged before English colonization. In the eighteenth century, the ideal English company official was an affluent diplomat who had equally good relations with Indian and European officials and strong knowledge of Indian culture. Cohabitation with Indian women was considered sophisticated and cosmopolitan. In the nineteenth century, as the English colonization of India intensified, the ideal of an English official changed. He now had to be an ambassador for English culture, representing and living by imperial example with his European wife and children. Interracial families were always contested and questioned among the English in India as they intersected with racial hierarchies, and their children inhabited ambiguous positions in the societal order.[78]

Cultural mixing in trading posts followed logic and power dynamics that often ran counter to colonial interests. European traders depended on the goodwill and interests of their trading partners, and it would, for example, never have been easy for Europeans to take their children away from the local families. In West Africa, where Europeans were stationed at their forts only with the permission of African rulers, cultural transmission—and mixing— was much more likely to happen on African rather than European terms. Yet, in both colonies and trading posts, interracial marriages, intimate mixing, and the resulting children of mixed descent functioned as catalysts for generating common practices around racial difference.[79]

Initially, negotiations over difference in interracial families in the early modern Atlantic world primarily followed lines of gender, class, and age— hierarchies that in different forms and specifics were recognized in most cultures. As they encountered and sought to understand each other, people from different groups recognized gender and class differences in modes of dress, occupations, and behaviors, and they used these recognizable signs of difference to communicate and understand each other across cultural differences. At times Europeans misunderstood cultural communication, ascribing the wrong meanings to gestures and behaviors that they thought they recognized as similar or even identical to their own. Yet even perceived similarities had the potential for opening up communication and interaction. In the intimate encounter that took place in cross-cultural marriages, gender and class played important roles in creating a shared space of perceived and recognized similarities: both sides recognized the marriage institution, but they also, of importance, agreed on gender and class assigning different roles, occupations, and social place for men and women.[80]

Ga and Danes were both accustomed to thinking of differences between people as inheritable and bound to cultural heritage (language, clothing, material culture, and so on), and they shared assumptions about gender and class that helped them recognize each other's social hierarchies. They agreed that women and men were expected to fill different roles in society, and they agreed that women were subordinate to men. They shared assumptions that wealth and occupation were measures of prestige that signaled distinction. The towns on the Gold Coast were stratified by wealth and occupation long before the Danes arrived. All along the Gold Coast, town populations consisted of distinct and varied occupational groups: traders, fishermen, priests, military men (*asafo*),[81] and so on. In distinguishing between different groups in the coastal towns, wealth and cultural markers associated with wealth were of paramount importance. The Danes came from a solidly stratified kingdom of landed gentry and commoners and could easily recognize social difference along lines of wealth and occupation.[82]

Danes and Ga also shared an understanding that wealth, prestige, and freedom were inseparably linked. The Danes at Christiansborg had not grown up in a society with slaves, but they would have been quite accustomed to only a few people in society having the "freedom" to travel or move as they wished. Throughout the Middle Ages there were strict rules regulating when and why people could travel or move away from the land they lived and worked on. Their labor in part belonged to the proprietor, who was responsible for collecting the king's taxes from individual farming families in the area he controlled. In 1733 these regulations were reinstated in a provision that prohibited all men and boys between fourteen and thirty-four (later between four and forty) from leaving the land they were born on without an explicit purpose as well as permission from their landed proprietor (*godsejer*). When the Danish men arrived in Africa they would have recognized that some people were more free than others, and that social status decided one's opportunities in life.[83]

Such distinctions were intensely important in the Atlantic slave trade, which depended on defining and maintaining social differences between people who were enslavable and people who were not for sale to European ships. On the Gold Coast, as in all other societies with slaves, distinctions between slaves and nonslaves had developed over the course of centuries. To the Ga and Akan distinctions between slaves and nonslaves followed lines of both ethnic difference and social class. People who had the social status of slaves in Gold Coast society were most often from a different ethnic group than their owners, whether they had been born on the coast to slave parents, or had been bought in one of the slave markets in the northern part of present-day Ghana or further inland (see Map 3). In Asante, as well as in Twi, *odonko* (used to mean "slave") literally means a foreigner, who has been bought, or, more specifically, a person from the north with tribal markings; the term carried (and still carries) very negative connotations. The Ga also adopted the Twi word *odonko* to designate "slaves from the north," while other slaves were called *nyon*.[84]

For the Ga, the difference between those who were for sale to European ships and those who were not was therefore essentially an ethnic distinction.

Enslaved people were considered "strangers," and whether they had been born slaves or bought later on in life, they did not have the same rights as other members of the kinship group they worked for. They were to some extent integrated in these kinship groups, but they did not belong to a family's lineage, and they had the lowest status in society. Only through adoption or marriage could slaves become "full" members of the family they worked for, and even then they might have had little chance of passing as freeborn. In particular slaves who had recently arrived from the north were easily recognized and were thought to be distinguished from other people by both physical and cultural characteristics.[85]

During the Atlantic slave trade, Danish traders at Christiansborg most often followed these Gold Coast distinctions between people who were for sale to European ships and people who were not. Danish traders understood the distinction between enslaved people from the north and people living on the coast, and they knew that people who did not have the status of slaves were to stay in the country.[86] But lines between slaves and nonslaves were not always so easily drawn. While the boundary between those who did and who did not have the social status of slaves in Osu was clear, there was another more varied group, human pawns, who sometimes also ended up on European slave ships. A pawn might, like a slave, end up working for a creditor for many years or a whole lifetime if a debt was not paid, but pawns continued to belong to the kinship group they were born into, and they had the status of free people. European forts on the Gold Coast pawned an increasing number of free Africans during the Atlantic slave trade, which gave European traders a powerful hold on African families—a dynamic we return to in chapter 4.[87]

In the social climate of the Atlantic slave trade, particularly as it intensified over the course of the eighteenth century, social differences between slaves and nonslaves in Osu were gradually racialized. As generations of Ga and Danish traders intermarried and produced new people and new meanings, they developed a common language and set of practices organized around racial difference. Racial distinctions between Euro-Africans and other Africans were never the only difference at work in defining social distinctions in Osu—class, gender, and other hierarchies of difference remained important—but they were all embedded in the same Atlantic world, where race was gaining strength in the eighteenth century. The growing group of Euro-Africans took advantage of this space that racialized difference had created and developed a hybrid culture that was specifically adapted to the trade.[88]

Discourses of racial difference were readily available in the Atlantic
world, and as Danish and Ga slave traders in Osu developed their practices
around racial difference, they drew on these Atlantic meanings attached to
racial difference. When Ga and Danes employed the Portuguese lingua
franca of the coast they simultaneously adopted centuries of Portuguese experience in racialist thinking. When Danes from the beginning referred to
Africans as "negroes" or "blacks" and to Europeans as "blanke," derived from
the Portuguese *blanco* instead of the Danish word for white (*hvid*), they were
participating in larger Atlantic discourses attaching meaning to racial
difference.[89]

Even before the early eighteenth century, a central feature of racialized
discourse was the linking of slavery and blackness, and Danish embedded-
ness in this discourse was perhaps most starkly expressed in the Danish practice of referring to certain Africans as "free blacks" or "free negroes."[90] If
"free" meant not enslaved, then everybody on the coast who did not have the
status of a slave was "free." Why, then, would it be necessary for the Danes to
draw attention to the fact that certain Africans were not enslaved? Presumably, either the Danes at Christiansborg had adopted the practice of referring
to Africans who were not enslaved as "free" from the plantation colonies in
the Americas, or they had brought it with them from home. In the collective
pool of knowledge in the overseas trading circles in Copenhagen, slave traders, planters, and administrators could easily share experiences and expectations from Africa, Asia, and America. Traders and colonists often came from
the same families, and they had much opportunity to learn from each other
in Copenhagen. However the practice emerged, it suggests that, in the eyes of
the Danes, all Africans were potentially enslavable, making it worthy of note
when Africans were "free."[91]

Though these early northern European traders made reference to racialized difference, they do not seem to have had a very clear sense of what racial
difference meant, or how flexibly racial characteristics should be understood.
Descriptions of West African women in travel accounts from around 1700
show Europeans grappling with and sometimes changing their opinions
about bodily racial difference. In the seventeenth century, travel accounts depicted African women as monstrous and physically different from European
women, whereas eighteenth-century accounts describe African women as
remarkably similar to European women physically. Indeed, at the turn of the
eighteenth century, West African women were sometimes depicted as so similar to European women that European men could choose to ignore their

skin color in the dark. In the Frenchman Jean Barbot's account from 1679, for instance, the women he met in Accra were beautifully dressed, good-humored, and skillful in the art of seducing European men: "I saw several of them richly adorned . . . in such manner as might prove sufficiently tempting to many lewd Europeans; who not regarding complexions, say *All cats are grey in the dark*."[92] Skin color was not a mark of essential difference; under certain (sexualized) circumstances it was easily ignored.

These unsettled meanings of racial difference are similarly evident in chaplain Johannes Rask's travel account. Rask stayed at the fort from 1708 to 1713, and his account sits in the transition period between the early modern view of Africa as the domain of witches and cannibals and the better-informed and more self-confident travel accounts of the eighteenth century. Rask often quoted travel accounts from the seventeenth century, but usually to correct them. For example, he observed that West African women's breasts did not sag as much as rumor had it: "I have not seen, anywhere on the Gold Coast, such ugly, extraordinarily hanging breasts as Dapper describes, apart from 2 or 3 at Del Mina. But in general they have well-shaped, moderately hanging breasts."[93]

Rask discussed a number of seventeenth-century understandings of skin color and held them up against other contradictory explanations, as if he was not quite sure which leg to stand on. For example, Rask recounted that African babies were almost white when they were born, but that then the babies were "smeared with palm oil or tallow into which has been mixed coal or soat" and laid in the sun for about fourteen days. But then in the following sentence, Rask contradicted himself by adding that African babies would also have become black without being smeared: "Negroes, or the Blacks, cannot give birth to white children, wherever in the world they live, so the blackness of their skin does not come from the great heat of the sun."[94] Why should African families then go through the trouble of smearing them and laying them out in the sun for two weeks? The contradiction suggests that Rask could not quite believe either that black skin was a product of culture or that babies were born with black skin.[95]

Rask's uncertainty about the nature and persistence of skin color also came out in discussions of the color of children of mixed racial heritage. Black skin seemed to disappear quickly when white men had children with black women: when a subagent at Cape Coast had two daughters with a woman of mixed Euro-African heritage, they were "so beautiful, white and well shaped . . . as if they had been born in London of the oldest English ancestry." In Copenhagen Rask had also encountered a young student, Verville, who was the son of a white man and a black woman, who could pass as white. According to Rask, Verville's skin was "somewhat dark," but not darker than many people with two white parents, and if one did not know that his mother was black, one would not guess it. Rask made sure to emphasize that this quick disappearance of black skin color happened only when white men had children with black women, and not when black men had children with white women. An Englishman had assured Rask that a child born of a white father and a black mother is whiter than one who is born of a black father and a white mother. The whitening of white men's children was of course also more relevant and important to Rask and other European men in these trading posts where there were very few white women—and those who were present were married to white men.[96]

The uncertainty about the meaning and persistence of skin color meant that any social distinctions Europeans attached to "Africans" collectively were relatively flexible, and not that they did not attach negative sentiments to "negroes" or "blacks." Rask, for one, described most West Africans he met in very negative terms. But, like skin color, such racial characteristics were presented as malleable. With class, education, and Christianity, Verville could easily pass in Copenhagen, and, in a similar way, Africans in Osu were to be judged by their class and their connections to Europeans—and later also their Christianity and education—at least as much as by their skin color. As in other areas of the Atlantic world in the early modern period, Danish men appear to have arrived in Africa with relatively vague and messy notions of what racial difference meant. Their large undifferentiated category of "Blacks" was not yet as full of meaning nor as rigid as it would become over the following centuries.[97]

Even though skin color and physical differences between people from different parts of the world had been studied and interpreted for centuries before any of the forts on the Gold Coast were established, the Danish traders at Christiansborg still arrived with relatively undefined and loose ideas of what racial difference between Europeans and Africans should mean. Unlike the Portuguese and the Spanish, who already had centuries of experience trading with Africans and buying, selling, and owning African slaves, Danes had next to no experience with Africans that would lead them to turn their ideas about racial difference into social practice. Even more important, these loose ideas encountered Gold Coast social hierarchies based on conceptions of ethnic and class difference that had developed over centuries and were therefore

much more solidified, and not surprisingly Gold Coast social hierarchies became more immediately important in defining difference in the slave trade.

However, as Danes and Ga intermarried and traded, the vague and unclear understandings of racial difference slowly solidified and became the
basis for a social hierarchy along racial lines. This process of developing social distinctions along lines of race was guided by the unequal power distribution in the Atlantic world. As the Atlantic colonial system emphasized and
strengthened racial difference, everything European gained value. Markers of
belonging to—or association with—the real beneficiaries of the colonial Atlantic system drew their prestige from the Atlantic world in which Europeans
and Africans lived on unequal terms. The two commercial systems that encountered one other in the Atlantic slave trade were never equally powerful,
and seen from an Atlantic perspective, Africans and Europeans did not have
the same opportunities to benefit from the colonial system that the slave
trade was a part of.[98]

In West Africa, in encounters around the slave trade, Africans had more
influence on everything from daily trading transactions to smaller and larger
political conflicts, but the European slave traders represented a much larger
colonial enterprise, one whose power and persistence did not hinge directly
on what happened in the local slave-trading business. When Danish men
died or were sent back to Denmark, new people were sent out. The Danish
slave trade was part of a colonial system, which over the course of the eighteenth century would become more and more profitable, as sugar production
in the Danish West Indies—St. Croix, St. Thomas, and St. John—took off.
Unlike African traders in Osu, the Danish traders shared a powerful sense of
economic and political security. This was the larger power hierarchy that
Euro-Africans in Osu would position themselves in and take advantage of, as
we will see in the following chapters.

Euro-Africans in Osu were of course not alone in taking advantage of the
power structures of the Atlantic colonial system. Individuals on all sides of
the Atlantic responded to the opportunities and pressures of the colonial system, and Europeans were better positioned than anybody else to take advantage of the economic opportunities. Frantz Boye, for example, managed to
draw on resources and family relations in several corners of the Atlantic
world, which situated him well to succeed in the Atlantic trade. He was still a
young man, as we know, when he was cassaret to Koko, and he continued to
build on his connections in Africa, but he could also draw on connections to
the Danish fort and to Europe. During a subsequent stay in Europe, in 1710,

he had married an Englishwoman, Johanna Smith, who was the sister of an officer at the customs house in London. When he returned to Osu as governor at Christiansborg in 1711, he was an experienced slave trader who could maneuver in both European and African slave-trading circles, and he did very well for himself until he was accused of private trading and called back to Copenhagen in 1717. Even after that, he returned to Africa in 1720 in the employ of the British Royal African Company (perhaps based on family connections in London).[99] In the local context of the Gold Coast, Africans and Euro-Africans set the terms for and initiated the cassare marriages, but the practice was also shaped by the larger Atlantic colonial system that the slave trade was part of. In that larger world, Africans did not set the terms for the mixing of cultures. In that larger world Europeans were positioned much better to take advantage of the opportunities opened by colonialism and slave trading.

We see the unequal conditions for participating in the Atlantic colonial system when we compare Frantz Boye and Koko Osu: while Frantz Boye benefited both from the cassare marriage and from his position as a European man in the larger Atlantic world, Koko and her kin's benefits and opportunities in the slave trade were restricted to their local world. When Koko's father became caboceer in 1711, he began receiving monthly payments from the fort and promised to trade primarily with them. As the generations passed, a number of slave-trading families like Tette Osu's would develop close ties with the Danes, and they would, in turn, benefit more than other Africans from the trade. They did not gain as much from the slave trade as inland kings, who could claim all captives taken in wars as their property and sell these captives to European slave ships, but caboceers also secured profits from the trade for themselves and their families. In return for these profits, African families established strong ties to European forts. They began to develop debts to the company. In fact, the last time Koko Osu is mentioned in the Danish sources it is for a debt of eight *rigsdaler*[100] owed to Governor Wærøe and assistant Sparre in 1735.[101]

CHAPTER 2

A Hybrid Position

At the fort school at Christiansborg in 1724, sitting in the small church room, Anna Sophie and her sister would have smelled and heard the slave yard just below. The church room was very poorly ventilated, with only three small windows, and at times the smell from the yard was so harsh that the chaplain had to send his students out to collect anise leaves and twigs to burn in an effort to mask it. Even if the children were to forget the business that had brought their teacher to Osu, the stench would have reminded them, along with the voices. Sometimes, when the trade was good, the voices of people imprisoned in the crowded space almost drowned out the words of the chaplain. When the slave yard was full like that, everyone was aware of the danger. The fort had to be well manned behind its thick walls; the slaves might revolt or someone could attack the fort trying to get the captives. They represented a tempting prize. With or without anise, the smell and the noise marked Anna Sophie and her sisters' privilege: they were not enslaved, they were free and baptized, and later they would be confirmed.[1]

From inside the church room, however, the school did not shimmer with privilege. The furniture was sparse, and the door was falling apart. The limited school supplies from Denmark quickly ran out; there were only a few tattered books and scraps of candles left. No great distance separated the schoolroom from the rest of the fort, or the fort from the world outside, for that matter. During class and at all other times of the day, as they sat there reciting the Bible and singing hymns in Danish, people going to see the governor would walk through the room on the way to his quarters. Sometimes they would stop and take a break or sit around and talk, smoking and drinking, in the classroom. Chaplain Elias Svane complained, again and again, that neither Europeans nor Africans had any respect for the church or the school, but the governor and the Secret Council ignored his protests.[2]

Anna Sophie's father, Christian Petersen Witt, was one of the growing number of "mulatto" soldiers at the fort. Witt's father had been governor of the old Danish headquarters at Frederiksborg, and after his father had left Africa, Christian was taken in at Christiansborg in 1688, along with another Euro-African boy. He was christened late, when he was thirty years old. Christian's daughters, however, were christened at a younger age. As small and unimposing as the church room was, Christian Witt must have thought that a Christian education and confirmation would be an advantage for his daughters. If nothing else, attending the school led to Anna Sophie's first marriage, to her assistant teacher, Ole Larsen Grue. Their marriage was brief and childless; Ole Larsen Grue died within a year, after which Anna Sophie took up with another Norwegian man, assistant Jørgen Bendixen Warberg. This time she could not get married in the church right away; Elias Svane had left the coast, and there was no new chaplain at the fort available to marry them. Her father reluctantly let Anna Sophie have a relationship with the Norwegian assistant anyway—on the explicit condition that he would marry her as soon a chaplain arrived on the coast. The chaplain's blessing appears to have been crucial for Anna Sophie's father.[3]

* * *

The hybrid Euro-African position inhabited by people like Anna Sophie and her father evolved in a field of tension among three groups of Atlantic players—the chaplains, the administration, and Euro-African families in Osu. These groups had distinct but overlapping interests in the cassare marriages. Danish protestant chaplains at Christiansborg, who were sent out to look after the spiritual well-being of Europeans at the fort, had a religious interest in the marriages and particularly in the offspring their congregation produced with African women. The administration at Christiansborg had an interest in hiring local people as soldiers and menial workers at the fort instead of relying on expensive and sickly northern Europeans; as Governor von Suhm put it in 1724, christening Euro-African children of Danish employees could help create a "substantial tribe for the Noble Company's service here in Guinea."[4] But neither chaplains nor administrators would have had any influence on the Euro-African children or families had these families not seen an advantage in having their marriages recognized by the Danish church or in sending their children to school at the fort. The story of how the cassare marriages became integrated in the fort hierarchy is therefore a story of how local Atlantic agents took advantage of and benefited from the Atlantic slave trade.

Across the world of European expansion, people of mixed European and American, Asian, or African descent played similar roles as intermediaries in trade and in colonial societies, and their positions in European social hierarchies were often predicated on or related to Christianity. How far newly converted people accepted or lived by Christian doctrine is almost impossible to determine. In the case of early Ga and Akan Christians, it is certain that Christian beliefs and practices were integrated into and adapted to African religion. Anna Sophie, her father, and many other Euro-Africans before and after inhabited hybrid positions between two cultures that were powerful precisely because they were hybrids. The cultural transformation initiated by the fort school and inclusion of Euro-Africans in the Christian congregation and workforce was therefore not the Christian cultural conversion that the chaplains were hoping for. What developed instead was a hybrid Euro-African culture, which borrowed from European material culture, words, and religion but remained embedded in the social world of Atlantic slave trading. Euro-Africans in Osu adapted European Christian culture to their purposes.[5]

In Osu, the cassare institution was an important catalyst for the production of this hybrid Euro-African culture. Both the fort administration and the chaplains expected Euro-Africans of Danish descent to become members of the fort community, or as chaplain Hagerup wrote to Governor Resch in 1765, education at the fort school would help Euro-African children become "useful members of our present republic."[6] In a broader sense this inclusion of Euro-Africans in the fort hierarchy helped crystallize a particular set of ideas about race. That some of the daughters of Danish men took up Danish language, clothing, and religious practice, and finally Danish husbands, and that the sons found a special place as soldiers at the fort, meant that Danish descent and the markers accompanying it conferred a special status. This distinguished them as the social superiors of other children of African mothers and strengthened the notion of European descent as a physically as well as culturally significant badge of superiority.

The practice of employing Euro-Africans at Christiansborg was not a coherent plan from the outset. In fact, early Danes in Africa appear to have had little idea of what to do as the number of Euro-African children grew following the rise of cassare marriages. At least one Danish governor envisioned that sons of employees would grow up to serve the West India and Guinea Company as soldiers or in other positions; in 1688 Governor Fensman made the following note in the daybook at Christiansborg about taking in Anna Sophie's father and another son of an employee: "Today at the request of *Afam*, one of our caboceers (he is married to Pieter Valck's former Negress), I have taken Pieter Valck's surviving son, who is about nine years old, into the service of the Noble Company in consideration of the fact that he was sired by a Christian, and ordered him to go to *Antoni* the mason to learn this craft, so he can later serve the Noble Royal Company: at least, if nothing else is possible, to use him in the same service as a soldier. . . . I also do [so] for Peter Witte's son]."[7] Fensman was taking the sons of employees in at the fort because they were "sired by a Christian." He did not claim responsibility for the boy because his father had been employed by the company, but because he was a Christian, and it is interesting to note that the company would take Pieter Valck's son in, even though his mother had remarried and her new husband had presumably adopted him. Pieter Valck's paternity must have been widely recognized in Osu, and perhaps his mother decided that sending the boy to learn a skill at the fort would be a good investment in his future.

Not all early governors were interested in taking responsibility for the children of Danish employees, however, whether Christian or not. In 1708, for instance, Governor Erich Lygaard seriously considered sending all Euro-Africans away from the coast. There were very few Euro-Africans at Christiansborg at that time, and he was responding to requests from the chaplain, Anders Winter, who wanted to christen a "Mulatto or drummer here in the service of the Company, *Jan De Wit*, who has enrolled as a soldier."[8] Lygaard wrote to the company in Copenhagen for clarification of the issue but added his own opinion as well: if Jan de Wit was christened, Lygaard thought, then it would be best to send him off to the West Indies or to Copenhagen instead of letting him stay on the coast, since allowing Christian Euro-Africans to stay in Osu could threaten the hierarchy of the trading post.

As an example of what might happen if Christian Euro-Africans were allowed to stay at the fort, Lygaard mentioned a Euro-African man from Cape Coast who had been permitted by the Royal African Company to stay after he had been christened. The man had no longer wanted to work for the company but had instead started trading directly with foreign ships on his own account, and "in the end [he] went so far that the Whites were his subjects and the English general could not get a Negro into the fort without this man's permission."[9] Interestingly, as we will see in the following, Lygaard was right that christening would open powerful opportunities for Euro-Africans. Lygaard's fear that Christianity would somehow erase any difference between Euro-Africans and Europeans at the fort—to the point that one would become powerful enough to subvert the power hierarchy—was, on the other hand, not warranted. At Christiansborg the social hierarchy at the fort quite smoothly integrated Euro-Africans in a distinct position, below European assistants and higher-ranking officers and above African "fort slaves."[10]

Sending all Euro-African children away from the coast would not have been a good solution in itself. Sending the children off without their families' consent was not an option, given the need to maintain friendships with African trading partners. Slave ships were the only ships that left the Gold Coast in this period, and it is hard to imagine that Ga and other African families would have been thrilled to see their children embark on European slave ships, whether they were headed for the West Indies or Copenhagen. Ga families in Osu seem to have been adamant that their girls—who could not be hired as soldiers at the fort—were not to work as fort slaves or be sent off to the West Indies. In 1727 Governor Pahl wrote: "To engage them [Euro-African girls] to serve here in the fort and use them as the Company's slaves is something, their black friends [kin] will not permit, nor that they journey to St. Thomas, and it cannot be done by force, since we can only expect palaver and harmful consequences from this."[11] The idea of sending all Euro-African children away could have emerged only at a very early moment of Euro-African interaction on the Gold Coast, when it was still possible to imagine a social hierarchy at the fort that was so clearly based on black and white that the presence of a single Christian Euro-African threatened to subvert the whole system.

As the fort administration developed a clearer stand on the question of Euro-Africans in the community, it became common and uncontroversial practice to hire Euro-Africans at the fort. Presumably, both administration and chaplains were also well aware that the practice of employing Euro-Africans was common in other European trading posts along the coast. At both the Dutch and the English forts, as at the earlier Portuguese and French trading posts, interracial marriages were common, and hiring Euro-Africans as soldiers equally so. However, according to Ludewig Rømer, the Danes were more dedicated to hiring soldiers who were, as he called it, "born under our fort" [meaning that they had Danish fathers] and christened."[12] Over the eighteenth century, the Danish administration and the Danish chaplains continued to negotiate and debate the cassare marriages, whether or not they should be blessed in church, and what to do about the Euro-African children, but most of the time they came to practical compromises that allowed for an integration of Euro-Africans in a well-defined middle position at the fort.

The church at Christiansborg and the fort school, which was established in 1722, were central in developing this specific position for Euro-Africans at the fort. From early on, chaplains at Christiansborg had an interest in and were sometimes in opposition to the cassare practice. While Frantz Boye was governor, for example, when he communicated with the company in Copenhagen about the cassare marriages, he suggested that the chaplains at Christiansborg were making the cassare marriages more complicated than they needed to be, and that "for that reason the English and Dutch nations have no chaplains here on the Coast."[13] Since the Danes had frequent contact with the other European forts only a few miles away, Danish employees were presumably well aware of the practices at these forts, but Boye's comment that the Dutch and English trading companies had decided against sending out chaplains specifically to avoid disruptive questions about employees' relations with African women is more dubious. Both the English East India Company and the Dutch West India Company had chaplains at their trading posts on the Gold Coast at different times in the eighteenth century, so, if Boye was right that there were no chaplains at the other European forts in his time, this was just a temporary situation.[14]

However, as Boye suggested, there does seem to have been a correlation between the presence of chaplains at Christiansborg and the attention paid to interracial sexual relations and marriage. The chaplains, not surprisingly, found the question of interracial intimacy more debatable than did administrators and traders. A congregation's social life was an important part of a chaplain's work, and extramarital sexual relations were a cause for concern in Africa, just as in contemporary Denmark. Throughout the eighteenth century chaplains therefore wrote to their bishops in Denmark about employees' relations with African women. They wrote for consolation or to ask the bishop how they should deal with a specific situation. They wrote about the growing number of children of mixed descent, and from 1722 they wrote about the schooling of these children in the church room at the fort.[15]

Unlike other employees at Christiansborg, the chaplains' work was ideological. They were sent out to oversee and regulate only the Christian congregation's social life and behavior, but in practice they also expected non-Christians at Christiansborg to follow the same set of rules. Whether it was excessive drinking or the use of fetish at Christiansborg that caught the attention of chaplains, they often felt compelled to address the problem, or at least to persuade their employer back in Denmark that they were doing so. The chaplains were sent out on behalf of the ecclesiastical authorities, the Protestant Danish church, and theoretically responded directly to the church and not the company in Copenhagen. In practice, though, daily authority rested entirely with the governor.

The chaplains' role at Christiansborg made them simultaneously central and marginal figures at the fort. In 1734 chaplain Erich Trane portrayed the congregation as "Noah's ark" and as "the ship of Christ until the end of the world" and prayed that God would help him do his work right: "I am all alone in this vast heathen country."[16] Trane was not the only Danish chaplain who felt alone at Christiansborg. Chaplains were outsiders, and they risked both ridicule and disrespect when they sought to enforce Christian norms. Chaplains wrote at length about their health and about the hardships of the job, the church, and the congregation. In the later part of the century several chaplains wrote back to the bishop asking to be relieved soon after they came out. They claimed that the climate was inimical to their constitutions and that they could not survive on the coast; the chaplains' otherness was presumably enhanced by the fact that they were different from most other men at the fort in rank, class, and education.[17] Besides some governors, a few bookkeepers, and later the doctors, the chaplains were the only employees at the fort with university degrees, and in principle the position ranked just below that of governor. Yet despite ridicule and outsider status the chaplains at Christiansborg had an important, though often roundabout, influence on the cassare institution and the hybrid position that Euro-Africans came to inhabit.

Chaplain Elias Svane's response to the marriages and his work on the coast was particularly important in establishing the fort school and a churchly response to the cassare marriages. Svane arrived at Christiansborg in 1721, and after only a few months on the coast he complained to both the bishop of Zealand and the company in Copenhagen about what he perceived to be sinful and disturbing practices at Christiansborg. In 1724, when the total number of employees at Christiansborg was around twenty-five, Svane protested that of the seven who had African wives—the governor, four members of the Secret Council, an assistant, and a soldier—five refused to regard the relationships as marriages in a Christian sense.[18] Svane did not discuss or mention how, when, or why the remaining two Danish men had chosen to have their marriages acknowledged by a Christian chaplain. It is likely that it was

Svane himself who convinced them to get married in the church, but in his letter to the company he paid much more attention to the men who had refused to seek a Christian blessing, because their marriages did not live up to even the basics of what Svane believed to be proper.[19]

Much about these arrangements disturbed Svane. Several of the men had more than one lover at a time, and they had no qualms about ending a marriage with one woman if they became interested in another. Sergeant Christen Hougaard sold his wife to a "Portuguese." Factor Hans Hendrick Sparre had left his wife in Quita and would no longer hear of her. Even the most "god-fearing" of the men plainly declined to take their wives with them when they left the coast, and they showed little or no interest in the education and upbringing of their Euro-African children. Instead, owing to what Svane called "old custom or their own convenience," they simply left their wives and children unsupported on the coast when their employment ended.[20]

Even men whom Svane had personally sought to prevent from cassaring, such as assistant and merchant Reinholt Nielsen Kamp, hastened to do so anyway. According to Svane, Kamp kept his marriage hidden from him right up until the "hasty celebration," when the bride "went from one town to another in her bridal array and finery accompanied by family and friends according to the custom of this country, and came strolling into this fort to be received with ceremony and beheld by all; [and] then he flatly refused always to keep her, and he still stubbornly refuses to do so." Svane presumably meant that Kamp had refused to promise to take his Ga wife with him back to Denmark when his time on the coast was up. Yet Kamp's marriage was clearly sanctioned by the secular administration at Christiansborg. Chaplain Svane appears to have been the only one not invited to the celebration, and after the ceremony Kamp and his bride were received at the fort and "beheld by all."[21]

This isolation of the chaplain from the festivities at the fort may have contributed to what Svane saw as a general mocking of the church. According to him, neither Africans nor Danes had *any* respect for the church, and the company's officials at Christiansborg did nothing to stop the rowdy behavior. Danish employees repeatedly set bad examples for the African slaves and workers at the fort, and Africans and Europeans alike performed fetish inside the fort. Governor David Herrn himself had even used "fetish" to swear in African workers, and when Svane complained to the governor, they had a small argument. In principle Herrn agreed with Svane that fetish was against the Christian religion, but "when someone is taken on as the Company's male or female slave, or if other Negroes must give their word to confirm or deny something, then the use of fetish is indeed necessary, and one cannot do without it."[22]

Svane's failed attempt to get the governor to stop swearing in workers with Ga religious oaths at the fort, and his exclusion from Kamp's wedding party at the fort, suggest the disjunction between secular and church expectations and authority at Christiansborg. If Svane were to have any impact on the social lives of his congregation he would have to conduct a difficult balancing act that accounted for both his religious principles and the practical reality of the slave trade. The company was interested in hiring Euro-Africans as soldiers, but they were first and foremost interested in Africans either as partners in slave trading or as slaves. Danes did not have any institutional means to force their will or culture on their African trading partners, and it was therefore not for the governor or the chaplain to decide which types of oaths were to be sworn when deals were made. Neither was it the chaplains' responsibility to be concerned with converting the local population in Osu—religiously or culturally. They were not sent out with a mandate to missionize and were therefore poorly positioned to persuade the governor or any of the slave traders that they should risk their friendship with African trading partners to achieve religious or moral goals.[23]

In the social climate of Christiansborg, Svane was realistic enough to conclude that interracial relationships were probably unavoidable. It was, after all, in Saint Paul's words "better to marry than to burn," and Svane therefore settled on what he considered the next best solution: to give the marriages a missionary purpose. By holding the Danish men to their Christian marriage vows, the chaplain could ensure that they did their Christian duty and took responsibility for the care and Christian upbringing of their children, and that their African wives were converted to Christianity. If only the men would "enter into their marriages after prior consultation with their chaplain and on good reflection," then much good could in principle come from the unions.[24]

He was also realistic enough to understand that it might be difficult for the Danish men not only to convert their African wives to Christianity, but also to make them give up their "heathen" ways. Danish men at Christiansborg were not exactly in a position to demand of free women in Osu that they should reject their religion and language and assimilate to Danish Christian ways. Svane therefore first suggested that the men buy and marry enslaved women, instead of marrying free African women, "because they could easily take such women with them wherever they wish" without asking their families for permission. Of enslaved women they could also demand that they give up their African religious practices, and hence more easily instruct them in Christianity. Finally, enslaved women could be bought and maintained "at far less cost," since "a female slave can be bought for forty rdl. or a little more at times, but the costume [bridewealth] of a free Negro girl costs far more, especially if she is to have a White [as husband], which makes it more and not less here, since his service and occupation is such as it is here."[25]

In Svane's vision, buying enslaved women and converting them to Christian Danish wives offered an achievable means to fulfilling a vision of domesticating the social world of Christiansborg. He was opposed to many of the social and religious practices that followed from his congregation's lives at Christiansborg, but he was not against slave trading per se. He did not discuss any moral implications of enslavement at all, but perhaps he shared the moral standpoint of many other European chaplains and missionaries in the early modern era: the slave trade could be defended as long as it had a missionary purpose, particularly since many Africans, in the chaplains' opinions, were better off being enslaved and christened.[26]

More than likely, Svane simply had not considered the moral implications of slavery. In the 1720s the Atlantic slave trade was not questioned as it would be half a century later, when generations of knowledge about the horrors of the trade, combined with Enlightenment ideas about liberal freedom amid an intensified slave trade, led to growing criticism. To Svane there would have been nothing inherently disturbing about enslavement. Indeed, as mentioned in Chapter 1, freedom and class were directly linked in Denmark, where poor and even middling farmers were restricted from moving or traveling without permission from the landed nobility.

But Svane's idea that Danish employees would be better off cassaring enslaved women did not display a very good understanding of the social and economic world of Osu. Cassaring a free daughter of a slave trader gave a better advantage in the trade, and this was typically what employees from Christiansborg did. It is possible that some men from Christiansborg were also cassaret to enslaved women, like some European men at the English and Dutch headquarters on the Gold Coast were, but none of the cassare marriages mentioned in the Danish sources were between European men and enslaved African women.[27] The sources on the marriages are sparse, and much happened that was not recorded, but when the status of a woman cassaret to a European man is mentioned it is always a free woman, which suggests both that these marriages were more common in Osu and that such marriages were more important diplomatically in the coastal society. Elias Svane's suggestion that the employees change their ways and marry enslaved women instead of free women also suggests that the latter was the common practice, and presumably this remained the case. Svane was quick to abandon the idea of cassaring slaves.

Svane did not, however, change his position on the marriages' missionary purpose. Like other Danish chaplains of his day, Svane expected the institution of marriage to help both to ensure his congregation's salvation and to regulate their social life. Svane's intent was to replace the African cassare marriages with Christian marriages, and he does not seem to have considered making any exception—for example, allowing for the cassare marriages to be African in ritual and practice or for the marriages to be temporary. Yet Svane's complaints set off a chain of events that led to an ambiguous compromise through which employees at the fort could be cassaret to African women with the blessing of the church. The way that this agreement was reached tells us a great deal about the intersecting, conflicting, but also overlapping interests that African and European traders and chaplains had in the interracial marriages.

Sometime in the 1730s, after Elias Svane had left Africa, the Danish administrators at the fort began referring to a dispensation allowing their employees to enter into temporary marriages with African women with the blessing of the church. Elias Svane never mentioned such a dispensation, but supposedly it had been given to him in a letter from Bishop Worm of Zealand in December 1722. When Svane left the coast in 1726, the story went, this letter was handed over to his successor, Christen Weigaard, and was later found among Weigaard's things when he passed away. After that it circulated on the coast for more than a decade.[28] Even after the putative letter was completely lost or destroyed, a remembered oral version of it lived on in the community as an official acknowledgment that allowed the cassare marriages to be sanctioned in church.

In 1747 chaplain Hans Jensen Flye described how previous chaplains had consecrated the marriages with African women and entered them into the church books. "The custom is such," Flye continued, that not only unmarried men had taken African wives, but also men who admitted to having wives back in Denmark. One said that he had a wife in Copenhagen, but that the company would not let him bring her to Africa, and "not long ago, they say, there were more people here in the same situation."[29] All that Flye's predecessors had done when a Danish employee had "taken a negress" was to publicly announce the union from the pulpit, that "N: had taken a negress of this name, whom he promised to stay with as long as he stays in the country, as long as she behaved and lived well."[30] At least one chaplain before him, Ole Dorph, had entered the couples into the church books. Dorph's successor, Meyer, whom Flye replaced, had not condoned temporary marriages but instead, in vain, tried to discourage the men from marrying African women. Flye concluded that it would probably be impossible to prohibit the cassare marriages, especially since a chaplain seeking to discourage the men would find no support from the administration at the fort.

The secular authorities at Christiansborg had of course unofficially been sanctioning and supporting the cassare marriages for decades, but the church's acceptance meant an opportunity to send Euro-African children to school at Christiansborg and to claim material support from the administration. In short, the dispensation opened the possibility for these children to position themselves as Christian members of the fort community, and given the dispensation's importance for the hybrid Euro-African culture that was to develop around it, it is interesting to follow how it came about.

The original letter from Bishop Worm was, as mentioned, apparently lost. Luckily for this story, in 1731, about nine years after it arrived, the letter was read aloud from the pulpit at the church at Christiansborg in support of a cassare marriage and was then copied in full into the Secret Council's letter copybook. The letter had been kept at Christiansborg for "such occasions," and an occasion had arisen. An employee at the fort, N. J. Bagge, had asked the residing chaplain, Niels Lange, for permission to cassare "a free negress" by the name of Sachiva. Chaplain Lange would not allow the marriage, claiming that Bagge was staying on the coast only for a short while, and Bagge therefore turned to the governor and the Secret Council for support. He promised to stay in the service of the company for three years and asked permission to cassare. The following Sunday assistant Reinholt Nielsen Kamp—who seven years earlier had so offended Svane by insisting on his own temporary cassare marriage—had Bishop Worm's letter to Svane read aloud from the pulpit in support of Bagge's cassaring.[31]

At first, it is hard to see how Bishop Worm's letter could be considered a dispensation permitting the Danish men to marry temporarily in Africa. To the contrary, Worm's words made it very clear that he was *not* in support of temporary marriages or Danish men leaving their wives in Africa. "I can only consider this a disgraceful and ungodly custom," Worm wrote to Svane, concluding that there was no defense for temporary marriages in scripture: "If it is not the heathen wife who leaves the Christian husband, but the man, who should be a Christian, who leaves his heathen wife, then I hold that these marriages, entered in such sinful manners, should not be blessed by you or any other God's servant. . . . For what God has joined together no man, and thereby not themselves, can separate."[32] According to Worm, Danish men who married African women were not to be received at the Lord's table unless their marriages were in accordance with Christian doctrine. The men were to promise to live and die with their wives, and to teach their wives and children about Christianity to ensure their salvation. Men who left their wives on the coast to go back to Denmark and get married again were "hore-karle" (literally "whore-men").[33]

However, after this long and sustained critique Bishop Worm's letter, as copied in the Secret Council's books, ended with a passage that seemed to leave an opening for the practice of the interracial marriages: "God commands that the man shall leave his father and mother and stay with his wife, but nowhere does he allow a man to leave his wife to return to his family and friends, when his wife wants to follow him."[34] This closing, "when his wife wants to follow him," is a much milder and more easily achievable version of the more extraordinary situation Worm had referred to earlier, "if the heathen wife divorces the Christian husband," and it is tempting to suggest that these last few words were added to Bishop Worm's letter by someone who had a more positive attitude toward cassare marriages. The pragmatic words seem oddly appended to the otherwise strong critique of the practice.

It is impossible to say how these words ended up in the last sentence of the letter that assistant Kamp had read aloud from the pulpit in 1731, but there were strong interests in having a church dispensation for the cassare marriages—both from the African families and the secular authorities invested in the slave trade. The Secret Council at Christiansborg may have reached a point where they decided to overrule the ecclesiastical authorities and to decide the matter themselves. Already in 1726, while Svane was still the chaplain at Christiansborg, Governor von Suhm had voiced a critique of letting bishops and chaplains alone decide the policy on interracial marriage. In a general letter to the company, von Suhm noted that other European nations on the Gold Coast had no problem permitting cassare marriages "without further conditions" and that it would be good if the Company could reach some kind of "middle way."[35]

Soon after, a situation arose in which the men at Christiansborg needed a dispensation they could refer to. In 1727 Svane's successor, Chresten

Heiggaard, forbade those of his congregation who were cassaret from taking the sacrament. He even, according to the presiding governor Friderich Pahl, came out publicly against the marriages in a sermon.[36] In response, Pahl explained, the men at Christiansborg offered to "assure the priest, in writing and orally, that they would take the Negresses with them if they would go with them; but if they will not go with them, that they may be free in accordance with the word of God" and that they would marry their wives in the church, if the wives had been christened.[37] The wording of this proposal sounds very much like the last sentence in the copy of Bishop Worm's letter in the letter-copy book: "when his wife wants to follow him." Bishop Worm's response to Svane's letters about the marriages does not suggest that he was about to bend the rules of Christian marriage to accommodate for temporary marriages in Africa, but the last clause, wherever it came from, opened up room for the "middle way" Governor von Suhm had requested.

This compromise reflects the inclination of the administration at Christiansborg to focus on what was practical for the company and their African trading partners. In von Suhm's opinion there was no way the cassare unions could live up to the Christian expectation of a lifelong marriage, since there was "no Negress who will be persuaded to go home [to Europe] with them," and, besides, von Suhm predicted, it would not be in the interest of the company either if the Danish men brought their African wives back to Denmark: "far less would it be welcome in our country." Von Suhm therefore asked chaplain Svane to ask the bishop for details on "what the ecclesiastical rules might have against this," but apparently the bishop did not give von Suhm the answer he wanted. At least he concluded from that answer that the church should not be deciding this matter alone: "it does not seem enough to us that the bishop instructs the chaplain here on this matter, since religion must be enforced by the secular authorities."[38]

The last words in Bishop Worm's letter were soon transformed into a full-fledged dispensation for Danish men to marry African women on a temporary basis. When Danish employees at Christiansborg approached Svane's successor Erich Trane for permission to marry African women in the 1730s, Trane asked them to make three promises: (1) that the husband would teach his wife Christianity, (2) that he would support any children that the union might bring and would educate them in the Christian faith, and (3) that he would publicly ask his wife if she wanted to come along when he left for Europe. Trane ended a letter to Bishop Worm with the remark that he hoped he had understood Worm's letter correctly, but Bishop Worm evidently did not deal with the subject any further before his death in 1737. The dispensation, whatever its origins, gained a long life: Ludewig Rømer's travel account from 1760 mentioned that the men on the coast still referred to a dispensation issued by Bishop Worm.[39]

In his description of the dispensation, Rømer remarked that none of the other Europeans on the Gold Coast employed "such ceremonies."[40] It is not clear what Rømer meant by this, but since it was commonly known that English and Dutch employees were also cassaret to women in Accra according to African marriage practices, Rømer probably meant that other forts did not share the Danish practice of solemnizing these unions in church. If this was what he meant, then he might have been right. The English and Dutch churches were less well established at those trading forts than was the Danish state church at Christiansborg, and English and Dutch chaplains do not seem to have had as established a practice of blessing the ceremonies in church. At least five marriages between Dutch men and African women did take place in the church at Elmina in 1752 and 1753, but this was after Rømer had returned to Copenhagen.[41]

This story of how Elias Svane's and Bishop Worm's negative responses to the cassare marriages led to a dispensation tells us about how the hybrid Euro-African culture was created. A European ideal, imported to the cultural encounter of the slave trade, was adapted and transformed to fit the needs of the African middle ground. Structures of European ideology (in this case religion) were negotiated with and accommodated to the local dynamics of the slave trade. None of the three Atlantic agents—the Euro-African families, the administration, or the chaplains—got all that they wanted, but allowing the temporary marriages turned out to be a practical compromise for all the involved parties. Christian Euro-Africans became part of the social hierarchy at Christiansborg, which satisfied both the administration and the Euro-African families, and the Danish chaplains became directly responsible for the "legitimate" (ægtefødte) Euro-African children of their congregation members. The fort school that followed was an important social institution in the small trading community, and it was central in establishing a unique position for Euro-Africans at the fort and in Osu. Like Anna Sophie and her sisters, generations of Euro-African children were integrated in the fort community and could claim their particular position in the social hierarchy of the Danish slave trade.[42]

This integration of Euro-African children had been central to the chaplains' approach to the cassare marriages from the beginning. Indeed, in his complaints to Denmark, chaplain Elias Svane was only indirectly interested in the cassare marriages; his biggest concern was that the Euro-African children fathered by his Christian congregation would "live here without any enlightenment about God and their own salvation." How, he asked the company directors, would they defend this to the Lord when the time came? To Svane, prohibiting or gaining control over the relationships his congregation had with African women was the first important step in ensuring that the Danish men take responsibility for their children, but he also suggested that the company send out an assistant who could serve as a school teacher. By then the administration was clearly also interested in development of a group of Christian Euro-Africans specifically trained and loyal to the Danish trading company, and they supported the idea of a school for the Euro-African children.

As early as February 1722 Governor David Herrn supported chaplain Svane in taking "all care to ensure that some small Mulattoes, boys and girls, may also be instructed in the true and saving faith."[43] In 1724 Governor von Suhm again assured the company in Copenhagen that the schooling of the Euro-African children, now with a more secular stamp, was a good investment. "The Noble Company can in time expect fruits from them: that you may have the fort manned by soldiers at less cost and by people who are used to this climate." Yet to make sure that the Euro-African soldiers would "serve [the company] faithfully" the governor suggested that a number of them be sent back to Copenhagen for further education in craftsmanship and Christianity and then sent out to Osu again.[44]

It was not quite as easy for the administration to find employment for the Euro-African daughters of employees. As the trading community in Osu expanded during the eighteenth century, the girls often became maids or servants in European or Euro-African households. Yet, to create a separate "tribe" of Euro-Africans to serve the company, as von Suhm had suggested, the women would be equally important as wives of future company employees and as mothers of children at the fort school. In any case, both governor and chaplain thought establishing a school at the fort was a natural course of action, since the children were sons and daughters of Christian fathers. The Danes may have been inspired by their Dutch and English contemporaries on the Gold Coast, who also attempted to establish fort schools in Cape Coast and in Elmina, though their attempts were not as successful as the Danish fort school.[45]

Even though Elias Svane and the other chaplains had no missionary mandate, their work at the fort school did have a missionary purpose. Seen from the perspective of the chaplains, children of Danish employees were members of the congregation, and their upbringing in the Christian faith was the church's responsibility. It was therefore not enough for the chaplains that Danish employees ensured that their African children were christened; the Danish fathers, and hence their chaplains, were also responsible for their children's education and support in general. In 1747 chaplain Flye reported to the bishop about the children's education at the school and complained that the fathers paid very little attention to their children at the fort. Even men who demanded to have their children christened by the chaplain would soon forget their promises and stop seeing to their children's upbringing.[46]

If the chaplains found the Danish fathers insufficiently involved, then the Ga mothers seemed altogether too involved. "They [the fathers] do spend a lot on them and their mothers," chaplain Flye admitted; "but it is impossible to get anywhere with their Christian education since they live with their mothers in Osu and there they learn nothing but the language of the country." The mothers did send their children to school at Christiansborg every day, but, Flye continued, since they could not understand a word of what the teacher was saying, they got far enough only to repeat the letters when the teacher pointed to them. A few boys had learned how to read a little by the age of fourteen or fifteen, but they still did not know the meanings of the words. "And when you speak to them in Danish they just shake their heads and can neither understand the question nor respond to it."[47]

How well the children understood the Christian faith they accepted at their graduation is impossible to say; their confirmation recitals may have been acts of memorization. Elias Svane for one expected that his students be able not only to recite their catechism and other biblical texts, but also to understand the meaning of what they were saying. "Even though they can read and learn all that one sets before them," Svane wrote in 1724, they "unfortunately can understand so little of it." A few of them spoke Danish well enough for Svane to understand them with patience, but very few of the children could confirm their Christian faith in Danish, and Svane was not ready to baptize the children until they were ready to confirm their faith. He wanted to defer "such a highly necessary and precious remedy as Baptism for their spiritual rebirth, the renewal of their lives and the seal on their salvation." Svane's insistence that the children understand the religion they were confirming—in Danish—meant that some of his pupils reached an older age before they were confirmed.[48]

Unlike actual missionaries (such as the Basel mission, which took over the fort school in the nineteenth century), the Danish chaplains were rather unsophisticated in their approach to missionary work. The later missionaries recognized the need to learn African languages, for instance, and they took time to translate the Bible and other religious texts to make them accessible. These earlier Danish chaplains, on the other hand, hypothesized a conversion process in which the children, being isolated as much a possible from their mothers' language and culture, would spontaneously adopt Danish religion and culture as soon as they understood the language. If only the children lived among Danes and spoke Danish, Svane wrote, "then there could hardly be any doubt that the children, since this greatest stone would be rolled from their path, would themselves become desirous of the knowledge of God."[49] The best thing Christians could do to persuade African children or adults to join the Christian congregation was to set a good example for them to follow. Isolating Euro-African children from the influences of Africa would not be an easy enterprise at Christiansborg, but Svane does not seem to have felt very restricted by the immediate impracticalities of his work.

Chaplain Svane would have preferred to have the children taken away from their mothers as soon as they could walk so that they could grow up at the fort. As it was now, the children grew up with their mothers surrounded by "superstition" (Ga religion) and speaking their mother's language, which according to Svane was "the root and birth of all evil and the greatest obstacle to all that is good and godly."[50] Instead Svane wanted both children and teachers to stay inside the fort at all times; they should not eat or sleep in Osu and should avoid contact with people in town as much as possible. Svane considered building a different schoolroom with a yard surrounded by walls high enough that nobody could climb over them "so that the children can stay there both night and day and thus be denied all opportunity of conversing with and mixing with the Blacks."[51]

The point of isolating the children at the fort was not only to prepare them for a religious conversion, but also to foster a broader cultural conversion. Inside the fort the chaplains could ensure that the children and their teachers were "kept to the fear of God and Christian customs, so that nothing should stick to them of the evil and vicious nature and habits of the heathens."[52] In a recognizable Christian missionary manner, Svane suggested that the school instill daily discipline to break the children of their habit of "running around almost like beasts and creatures without reason when they eat and drink." Instead the children were to be carefully supervised during their meals and "their morning, evening and table reading, and they must also be present in the church at the ordinary hours of prayer."[53]

The nature of the slave trade, in which the European traders were dependent on African trading partners, did not, of course, lend itself to a system that kept Christiansborg and Osu strictly separated. To the contrary, the fort and the town community were steadily growing together, with many family and friendship contacts connecting the two communities, and the idea of isolating the children remained but a loose suggestion in the chaplains' letters to their bishop back home. The chaplains would have had no way to force them to attend the school or accept such isolation from African kin. In the case of Elmina, Akan matrilineal family structure can probably explain some families' great influence over the Euro-African children, but in the case of Osu the patrilinear Ga families seem to have had just as much influence over the upbringing of their children. When mothers of Euro-African children sent their children to school at Christiansborg, it must have been (or seemed to be) in their own interest.[54]

The key to understanding the attraction that christening and the school held in the small community is that this institution meant much more than Christian names and clothes. Though it wasn't the physical wall between Christiansborg and Osu that Svane imagined, the school *did* instate a growing cultural and social distinction between Euro-African children, other children growing up in Osu, and Africans at large on the coast. In that sense, the chaplains indirectly provoked a cultural transformation, though not in the way or to the extent that they had intended. Instead, they supplied Christian Danish cultural markers—clothes, words, and practices—which Euro-Africans adopted and made their own.

These cultural markers represented the larger Atlantic world. They represented wealth, power, and trading connections to Europeans: all valuable cultural and social capital on the Gold Coast. These markers came with the schooling, but they could also easily be detached from its European context and develop a life of their own, as apparently happened a few generations later at Cape Coast. When the English missionary Thomas Thompson arrived in Cape Coast in the early 1750s, he found a community of Christian Euro-Africans who considered their European heritage and their Christianity an "honorable distinction," but who showed very little interest in participating in an actual Christian congregation.[55] In that case the European cultural markers signaled belonging in a Euro-African subgroup, which was distinct from church membership.

In Osu, European cultural markers also had a life well beyond the institutions and the culture they represented, but they remained attached to the specific hybrid position that the school and inclusion in the fort congregation made possible. Being able to claim such a position gave people a better chance of being hired at the fort, as well as a better chance of marriage to a high-ranking Danish employee. The fort school may not have lived up to the chaplains' high expectations of cultural conversion, but its pupils did become acquainted with Danish practices. Through the daily routines at the fort, they were socialized in the ways and culture of Danish men—of their fathers and of possible future husbands. In broader terms, the schooling meant inclusion at a higher level of the social hierarchy than for other Africans at the fort and in Osu. Over time Euro-Africans who attended the school got a better-than-average share of European trading goods, trading contacts, wages, and European marriage partners. Euro-African families who intermarried with Europeans developed what we could call a hybrid Euro-African culture, which helped them benefit further from the Atlantic slave trade.

To understand the Ga and Euro-African families' interest in sending their children to the fort school, we should also consider the material support that followed from the schooling. At Christiansborg, the chaplains and their school had more than the ideological backing of the Danish state church and the trading company; they had monetary support as well—an economic incentive that was apparently not part of the plan for the congregation Thompson was setting up in Cape Coast.[56] In the Danish case, entering the fort school and gaining status as Christian Euro-Africans meant more direct access to material resources. For one, mothers who were cassaret to Danish employees and sent their children to school at the fort became eligible for support for themselves and their children from "the poor mulatto children's chest," or simply, the "mulatto chest"—a monetary relief fund that was established around the time that Svane's school at Christiansborg was started in 1722. By 1726 Governor von Suhm suggested that men who had children on the coast should be required to leave a sum of money for their children's support before they returned to Denmark. Three years later, in 1729, Governor Wærøe remarked that he was pleased to hear of the company's support of the idea that the men who took African wives "should set aside something each month from their salary."[57]

For the next 120 years, until the Danes left Christiansborg in 1850, it was a well-established practice for Danish employees at the fort to make payments to the "mulatto chest." In the 1780s Isert described how only men who were cassaret made monthly payments to the fund. When they entered the union and when they left the country they paid a half month's salary, and while on the coast a monthly 4 percent of their salary.[58] Correspondingly, the pay lists from Christiansborg show individual monthly payments to the fund and some employees making extraordinary payments in connection with cassare costume [bridewealth] or the cassare parties. But books from the Secret Council also show that fines for minor offenses were paid to "the poor mulatto children."[59] In the early nineteenth century, when Monrad described the "mulatto chest," all European men employed at the fort made payments to the chest according to their wages, and according to Monrad these funds primarily supported the school run by the chaplain in the new church, though the chest also supported wives of Danish employees and their children. Monrad indicated that the monthly payments to the children were a direct incentive for Africans to cassare Danish employees: "Is a negress so fortunate to give birth to a mulatto child, then she will have her livelihood from this chest until the child is grown."[60]

Other sources imply that the Danish men not only paid to support their African children but also made direct monthly payments to their wives. Governor Friderich Pahl's estate owed his wife, Auchue, fourteen months of "wages," which came to 28 rdl.; Auchue's second Danish husband, surgeon Johan Rudolph Muxol, similarly departed this world owing 4 rdl. "to his negress [Auchue] for two months salary."[61] Half a century later Isert also mentioned that employees supported their wives with monthly dues, and around that time there are also a few references to African and Euro-African women receiving "wages" (gage) for being cassaret to European men.[62] These types of monthly payments to wives are not mentioned as often as payments to the "mulatto chest." However, payments to this chest were drawn from the wages of the employees and are therefore listed in the wage lists, whereas payments made directly to cassare wives may not have been recorded, in which case they may have been more common than it seems.

This monetary support must have made a difference to families in Osu, who most often had no monetary income. In 1747 a chaplain remarked that some women in Osu wanted to send their children to school only if the fort also paid for the children's food during the day. In 1765 chaplain Hagerup suggested that monetary relief could be used to persuade an African wife of a Danish employee to send her daughter Jacobæa to school at Fredensborg.

The girl's mother had been cassaret to a Danish employee who had traveled back to Europe, leaving her pregnant. The mother had taken employment somewhere else for some years but had returned and now lived at Fredensborg. When merchant Bjørn discovered this, he informed Hagerup about it. He then ordered the schoolteacher at the fort, Dressing, to admit the girl to the school, and in case the mother or the family should resist he ordered Bjørn to attend to "food money" as well as clothes for the girl.[63]

The chaplains made distinctions between Euro-African children and other Africans in Osu, but they also emphasized and paid attention to social class difference within the school. Hagerup, for example, described how he wanted the children divided into three groups according to how much support they needed: (1) those who had both father and mother on the coast, who should be supported fully by their parents, (2) those living under "medium" conditions, whom the church would clothe but whose parents were also asked to support them, and (3) those who were "nødlidende" (destitute), who received food, clothes and monthly payments from the chest.[64] And as chaplains like Hagerup distinguished among African children who were deserving of varying degrees of support, schooling, and clothes, they established social distinctions between them. In the small trading community material support of course made a difference, as did the midday food and the clothes. The prestige and privilege attached to and associated with European culture was creating social differences.

Christianity and schooling at the fort gave Euro-African children the opportunity for integration in the fort hierarchy and possible marriage to high-ranking assistants and traders. Christian Petersen Witt might have had these opportunities in mind when he sent his daughters to the school. But claiming this position in the higher ranks in Osu and at the fort might also limit a woman's marriage options. In fact, some families were directly opposed to their children attending the fort school because they thought it would diminish their chances of marrying Danish men. In 1747, for example, chaplain Flye described how some mothers of mixed girls in Osu refused to send them to school, since it would cause their daughters to "waste their happiness" if they went to school and were christened. Some men apparently refused to settle with girls who had attended school and been "brought up" at the fort, since they knew that they would have to marry them in church. According to Flye, several girls who had gone to school while Elias Svane was on the coast had not found any European men to marry and had instead been forced to "take employment" on slave ships that sailed up and down the coast to trade. If a young woman was not christened, on the other hand, and kept living "like a black woman," then she had a much better chance of "being entertained by a white."[65]

This concern is also mentioned in sources from Elmina. In 1746 the African chaplain Jacobus Capitein at Elmina noted that Euro-African girls had a harder time "finding a common-law husband" if they were christened. Likewise, in 1768, chaplain Philip Quaque remarked that the European men employed at Cape Coast Castle feared that they would lose their "wenches" if they were christened. The language of "common-law" wives is not used in the Danish source, and neither is the term "wenches," but there is the same sense that two different types of cassare marriages existed: those between christened Euro-Africans and higher-ranking assistants and traders, which were sanctioned by the church; and those between African or Euro-African women who had not attended the school or been christened and Danish soldiers and other lower-ranking employees at Christiansborg.[66] Only a few marriages fit in the first group, in part because only a small number of Euro-African children attended the fort school. The church efforts to control the marriages, the dispensation, and the church school "caught" only a small number of the Euro-African children; throughout the century there were still many Danish employees who were cassaret or had unofficial relationships with women, without the blessing of the church, and their children often did not attend the school.

For a small group of Euro-Africans, however, it seems that claiming this Euro-African Christian position was both deliberate and crucial. To Christian Petersen Witt, for example, it was of great importance that his daughter be married in church, and he may have had several different reasons to insist on this. For one, Anna Sophie had become pregnant while living with assistant Warberg, and by the time chaplain Niels Lange wrote to the bishop of Zealand and the directors of the trading company in Copenhagen to ask what he was to do in such "casibus," she had given birth to a "beautiful white baby girl." Christian Petersen Witt therefore might have had both religious and practical reasons. He may have believed in what the Danish chaplains had told him about Christian marriage as the only moral way, but he probably also knew how the Danish hierarchy worked and was seeking to ensure that his daughter would have the educational and cultural means to gain a powerful position in the Euro-African slave trade.[67]

Money was also at stake. Witt seems to have presumed that getting married with the chaplain's blessing would give Anna Sophie the right to claim inheritance if her husband should die. Soon after Jørgen Warberg died, Christian Petersen Witt did in fact claim 80 rdl. inheritance from Warberg's estate on behalf of his daughter, on the grounds that the deceased had promised to marry her. The administration wrote to Copenhagen to ask how they should respond to Witt's claim. "It is true enough that she is a free Mulatta, born of a Mulatto father and a Black mother," the administration noted, but this did not automatically make her an heir to her European husband's estate.[68] In the case of Anna Sophie's inheritance the Secret Council requested advice from Copenhagen on what to do. There are no other cases of an African wife mentioned as an heir to her European husband's estate in the sources from Christiansborg before the end of the eighteenth century, when some of the men started mentioning their Euro-African families explicitly in written wills.[69]

With his insistence that Warberg marry Anna Sophie with the blessing of a Christian chaplain, Christian Petersen Witt was trying to secure a particular future for Anna Sophie and her child. Getting married with the church's blessing would distinguish her from both the enslaved Africans in the dungeons at Christiansborg and other Africans in Osu. Such a marriage would also be a ticket to a particularly powerful position in the social hierarchy at Christiansborg. In itself, a rudimentary education in reading the Bible in Danish would probably not have been considered an attractive asset by parents and kin of Euro-African children, but graduating from the fort school with a Christian confirmation gave cultural capital in a world organized around slave trading in the colonial Atlantic system. Cassaring a man from Christiansborg of course meant access to European goods and a profitable trading connection, but from the 1720s on, having the marriage blessed in church could also mean that her children would have access to education and future employment at the fort. She would have financial support for them, and, to a lesser extent, direct support for herself. Such benefits, in theory at least, followed from a cassare marriage only if the woman agreed to adopt Christianity and to send her children to school at the fort. By sending their children to school at Christiansborg, parents and kin in Osu must have hoped and expected that the children would marry higher-ranking Danish assistants and that they would become part of the community at Christiansborg, though, of course, the schooling was not a guarantee of access to European marriage partners.

When Euro-Africans opted to send their children to the fort, they helped the chaplains in their otherwise futile attempts to regulate the social environment at the fort and in Osu. The chaplains' work was based on the same ideological structure of Christian mission that contemporary missionaries brought with them to the Danish West Indies, where their impact on the colonial society was much more immediate. Svane and the other Danish chaplains' efforts shaped the precolonial trading port much more indirectly but in long-term structural ways, as generations of people in Osu attended the fort school and received material support or wages from the administration at Christiansborg. It was a cultural transformation taking place within the ideological and economic structures of the Atlantic plantation system, but it was negotiated in the local world of Osu, and the culture produced was a hybrid.[70]

Inclusion in the congregation at the fort did not mean that Anna Sophie, her sister, her father, or any other Euro-African in Osu was or became "European" or "Europeanized." Anna Sophie attended the church school and was married to employees at the fort, but this did not mean that she lost her ties to her father's or to her mother's kin, or that she stopped being "African." Anna Sophie's mother came from Aprag, a few miles from Osu, by the Dutch fort, and her African kin—there and in Osu—were much more important in shaping both her childhood and her later life than the few Danes at Christiansborg. Indeed, Anna Sophie's personal story, if we follow her for a few more years, suggests that she was at least as well connected outside as inside the Danish fort. Just how hybrid and intermediary her position was comes out clearly in the sources from the 1730s, when Anna Sophie was cassaret to her third Norwegian husband, Cornelius Petersen, and became a central player in the politics of the fort and in a larger political conflict between Osu and Aprag.[71]

Anna Sophie was cassaret to Cornelius Petersen before she turned twenty. Her third marriage was, like her first two, relatively brief, but at least Cornelius stayed in Africa with Anna Sophie for fifteen years, until 1744, when he was charged with attempted mutiny—an accusation he did not deny. The main complaint raised by Sergeant Cornelius Petersen and the other soldiers accused of the mutiny against Governor Billsen was that he had refused to give them their monthly wages in trading goods, as was the custom. Instead he had paid them in *cowries*,[72] which were worth less than goods in the coastal trade. The soldiers, along with "the whole garrison," elected a new governor—first Joost Platfues, who claimed he was too old and declined, then assistant Klein.[73] The mutiny failed, Governor Billsen retained his position, and Cornelius Petersen was charged as one of the main perpetrators of the mutiny. He was arrested but managed to escape to Aprag through the help of Anna Sophie's father, Christian Petersen Witt. In Aprag, Cornelius "ate fetish with the Dutch negroes," who promised to protect him and send him off down the coast instead of turning him in to the Danes. However, as Cornelius Petersen tried to escape he was caught by *remidors* (canoe rowers) from the Danish fort, arrested, brought back to Christiansborg, and later shipped off to the West Indies.[74]

But this was not the end of the story. Anna Sophie was able to use her connections in Aprag to start an armed conflict over her husband's treatment. At the end of December 1744 "the Dutch"—meaning people living in Aprag by the Dutch fort—closed the roads to Osu and demanded to know who had betrayed Cornelius and given him up to the Danes.[75] There were also rumors that Anna Sophie used witchcraft and poison to get her husband freed. In 1748 Friderich Svane claimed that Anna Sophie was "notorious all over the country for her designs on the life of Mr. Billsen and all his supporters" and explained that she had poisoned first Billsen and then several other men to get her husband out of prison.[76] Whether or not Anna Sophie actually went to such lengths to save her husband, rumors of poison make her sound like a powerful woman. Four years later, when Cornelius Petersen showed up in Copenhagen, planning to return to the Gold Coast on "foreign ships," the presiding interim governor Joost Platfues promised he would see to it that Anna Sophie was removed from the area. Platfues did not mention how he was planning to do so while keeping up his connections with her and her kin in Aprag.[77]

It was not Anna Sophie's connection to the church school or her Christianity that made her dangerous to the administration at Christiansborg, but rather her hybrid position with access to both the fort and the African community. She gained access to the fort via her marriages to its employees, and she thereby tied affairs at the fort to her kinship group in Aprag and Osu. But these ties could threaten the power hierarchies within the fort, which in the eyes of its rulers was highly problematic, given that Cornelius was just a mutinous sergeant. In a rare moment, the administration at Christiansborg openly criticized the cassare marriages as they shipped Cornelius Petersen off to the West Indies. Governor Hackenburg, Joost Platfues, and Ludewig Rømer wrote to the company directors in Copenhagen and recommended that in the future they "forbid (for the sake of our successors) any White in the service of the Noble Company to marry a Mulatta or native woman, since they thus become related to our Negroes, and it is dangerous for the government to punish a subordinate as the offense merits if he has such extensive family ties."[78] Ironically, all three members of the Secret Council signing the request to forbid the cassare marriages were themselves cassaret to women in Africa.[79] It seems that such relationships were problematic only when men who were not supposed to be influential at the fort were cassaret to daughters of powerful trading families.

The administration at the fort thereafter sought to control, or at least influence, who was cassaret to whom. Later in the century, for example, Governor Hachsen accused assistant Marcus Svane and assistant Jørgen Sonne of conspiring against him by cassaring "without the prior knowledge of the governor and much against his will and permission."[80] Like Koko's husband, Frantz Boye, and Anna Sophie's husband, Cornelius Petersen, Sonne and Svane had gained powerful positions in the Accra area by cassaring. It was therefore in the administration's interest to seek some control over the cassare marriages. The governor normally had to approve of the marriages. The administration did not seek control over the marriages to ensure that couples lived up to Christian doctrine or expectations, as the chaplains would have liked to see them do, but to ensure that connections with powerful families in Osu and beyond remained with the proper people.[81]

Euro-Africans like Anna Sophie and her father, who had access to the fort and to important kinship groups in Osu and Aprag, inhabited a powerful hybrid position in the cultural encounter of the slave trade. The story of Anna Sophie's husbands is strikingly similar to earlier cassare marriages, such as those of Auchue or Koko, in which African families negotiated and took advantage of the Atlantic slave trade by marrying their daughters to Danish employees. The difference is that while Anna Sophie and her father drew on and situated her in her African kinship network, they simultaneously employed a Danish name, christening, and education at the fort school to position her in the social hierarchy at the fort. She had access to the social and cultural advantages of being connected to the Danish fort, but her position came from being an intermediary with ties to both Africans and Europeans.

Anna Sophie and her kin in Aprag seem to have been particularly powerful in relation to the Danish fort, so it's not surprising that some people in Accra were unhappy with the influence they had. Along with the rumors of poison and witchcraft, after Anna Sophie's third husband was shipped off to the West Indies, Ludewig Rømer also related a story about how Anna Sophie had been rejected by the Labade oracle, Giemawong, to whom she had sought to sacrifice a bottle of brandy. He had not only refused her offering but damned her, saying, "your memory shall be obliterated." The news of this incident had quickly spread to Osu, three-quarters of a mile from Labadi, where "many blacks" told Rømer about it. So many people at Christiansborg knew the story that Anna Sophie did not dare show up at the fort for an entire year—a period during which she may have lived in Aprag.[82]

Because Anna Sophie managed to juggle her connections to Aprag, Osu, and Christiansborg, she and her kin were well situated to invest in the Atlantic slave trade and the larger colonial system it represented. When her kin sent her to school at Christiansborg, when she was christened and wore the European school uniform, her kin gave the chaplains at Christiansborg a chance to influence the community in Osu that they would not otherwise have had. But it was not at all, as Svane may have thought, an inherent superiority in Danish religion and culture that gave the chaplains the power to shape the social world of Osu. If and when Euro-Africans gained power and influence by adopting Christianity and attending the fort school it was thoroughly embedded in the power negotiations and relations of the Gold Coast. The church at Christiansborg represented the larger Danish Atlantic system, which was, in Anna Sophie's lifetime, becoming more profitable and established.

The unequal power relations between Europeans and Africans participating in the Atlantic slave trade are evident in the way some Euro-Africans, like Anna Sophie's father, for example, worked up increasing debts to the European fort. Unlike Koko and her family a generation earlier, Christian Petersen Witt was directly connected to the Danish fort. He was a lifelong employee at the fort. He was first hired as a soldier in 1708 and was later reemployed as drummer in 1718, and he stayed employed at the fort in various positions until he was listed as "pensioner" with 8 rdl. a month in 1753. In 1724 he owed the company 1,120 rdl., which was three times as much as the second largest debtor. He was probably going to be working for the Danes at Christiansborg as long as he stayed in Osu.[83]

Claiming a position in the social hierarchy at the fort gave Euro-Africans access to trade, employment, and material support and advantages, but it also gave them the educational and cultural means to distinguish themselves from other Africans, as people belonging to a specific intermediary group that was both African and European. In return, accepting this position in the European social hierarchy, Euro-Africans became invested in a hybrid culture of specific practices and material possibilities that followed from the slave trade.

This Euro-African hybrid culture was never a full "system" of cultural practices, with distinct language, dialect, or habits. Given another century or two, perhaps it would have been. As it was, it was too young a culture. Even at the end of the century, when Euro-African families lived in European-style stone houses, they lived in ways that would have been more familiar to their African neighbors than to Europeans. In Anna Sophie's generation Euro-African children might have spoken a few Danish words, worn some Danish clothes, and known a few Danish adults (including their fathers, the chaplains, and their teacher at the fort school), but the chaplains constantly complained how little their students understood of the Bible and how they stared with blank expressions when spoken to in Danish, or repeated the chaplain's questions instead of answering them. Perhaps the chaplains were right. It would not be surprising if Anna Sophie and many students after her had only a very rudimentary knowledge of Danish language and culture. Danish had very limited use; Danes themselves relied on the Portuguese lingua franca as well as Ga phrases and practices to get by on the coast.

Yet the markers and distinctions displayed by Euro-Africans in Osu were signs of a developing hybrid culture. The adoption of these markers happened in ways that are familiar to us from anthropological thinking about how culture works; the adoption of European markers of culture was not random, but part of a process in which individuals responded to their social environment, to the hierarchies of power that structured their worlds. It took place in a field of intersecting European economic and religious interests, the slave trade, and the Danish chaplains' religious and cultural doctrine. When the Danish administration preferred to hire Christian Euro-Africans, and Danish chaplains educated and economically supported Euro-Africans because of their European heritage, they borrowed power from these larger economic and religious structures to create a social position, which privileged some Africans and helped them distinguish themselves from other Africans.

Anna Sophie's hybrid position in the slave trade and the hybrid culture that followed was not a product of a well-established, inflexible racial or ethnic hierarchy arriving from the outside. The position was shaped by the unequal power balance of the Atlantic world, and it was created by local practices of slave trading. The choices that Anna Sophie and her father made were far from "open." They were, like all human choices, structured by the social world. Once the slave trade became the motor of the local economy, individuals could choose only how to respond to its structures and conditions. They could not opt out. And within these structures, some families chose to invest in the slave trade, and some—namely those with European heritage and names—could use their heritage to claim a Euro-African position as intermediaries and traders. The cassare marriages of Anna Sophie and her grandparents were central in the creation of her hybrid position. It was a position shaped by European trade and religious interests, but it took place and form in the intricate cultural production of practices and generations of people in the Euro-African marriages and families.[84]

CHAPTER 3

"What in Guinea You Promised Me"

On the morning of the last day of October 1765, sugar refiner Ludewig Ferdinand Rømer had an appointment in the Church of Our Lady Cathedral on Nørregade in Copenhagen. We can imagine him leaving his home in Nyhavn 11 and walking across town rather pleased with himself. Copenhagen was booming. Every year new expensive buildings were being built, and the sugar business that had made him his own fortune was going well, but perhaps he was particularly pleased this morning as he was going to celebrate the christening of his good friend Carl Engman's first daughter, Christina Sophia Engman, and to become one of her godfathers.[1]

He passed by shopkeepers opening their stores and horse-drawn carriages carrying goods and people down to the market squares. The three-story buildings lining the street kept most of the sun out, but this late in the year, at this hour, not much sun would have made it to the street anyway. Perhaps he walked down Gothersgade and passed the building where he rented a room the first time he returned from Osu in 1745. He had been at a low point then: he had lost all of his belongings, including everything he had brought back from Africa, in a shipwreck off the coast of Norway. But he had made his way up from that rented room in the basement under the butcher shop, and been sent back to Christiansborg—this time as senior trader—the following year. When he returned from Africa the second time, in 1749, he was much more successful. Within a few years he had established himself with a wife, a growing family, and a profitable sugar refinery. Now he was about to stand up before God and his countrymen as a man of some importance, side by side with Christina Sophia's other godfather, chamber councilor Johan Friedrich Reindorph.[2]

Reindorph, Engman, and Rømer were publicly bound by their prominence as traders and royal officials, but they also shared an intimate bond that few of the other guests assembled in the cathedral would have been aware of, and about which none would have dared speak openly. All knew that Reindorph and Engman, like Rømer, had both been stationed at Fort Christiansborg on the Gold Coast. Few, or none, would have known that both Engman and Reindorph had been cassaret to the same woman, Ashio-kai Wondo, daughter of Adovi, the most powerful caboceer in Osu. Adovi had first secured his connections to the fort by having Ashiokai cassaret to August Friderich Hackenburg, a successful assistant and trader who served as interim governor at Christiansborg in 1745, then to Engman, and later to Reindorph.[3]

After both men returned to Copenhagen, they must have had much to talk about: sugar prices, politics, news and gossip from the royal court—and slave trading. These were conversations in which many Danes could take part. But the more intimate memories and stories of family and social life in Africa that Johan Reindorph and Carl Engman shared must have been hard for outsiders—those who had not been to Africa—to understand. How, for example, would Carl Engman have explained the sons he left in Africa? Besides being cassaret to Adovi's daughter, he had been cassaret to a Euro-African woman in Osu, with whom he had three sons. As Engman stood there in the cathedral beside his Danish wife and daughter, with his fellow men from the coast standing witness, perhaps he thought about the children who were not there with them. Or perhaps he was so used to living with these distant memories that they were easy to keep at bay. The distance between Osu and Copenhagen was vast, but across the Atlantic distances, families and people remained deeply entangled. When two of Engman's African sons arrived in Copenhagen a decade later, they were probably harder to ignore.[4]

* * *

Euro-African families in Osu invested in and responded to a broader history of an expanding sugar-plantation system in which both Copenhagen and the Danish West Indies played critical roles. Indeed, throughout most of the eighteenth century, the Danish trading posts in Africa were administered by the same companies that controlled the Danish West Indies, and between them, interests, investments, important families, owners, and employees overlapped. The small social institutions of Osu's school and church, along with the rest of the Danish slave trade, and Christiansborg itself, were essentially adjuncts to the plantation colonies in the West Indies, the more profitable parts of Denmark's overseas activities. The not-always-profitable slave trade persisted because it was supported by the Copenhagen backers of the Danish sugar colonies in the West Indies, for which its human commodities were indispensable.

The opportunities that opened for Euro-Africans at Christiansborg during the era of the slave trade did not transfer to this larger Atlantic colonial world. Neither did the family connections. When the men from Christiansborg returned to Europe—many of them to Copenhagen—they did not bring their African wives and children. In a few rare cases employees from Christiansborg brought a son or two back with them or sent for them later, as when Carl Engman's sons came to Copenhagen in 1775. But men never brought their African wives to Denmark, and a look at how these women might have been perceived suggests that an integration of Danish men's families from Osu would have been difficult at best. If and when Africans traveled from the coast to Copenhagen in the eighteenth century, they were no longer seen as equal trading partners or family members, and they needed Danes' and other Europeans' help, support, and protection against the risk of enslavement. They were at least as dependent as their fathers had been when they first arrived in Osu.

In Copenhagen, Atlantic colonial understandings of Africans and their roles in the larger history of plantation production set limits on what actual Africans could and could not do. In the collective pool of knowledge in Copenhagen, information about the slave trade and Africa was mixed with experiences and news about the growing sugar plantations on St. Croix, which meant that specificities of individual African friends and family members was mixed with the generic and deprecating broad category of "negroes" on which the plantation system depended. Particularly as the eighteenth century progressed, African descent of any visible degree became increasingly associated with slavery. In Copenhagen Danes were not under pressure from African trading partners to overlook racial difference and make distinctions along lines of class, ethnic belonging, or heritage. They were, instead, under pressure from the plantation system to strengthen and uphold a clear link between Africans and slavery, which meant that Euro-African wives and children would have been difficult to integrate, whether they had Danish names and heritage or not.

Even employees from Christiansborg, who in Osu considered their African trading partners family and friends, were fully aware that outside the Gold Coast context Africans were much less likely to be considered wives, brothers-in-law, or sons than potentially enslavable subordinates. This did not mean, however, that employees from Christiansborg could simply cut their ties to their African families when they settled in Copenhagen, even if they wanted to. Some brought golden amulets, cowries, brandy, and souvenirs back with them. The lucky ones also came back with wealth. But they all must have returned with memories of the slave trade, of their social worlds in Africa, and of their wives and children. Osu remained present in the lives of Danish employees from Christiansborg long after they returned to Copenhagen.

Moving the focus of this story to Copenhagen, shows how Christiansborg was embedded in a larger material world that was fundamentally unequal. Profits accrued to many actors in the world of the Atlantic slave trade, but most of the wealth flowed in the direction of European capitals such as Copenhagen.[5] Danish traders in Osu were economically and ideologically backed by the relatively powerful state and economy of the Danish crown, the investors in Copenhagen, and the West Indian plantations. In this larger system, Christiansborg's value lay in the access it provided to slaves who could service the more profitable plantation colony. Indeed, over the course of the eighteenth century, the discrepancy between the small profits that flowed from the slave trade itself and the much larger profits to be made from colonial sugar production became still more obvious in the growing Danish sugar industry and in the large and impressive private residences that sprang up in the center of Copenhagen, funded by sugar. Industrial profits from the refinement of sugar contributed in important ways to the industrialization of Copenhagen. African merchant profits from the slave trade, by contrast, were temporary and vulnerable, since they were generally not invested in industrial production or social infrastructure and often spent on luxury goods, weapons, and alcohol (Figure 3).[6]

The profits from sugar production and the prestige of the colonial enterprise meant that the Danish king and investors in colonial companies were willing to subsidize the slave trade, even over decades of losses. Travel writer, slave trader, and later sugar refiner Ludewig Ferdinand Rømer, for one, held that the slave trade, with its assurance of a labor supply, was "the driving power behind the entire West Indian trade" (Figure 4). He was keenly aware of how the "triangular" trade and plantation system had developed and how important the slave trade was to sustain a Danish sugar-producing empire. "Before I go any further," he wrote in his 1760 travel account, "I must first

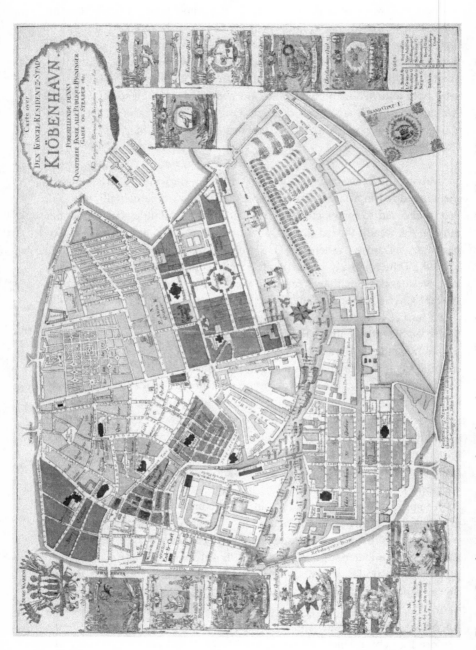

Figure 3. Copenhagen, 1769. During the eighteenth century Copenhagen grew, prospered, and boasted long-distance trading, as this map with an oversized fleet of both warships and trade ships suggests. Royal Library, Copenhagen (Kort- og billedsamlingen).

Figure 4. Ludewig Ferdinand Rømer (1714–76). Frontispiece of his 1760 travel
account. Royal Library, Copenhagen (Kort- og billedsamlingen).

introduce the reader to the Guinean slave trade ... since, without Guinean slaves it would not be possible for us to obtain West Indian products."[7] At first, Rømer explained, Europeans thought the West Indian island colonies could be inhabited by European farmers, but they soon realized that they "died like flies" because of the climate. The European colonial nations were in a dilemma until they found "the perfect solution" in buying African slaves: "This opportunity [buying Africans to work in the plantations in the west] created the great and famous Guinea trade, which has brought many advantages to those nations seriously involved in it."[8]

In Copenhagen those advantages were becoming increasingly visible as sugar production grew in the second half of the eighteenth century. Since the acquisition of St. Croix from France in 1733, the number of sugar plantations under Danish authority had been growing steadily and had created a need for more enslaved labor. Planters and investors in the West Indian plantations complained that the West India and Guinea Company was supplying too few slaves, and West Indian investors pressured the king to dissolve the West India and Guinea Company and turn the trade over to private merchants, who would invest more in it.[9] The king's administration agreed to do a minimum of maintenance and management of the trading post, but to leave the trading itself to private traders. This transfer of authority did not occasion many direct changes at the forts and factories in Africa, but the influence of private interests in the trade meant that the plantations and the slave-trading posts were more directly connected than ever to an increasingly powerful sugar network.[10]

In Copenhagen, that network was not only powerful but intimate, for colonial investors and slave traders never lived far apart. Compared to London, with its one million inhabitants in 1800, the Danish capital was small: only about one hundred thousand at the end of the eighteenth century.[11] But Copenhagen was politically and economically important as the capital and home of the royal court and as a commercial center in a small empire built on trade. It was where the merchants and the investors lived, where most of the merchandise and colonial goods were brought in, and where ships left for Africa and many other corners of the world. Many of the richest and most influential families in Copenhagen were connected to the Danish West Indies and to the slave trade in Africa, and as the eighteenth century progressed these families accumulated a large share of the profits from the trade, from the plantations in the West Indies and from the refining of colonial products in Copenhagen. Inside the crowded city walls everything was within walking distance. The ships leaving for Africa anchored out in Christianshavn, and most men traveling to or from the Danish overseas possessions lived either there or in the city center.

The Danish sugar industry really took off in the second half of the eighteenth century. Until the 1750s the West India and Guinea Company had a monopoly on sugar refining in Denmark, but during an economic boom in the 1740s, when the sugar production on St. Croix expanded substantially, the company's refinery could no longer manage to refine enough of the sugar brought in from the West Indies. After 1750 a few "provincial" sugar refineries were established in Norway and Denmark, but all sugar refining was still to be kept in Danish hands, and all import of foreign raw sugar was forbidden. In short order the Board of Commerce judged that the sugar industry was now well enough established that it would benefit from allowing investors to establish more sugar refineries, and the company's monopoly on sugar refining in Copenhagen was lifted in 1754. In the century to follow, sugar production was tremendously important for the economic development of the city. At times the export of refined and unrefined sugar made up 80–90 percent of the net worth of all exports of industrial products from Copenhagen, and profits from sugar became the primary capital for many important commercial houses in the city.[12]

Ludewig Rømer's story, like Frantz Boye's, demonstrates how connections in both Africa and Europe could ensure a powerful position in the Atlantic world. Rømer was one of the first to open a private sugar refinery when the monopoly was lifted in 1754. He had returned to Copenhagen from the coast in 1749, married Anna Catherine Wedderkamp, the nineteen-year-old Danish daughter of a municipal surgeon, and had a son, George Friderick Rømer, who was christened in St. Petri in Copenhagen in 1752. In the following years he and Anna Catherine had a total of fourteen children. Even as he became a central figure in the trading and sugar circles in Denmark, though, he maintained connections with Osu, sending gifts and letters to old friends and trading partners. Rømer's expertise in the slave trade made him his first profits and taught him the centrality of the trade in humans to uphold the sugar-producing economy. Later on, as a successful sugar refiner in Copenhagen, his connections both to investors in the West India and Guinea Company and to chamber councilors in Frederik V's administration helped him succeed in the capital of the small Danish Atlantic world.[13]

A subculture of former and future employees from the overseas trading posts and colonies soon developed in Copenhagen. Some had grown up in the city, others in smaller Danish merchant towns, and the rest in the country or in smaller towns or villages. Many, like Ludewig Rømer, who was originally from Oldenburg, settled there when they returned from their overseas employment.[14] In any case, they all came through the city on their way to Africa, and the economic boom in the second half of the eighteenth century, which Danish historians have termed "the flourishing [*florrissant*] trading era," attracted people from near and far.[15] Soldiers met sailors in pubs, while company assistants, merchants, and planters frequented the same wine bars in Christianshavn, Nyhavn, or Nyboder. Younger sons and nephews of West Indian planters might become surgeons or chaplains at Christiansborg, and men who had stood a term in Africa would later take employment in the Danish West Indies, in another of the Danish overseas possessions—Norway, Iceland, Greenland, Trankebar in India—or, if they had done well enough, in the administration in Denmark. In between assignments or when they had left overseas service, company employees from Africa settled in the same streets as employees from the West Indies and married into the same families, or as Ludewig Rømer put it: "Our governors marry the widows or daughters of rich planters."[16] It does not seem to have mattered much that many of these men returning from Africa were already married and had children in Osu. At least not on the surface.

Returning from Africa and marrying into Danish families was of course easier when African wives of Danish employees did not come back with their husbands, and that alone goes a long way toward explaining why no African wives came to Copenhagen. As we have seen, the men at Christiansborg were supposed to ask their African wives if they wanted to go with them when they left the coast, but there are no references to Danish men actually doing so, and no evidence of women from Osu coming to Copenhagen at all. In the case of employees who were already married in Denmark and had taken a second wife in Africa, it would of course have been problematic to bring a second wife back to Copenhagen, since both bigamy and adultery were grounds for divorce in eighteenth-century Denmark. But in the case of men who were married for the first time in Africa—which was the case for most of the men who were cassaret in Osu—we must look for other explanations for why African wives did not come to Copenhagen.

It seems likely that African wives were simply uninterested in going or indeed refused to go, and that their kin would have been against them going. One English source from Cape Coast Castle suggests that African wives of

European employees were unenthusiastic about following their husbands to Europe. In his travel account from 1735 John Atkins reported how an English governor in Cape Coast wanted to take his "consa" (as the English called an African wife) back to England with him. Atkins noted that Africans at Cape Coast considered a consa a temporary wife, and that the women normally were not obliged to follow their husbands back to England, "which is looked on as Slavery." In what sense people on the Gold Coast considered it a form of slavery to require consa wives to follow their English husbands back to England is not self-evident. Did Atkins mean that they associated the immediate act of boarding a slave ship to travel to Europe with slavery? This would make sense, given that it must have evoked frightening associations to board these ships—most Africans did not return once they were on board a European slaver. Or was it, more generally, the prospect of a European man taking his African wife away from her kinship group?[17]

In the specific case that Atkins was describing, the governor had actually asked his African wife to follow him back to England, but she refused to go. Even the fact that the governor was going to take their four children with him could not persuade her to follow them. Atkins did not mention whether she also associated following her husband to England with slavery; instead, he reported her reasoning as if she were afraid of being culturally out of place in her husband's home country. Wearing African clothes, "always barefoot and fetished with Chains and Gobbets of Gold," and not knowing "how to comport her self with new and strange conversation," Atkins explained, she feared that she would be out of place in England and that her awkwardness would alienate her husband from her once they were back in his home country.[18]

Atkins's anecdote offers a unique glimpse—albeit at a remove—into the thinking of a Euro-African woman, who was aware of the cultural distance between the Gold Coast and northern Europe, and who had thought about what transitioning to such a different English culture would mean for her and for her relationship with her husband. Her clothes, her jewelry, her trouble "comporting" herself in conversations and company would make her integration in English society complicated. She seems to have been well aware that clothes that in Gold Coast society marked her as European or different from other Africans did not make her English enough to pass in England.

As Ga women had been living with European men for generations, many other women on the Gold Coast probably gave thought to what it would mean to follow a European man to his home. Did many of them similarly recognize their intermediate position as different from other Africans and yet not at all European? What did they think about that faraway world that their European husbands, and sometimes sons, traveled to and often did not return from? It would not be surprising if they were hesitant, but the lack of other references to what eighteenth-century Euro-African women thought of traveling to Europe with their husbands discourages generalization.

It is also likely that Danish men resisted bringing their African wives to Copenhagen and that it would have been difficult for them to settle in the city with their African families. A few Africans, enslaved and free, did end up in Copenhagen, and their stories give a sense of how difficult it might have been for Danish men to imagine bringing their African families home, as well as why African women might have been hesitant to go. The fact was that Africans would not have been easy to integrate in the city. Recall, from the previous chapter, how one governor from Christiansborg already in 1726 plainly dismissed the thought of African wives coming back with the men, since, in his opinion, neither the company nor the general opinion in Denmark was in favor of Africans. It would, Governor Suhm wrote, "hardly be to the advantage of the Company . . . if Negresses were dragged home with the ships; far less would it be welcome in our country."[19] Judging from how hesitant the company was to pay for employees to bring their Danish wives to Africa, they would probably also have resisted supporting African wives of their employees in returning to Denmark. The governor's larger claim that the African wives would not be welcome in Denmark is even more interesting. How would the general population of Copenhagen have received African or Euro-African wives in the eighteenth century?

The number of Africans of any status or descent in Copenhagen was never great, but there appear to have been more people of African descent within the medieval city walls of the eighteenth-century city than ever before or for a long time after. Many people, both Europeans and Africans, stayed only for short periods in Copenhagen before they left for other Atlantic shores. Employees from Africa often sailed back to Denmark via slave ships bound for the West Indies, where some stayed for a time before continuing home on ships loaded with sugar or other goods bound for Copenhagen. Popular perception has it that European ships sailed in a triangle between the three continents, but few Danish ships actually sailed a triangular route from Copenhagen to Africa, on to the West Indies, and then back to Copenhagen. Ships sailing between Africa and America seldom sailed to Europe; by the eighteenth century slave ships were specialized in carrying imprisoned human cargo and would have been less practical for sugar transport. People, however, often sailed on one ship from the Gold Coast to the Danish West Indies, then from there boarded a different ship to Copenhagen, and finally sailed the last leg back to Africa on a third ship. Soldiers from Christiansborg were employed as sailors on slave ships on their way across, and employees returned to Copenhagen by the way of the West Indies, which meant that a number of people from both Africa and the West Indies ended up in Copenhagen.[20]

One man from Osu who came to Copenhagen was Anna Sophie's father, Christian Petersen Witt, and his story suggests some of ways that Africans— Euro-African or not—traveled the Atlantic world under different conditions than Europeans. Unlike Frantz Boye, who maneuvered rather smoothly in the Atlantic system, getting married in England on the way back to Copenhagen, and returning to Africa several times, Christian Petersen Witt had trouble even getting started. He asked the Secret Council at Christiansborg for permission to travel to Denmark many times, without success, before Governor Wærøe announced to the company in 1730 that he would send Witt to Copenhagen: "A mulatto who was born here below the fort and who has served the Noble Company as a soldier and lance-corporal for thirty years . . . has previously often applied to the governors for permission to travel to the home country and return again with the first ship. . . . Since he has once more requested the same thing from the governor and the Secret Council, it has been permitted him, because he is an old man and has always been used in the palavers of Whites and Blacks here at the fort."[21] The governor's idea was that Christian Petersen Witt could serve as a type of ambassador from the coast and tell the company in Copenhagen all they wanted to know about the trade. "He also has a good memory," the governor added, and he proposed that Witt would be able to tell them all about the fort "since the Company first got here until today."[22] He was to be given 4 rdl. a month while traveling and in Copenhagen, and Wærøe felt that there was no risk of Witt staying in Europe, since he was married and had two daughters in Osu. It is fascinating to ponder what Witt could have told about growing up in Osu in the early eighteenth century, but unfortunately in 1733 Governor Wærøe remarked to the company that he was surprised that Witt had not been of greater help to them.[23]

When two of Carl Engman's three African sons were sent to Copenhagen from Osu in 1775, it was with the explicit purpose of serving the company: they were to "learn a profession" and then return to Osu. According to a general letter from the Secret Council, the two boys traveled along with one of former governor Hackenburg's sons, hired as sailors on the Danish slave ship going from Osu to the Danish West Indies. The letter from the council explained: "Since there is a great deficiency of manpower on the snow Ada's crew, they were required to let the mulattos travel with the ship, to do service on the way."[24] They came to Copenhagen in part because they were the sons of former governors, but primarily because of the service they would be able to render the company, both during their passage and after their return to Osu as skilled workers, after learning "a profession."[25]

It would be interesting to know how Carl Engman and his Danish wife and daughters received the two Engman sons from Osu. They did not live in the Engman household in the census from 1787, but at that point Carl Engman had passed, and his widow lived with her unmarried daughters, two "renting" women, one of whom must have been an older sister, and two maids.[26] Perhaps the Engman sons were taken in by Rømer to work in his sugar refinery. Or maybe they lived somewhere else during their stay in Copenhagen. Chances are that their integration in Copenhagen was not so smooth, though similar examples of sons of Euro-African descent coming to England from Jamaica, for example, show that sometimes families were quite ready to welcome their mixed relatives from overseas. But there does seem to have been a certain hesitation in speaking too openly about Euro-African sons brought to Copenhagen.[27]

In 1763, for example, Ludewig Ferdinand Rømer requested permission from the Chamber of Customs to have a Euro-African boy by the name of Ludewig Ferdinand sent to Copenhagen. It is tempting to suggest that this Euro-African boy was Rømer's son, even though he himself described the boy as a fatherless child whom he had adopted and educated in Christianity. The names they have in common is the first hint. Rømer's first son born in Copenhagen was also given his name. The names alone would not be enough; it was not unheard of that African children adopted by Danish men took their names, as Friderich Pedersen Svane was named after his teacher and chaplain Elias Svane. But there are indications that Rømer was cassaret and had children in Africa. In his "relation" of 1748 Friderich Pedersen Svane, for example, claimed that Rømer, "after putting aside his former Negress, has taken a Mulatta for himself."[28] Given that most other traders who stayed as long and were as successful as Rømer had relationships with women in Osu, it is a possibility. In his own travel account, when Rømer claimed that everyone had a wife in Africa, he did not leave himself out. Perhaps a final indication that Ludewig Rømer left descendants in Africa is the fact that there was still a man named Ludewig Rømer in Osu in the 1830s.[29]

The Secret Council at Christiansborg openly announced that Engman and Hackenburg's sons were sent to Copenhagen, but even then they did not primarily come to the city to be reunited with their Danish fathers or families. They came because they could be of good service to the company. This was also the case for the better-known examples of Christian Protten and Friderich Svane, two Euro-African boys who came to Copenhagen from Osu in 1727 with their teacher Elias Svane. (Friderich Svane had been given his teacher's name but was not Elias Svane's son; his father was a soldier at Christiansborg.) These boys were brought to Denmark to be trained in Christianity to then be sent back to Osu as teachers. Both Friderich Svane and Christian Protten came from important families in Osu, and how the Danes at Christiansborg justified sending them off without their families' permission is not clear, nor is it clear if there were any repercussions. According to Protten, his family did not let him go voluntarily. When he was rowed out to the ship they stood on the beach hoping that the canoe would sink and he would come back.[30]

In any case, when the two boys arrived in Copenhagen they were, like other Africans arriving in Europe in the early modern period, perceived as exotic and different. Both of them later added "Africanus" to their names, and there is nothing that suggests that they simply blended into the city and passed for white, as Rask suggested happened to Verville earlier in the eighteenth century. Indeed, they are supposed to have been baptized in the Garrison Church in Copenhagen in 1727, soon after they arrived, in what must have been a publicized and well attended event, since the Danish king was serving as witness (godfather). Later in the century a number of such ceremonial baptisms of people from Danish trading posts and colonies took place in Copenhagen. Whether the persons being baptized were from the West Indies, Tranquebar, or Africa, their darker skin color and, presumably, their subaltern status in relation to the people who had brought them to Europe led to these broad and generalizing strokes in the public announcements of their baptisms.[31]

Christian Protten and Friderich Svane's individual life stories indicate that living in an intermediate space between Africans and Europeans was not quite as easy in Copenhagen as it was in Osu. They both studied theology at Copenhagen University and lived at Regensen, one of the university's dormitories. Svane was sent back to Osu in 1735, while Protten stayed in Copenhagen a time longer, met up with a Moravian missionary, Count Zinzendorf, and joined their mission. A few years later he ended up as teacher at the fort school at Christiansborg anyway, but was then called back to Europe by the Moravian mission in 1741, and in 1746 he was married to another Moravian missionary, Rebecca, who was a West Indian widow of a German missionary (Figure 5). In the years following, Protten traveled between Europe and Africa several times. His second term as teacher at the fort school ended when he accidently shot one of his pupils, but he was rehired a third time after pleading his case in Copenhagen.[32]

In his 1764 application to be sent out as teacher a third time, Protten described the Euro-African children at the fort as "this lineage [*slægt*] [that] is neither Christian nor Heathen, but like the color a mix of both." This seems to be an apt description of the children at the fort, many of whom would grow up to be (like the successful Anna Sophie) connected to and situated in both European and African religion and culture. But perhaps it was as much a description of Christian Protten himself, and of Friderich Svane, who never stopped being African—even when they were fully embedded in the Christian church and the Moravian mission. The word "neither" that he used in this quote is important in that case. How can a mix of both end up being neither of the two? Euro-African Christian Protten does not seem to have been very at peace with himself in Copenhagen in the 1730s and 1740s. Even in Osu, Protten was not easily integrated when he returned. Late in his life he had a series of conflicts with Governor Resch and Esau Quist—once when he refused to move from the rooms he occupied at the fort to some other rooms, and again when he was arrested for shooting in Osu in the night and threatened the governor—and the last years before he died in 1769 were rather troubled.[33]

Friderich Svane's life was not much easier. After graduating with a degree in theology he married a Danish woman, Catharina Marie Badtz, daughter of a cabinetmaker, and went to Osu to teach at the fort school from 1735 to 1746. According to his long "declaration" about his time at the fort, he arrived to find his mother, sisters, and brothers in a "poor and miserable condition," needing more help from him than he could expect in return. At first he did not have a job at the fort, but his Danish wife, who, again according to him, had not been brought up to "idleness and laziness," immediately started to work. The following year he was hired as catechist at the fort and stayed in that position until he fell out with Governor Christian Glop Dorph, and ended up being arrested and sitting in "the black hole" (the dungeon) for half a year in 1742–43. In 1746 he returned to Denmark, where Elias Svane helped him obtain a position as teacher and catechist in a small town on Zealand,

Figure 5. Christian (1715–69) and Rebecca (1718–89) Protten with their daughter
Anna Maria, born in 1750. Painted by Johann Valentin Haidt, ca. 1751.
Unity Archives, Herrnhut.

not far from Sorterup, where Elias Svane was chaplain. In that position Friderich Svane had a number of conflicts with both the chaplain and the bishop
he worked for. In 1757 his only son died, and in 1770, when he was fifty-seven
years old, he applied to be sent to Osu again as missionary. He did not get
permission to go and stayed in his position as catechist in Havrebjerg until he
was too blind to work in 1785. He died a few years later.[34]

Though it is difficult from this brief sketch of the lives of Christian Protten
and Friderich Svane to judge how Euro-Africans were perceived and positioned in Copenhagen, it is clear that their intermediate position in the Danish metropole did not make them either as useful or as privileged as
Euro-Africans who remained in Osu. Euro-African women—wives or
daughters—would presumably have been similarly unable to transfer their

important positions in Osu to the larger Atlantic world. When Africans traveled in the Atlantic world Europeans met them with very different expectations and assumptions than they were met with in the local trading encounters on the Gold Coast. Beyond the immediate circumstances of Gold Coast trading society, they could not as easily be friends, trading partners, or kin.

The ever-tighter Atlantic connection between blackness and slavery restricted Europeans' imagination of the roles Africans could play. In Copenhagen, Danish investments in a colonial system were specifically tying meanings of power, sugar, and wealth to Africa and to Africans. Europeans had made links between slavery and blackness long before the eighteenth century, which influenced early European participation in enslaving Africans. But the period of Atlantic slavery was also marked by an ever-deepening linkage of slavery and blackness, and this process happened not only on European slave ships, but in European art, literature, and travel accounts, and in every corner of the Atlantic touched or affected by the Atlantic slave trade and plantation system. In short, the pressure from Atlantic European assumptions of a correlation between blackness and slavery was increasing in the eighteenth century, and in Copenhagen this meant that visiting Africans were likely to be associated with slavery.[35]

When Africans traveled the Atlantic world they were therefore under pressure to prove that they were not slaves. Consider the case of one Quau from Osu, who "presented his fate [skæbne]" in a letter to King Frederik V in 1760. Quau was a nephew of the broker Soya and had served as a soldier at Christiansborg, until he was accused of stealing a pair of silver buckles. He offered to "eat fetish" to prove his innocence, but the administration turned down his proposal. Instead, even though his uncle Soya offered to replace him with two slaves, the Danes at Christiansborg sold him to a slave ship bound for the West Indies. Luckily, Soya convinced a Danish merchant to buy Quau for him and bring him to Copenhagen, which is how the young man came to implore King Frederik V to take pity on him, buy his freedom, grant him a small stipend for food and shelter, and allow him free passage back to Africa.[36] Quau's request was apparently successful, since the following year Ludewig Rømer thanked the king for having "freed" Quau and giving him a weekly allowance while in Copenhagen. Still, even though Quau—as he pointed out in his letter to the king—had not only been living as a "free subject" in Osu, came from an important family on the coast, and was himself a "big man," his fate in Copenhagen remained less than perfectly secure. On Quau's behalf, Rømer requested that the king give Quau written proof that he was now a free man, as if he were in constant danger of having his freedom taken away again.[37]

One of the cultural practices that helped attach meaning to blackness in the minds of people in Copenhagen—particularly the better-off merchants and colonists with connections to the royal court—was the established tradition of including a black slave, servant, or attendant in royal or aristocratic portraits. Commissioning portraits with black slaves became increasingly popular in Europe from around the mid-seventeenth century, signaling prestige, wealth, colonial expansion, and powerful whiteness in opposition to black servitude. In the seventeenth century Queen Anne was famously painted in England with a black groom, and by the eighteenth century, the practice was well established in Copenhagen (Figure 6).[38]

In the second half of the eighteenth century, slavery was also discursively associated with blackness through the emerging debate about the morality of the Atlantic slave trade. Unlike earlier in the century, when Elias Svane unapologetically proposed that his congregation at Christiansborg marry enslaved women who could be more easily converted to Christian religion and culture, some voices were beginning to question the morality of the slave trade. This led others to feel that they needed to justify the trade. We can see how this debate contributed to the link between slavery and blackness in a foreword that bishop and professor of theology Erik Pontoppidan wrote for Ludewig Rømer's 1760 travel account. Responding to "a certain Christian-minded person of rank" who had recently revealed "serious doubts" about the Christian morality of the slave trade, Pontoppidan admitted, "It might seem that the spirit of Christianity would not permit the practice of trade in human beings created, just as we are, in the image of God," but then he went on to make a case for the moral virtue of bringing enslaved Africans to the West Indies. Pontoppidan's argument, familiar from eighteenth-century abolition debates, centered on Atlantic slavery as a way to help Africans to gain what Europeans perceived to be a better understanding of God, to be "liberated in Christ," and to earn a generally better life in the West Indies.[39]

Similar debates about the morality of the slave trade would of course eventually lead to the demise of the trade, but in the meantime it also contributed to linking blackness to slavery in the minds of Europeans. As both sides debated "the nature of Africans" and whether "Africans" were better off on one or the other side of the Atlantic, Danes and other Europeans were

Figure 6. King Christian VI's daughter Princess Louise of Denmark with Ernst
Ludwig Andrea, a young boy from the Danish West Indies, 1749. De Danske Kongers
Kronologiske Samling, Rosenborg Castle, Denmark.

learning about Africa and, in the process, collapsing all black people they heard of or saw in the streets of Europe into one large category: "the negro." Such a broad category was not disturbed by intimate and familiar relations that Danes forged in Africa, at least so long as these were not brought back to Denmark. An African wife or child, avowed as such by a prominent Danish man, might present difficulties. But salacious rumors about such men's social lives in Africa could probably circulate in Copenhagen without fundamentally challenging the overall Atlantic perception of Africans.

It appears that the Secret Council at Christiansborg was not particularly worried that rumors about interracial intimacy in Africa were circulating in Copenhagen. One rumor, for example, revealed that Christian Jessen had a child with an African woman. In 1750 this rumor caused Jessen's Danish wife, Charlotta Sophia Amalia Schwier Jessen, to write to the Danish king, seeking permission to divorce Jessen. To get a divorce she needed to prove her husband's infidelity, and she therefore wrote to the administration at Christiansborg in Africa requesting the necessary evidence: "It is unfortunately notoriously known that my husband Christian Jessen . . . has procreated a child with a mooress," she began her letter, and she asked that the administration secure a statement from Jessen about the case, as well as a document from the midwife who received the child and a transcript from the church book proving that Jessen was the child's designated father.[40]

The administration's answer to Charlotta Schwier was rather mocking. After Jessen signed the forwarded summons he was allowed to repatriate if he wanted to, but he instead requested to stay in Africa. As to the documentary proof she had asked for, the administration replied that a transcript from the church book was impossible, since there had been no chaplain at the fort at the time, and it was not even certain whether the child had been baptized. A certificate from the midwife was equally unobtainable, since "it was a black [midwife] . . . and no testimony can be taken from this woman without, according to their country's customs, eating fetish, which is considered unnecessary, since Jessen has already confessed."[41] Subsequent letters from Christiansborg do not mention the case any further, and Jessen apparently suffered no punishment from the company for having a child out of wedlock. To the contrary, a year after his wife's letter to the administration Jessen was promoted to chief assistant and third voice in the Secret Council, since he had always behaved "properly and well."[42] The case of Jessen's wife indicates that knowledge about intimate relations among Danish men and African women was part of the larger circulation of rumors and information in

Copenhagen. Osu was becoming an integrated part of Copenhagen con-
sciousness, often in indirect ways.

Outside Africa in other corners of the Atlantic world, Africans and Europeans seldom met as equal trading partners, and African women were not
considered proper or even possible marriage partners. Copenhagen represented a very different local Atlantic context than Osu, and by following the
men back to where they came from, we might better understand the nature
of the pressure that the Atlantic system put on Osu in the shape of racial hierarchies. In Copenhagen, Atlantic versions of what racial difference should
mean overpowered Gold Coast distinctions between free and enslaved based
on ethnicity and class rather than race.

We see the clash of different perspectives most clearly when the Danish
slave traders left the Gold Coast and had to translate or defend the positions
they took in Africa and tried to get the administration in Copenhagen to
understand how Europeans should act when they were slave trading in Africa. Diplomatic concerns of the slave traders were not always easily understood in Copenhagen, and European slave traders living in both European
and African contexts shifted between African and European ways of making
distinctions between Africans. As traders in Africa, they routinely distinguished among Africans belonging to different social groups, but in Copenhagen they at times collapsed all Africans into a large, undistinguished
category of "negroes" or "Africans" and seemed to forget those previously
crucial social distinctions.

This difference between the Gold Coast and Copenhagen becomes clear
in a number of cases where Danish slave traders defended their African trading partners in confrontations with European slave ship captains. According
to the "local" Danish slave traders, captains, who were in Africa only until
their ships were loaded with enslaved Africans, could be inconsiderate or directly rude when dealing with Africans. Traders therefore asked the company
to ensure that captains behaved diplomatically when dealing with African
traders. Even smaller disagreements with African traders could harm the
trade. As Governor Joost Platfues put it when he complained about two captains in 1749, "we would not dare to report such trivial matters if they did not
have such a great influence on our trade."[43]

On the coast of Africa, where the trade depended on maintaining good
relations with Africans, treating African caboceers properly when they came
on board a Danish ship was a must, and this was apparently what Captain

Erichsen had failed to do. According to Governor Platfues and two other ex-perienced traders, Erichsen received a caboceer, Qvansang, on his ship when he was at anchor about eight miles from Christiansborg. The caboceer re-ported to Captain Erichsen that he had millet and a couple of slaves for sale, but while the two traders were meeting on the Danish slave ship, Captain Erichsen falsely accused Qvansang of stealing from him, even drawing his sword and threatening to kill the caboceer if he did not return the stolen goods. In his letter of defense Captain Erichsen objected to the accusations and told a different version of the incident, in which the captain held that he never had the slightest controversy with "any negroe," but to the contrary al-ways parted in friendship.[44]

In this case, the traders took Qvansang's side. Platfues, Engman, and Rømer requested that, in the future, directors make sure that captains in Africa "treat a negroe like a negroe."[45] In postcolonial times this request sounds like an injunction to Europeans to keep Africans in a subordinate position, but in the context of trade on the Gold Coast it meant rather that Europeans dealing with Africans along the West African coast should be more culturally adept than captain Erichsen had been and deal appropri-ately with African trading partners. Threatening to kill an African trading partner with a drawn sword because he might have stolen a handkerchief was not good practice.[46]

Platfues's complaint about Erichsen and the captain's defense demon-strate the traders' closer relationship with African traders. In the letter from the traders Qvansang is mentioned several times, and they refer to him as "Caboceer Qvansang himself," which suggests that they saw him as an im-portant person on the coast. In Erichsen's response to the complaint, by con-trast, neither he nor two witnesses from his ship could remember the caboceer's name. They recounted how "the negroes" had claimed that the man was a caboceer and a big man on the coast but left some doubt as to whether he was actually important.[47] To Captain Erichsen, threatening Cabo-ceer Qvansang was an event of little consequence—an anonymous dispute with a nameless African. In the context of the Atlantic system, in which slave ship captains were supplying sugar plantations on St. Croix with enslaved labor from Africa, it was much more common to use impersonal racial cate-gories such as "the negroes" to describe Africans. Captains may have been somewhat more diplomatic when trading on the African coast, but once they left Africa they were in charge of a "floating dungeon," all of whose prisoners were Africans.[48]

To Danes at Christiansborg, on the other hand, Africans remained in a wide variety of relations: trading partners and competitors, slaves, wives, relations, friends, sons, and daughters. In this context, racial distinctions that drew the line simply between white and black and thereby allowed for grouping all Africans together in one category were not functional. It is therefore puzzling that the traders would fall back on a category like "a negroe" in their remark about "treating a negroe like a negroe." In the context of Christiansborg, there were many ways to treat Africans; why didn't they request that the captains should treat a caboceer like a caboceer? They had no trouble being specific about Qvansang in the rest of their letter. The answer could be that when the traders employed this generalizing category, "a negro," they were addressing the Chamber of Customs in Copenhagen, and for that purpose finer distinctions between Africans were not necessary. They knew the expectations and rules of both Osu and Copenhagen.

When Danes left Christiansborg they entered a sphere in which making generalizing statements about "the negroe" was common practice. In a similar way Ludewig Rømer occasionally employed a large undistinguished category covering all Africans in his travel account from 1760. In general he was very aware of Gold Coast differences between free and "enslavable," as described in Chapter 1. But in his travel account, which was written for the reading public in Europe who did not know much about the Gold Coast, he sometimes described the slave trade in ways that would have made more sense for Europeans than Africans. He referred, for example, to a conversation about the slave trade that he had with an old man in Osu. The old man said: "It is you, you Whites . . . who have brought all the evil among us. Indeed, would we have sold one another if you, as purchasers, had not come to us? The desire we have for your fascinating goods and your brandy, bring it to pass that one brother cannot trust the other, nor one friend another. Indeed, a father hardly his own son!"[49]

This fascinating and rare "direct" quote from an African trading partner in Osu probably says more about Rømer and the audience he was writing to in Copenhagen than it does about how Africans thought of the slave trade, because Africans in general of course did not simply "sell one another," but made social distinctions between people who were for sale and people who were not. The earlier quote from Rømer, in which he described people north of the Gold Coast as somehow less human than people on the coast, suggested that he was well aware of African social distinctions that made some people more "enslavable" than others, and yet in this purported quotation of a representative of "the Old negroes on the Gold Coast" he collapses all Gold Coast people into one category of people who "sell one another." It is possible that the old man Rømer was quoting had seen brothers who could not trust each other in the slave trade—particularly as lines between free and enslaved became threatened by the intensified Atlantic trade in the later eighteenth century (to which we will turn in the next chapter)—and he had most likely seen many evils produced by the Atlantic slave trade. Yet Rømer's wording echoes a European generalization about the "nature of Africans," which indicates how categories of social distinction, notably race, operated and changed according to their local social practices. In Copenhagen, Atlantic expectations about racial difference had a more immediate power than they did in Osu.

Atlantic expectation about race, linking blackness to slavery, also overpowered Gold Coast distinctions between free and enslaved in a conflict between two former "coast men" in Copenhagen in 1764. This conflict between former governor Jessen and trader Johan Friedrich Reindorph, now a chamber councilor, started in Africa as a case in the Secret Council at Christiansborg but made it to Copenhagen, where it produced a written complaint in the Chamber of Customs. The immediate points of contention had to do with the question of who had the right to call themselves "mægler" (broker) in Osu, but more broadly Jessen complained that Reindorph had interfered too much in the company's business on the Gold Coast. Reindorph in turn accused Jessen of having acted carelessly toward African trading partners. The case allows us a unique glimpse into how Danish men, who were familiar with several of these local historical contexts, alternated between different understandings of race depending on which context they were speaking in, and how being considered free on the Gold Coast did not necessarily extend to the rest of the Danish Atlantic system.[50]

To support his complaint about Jessen's conduct in Africa, Reindorph called five former company employees as witnesses: Ludewig Rømer, Esau Quist, Carl Engman, Joost Platfues, and the chaplain Arp Lütken Kop. These were hardly average employees at Christiansborg. They had all stayed in Africa longer and had more influence on the political life at Christiansborg than most Danes; Engman and Platfues had served time as governors, and all five had been members of the Secret Council. These men had broad experience with trading in Africa, and, except for the chaplain, they had all been cassaret to and had children with women in Osu. Reindorph's questions to them demanded detailed inside knowledge about the political and diplomatic context of the slave trade, and few people in Copenhagen in 1764 could have known as much about slave trading at Christiansborg as they did.[51]

One of Reindorph's questions was about a woman who had been bought as a wife but sold as a slave. He asked, "If any of them, especially Mr. Quist, knew that interim Governor Jessen had bought a free negress from Crobbe [Krobo] of the negro Okue, and afterward sent her away with Captain Jens Knie, and what consequences could have or did follow from such action?"[52] Rømer replied that he did not know whether Jessen had bought a free woman from Krobo. Carl Engman claimed that he had heard of the case only after he returned to Copenhagen but continued that if it was true that Jessen had bought a "protected negress" from Krobo then it would have been very careless of him, since "Crabbe [Krobo] are a dangerous people, who in such case would seek and get satisfaction." Both Joost Platfues and Arp Lütken Kop agreed with Engman that the people in Krobo were dangerous and would take revenge if any of their women were sold or bought "unjustly."[53]

Reindorph also told his own version of the story to the Chamber of Customs. He described how Okue, who was a "bad," "drunken," and "raunchy" man, had married a woman in Krobo after the customs of the country, and then, after his return to the coast, sold her to Jessen to buy spirits. Jessen had, according to Reindorph, seen a chance to get a good slave woman for very little, even though "he and everybody else knew" that this woman was free and could "neither be bought nor sold." Jessen therefore kept the woman hidden in his quarters until he took her to Captain Knie's ship during the night, where he sold her as a slave to be sent to the West Indies. Jessen's conduct was discovered by people in Osu, who contacted Reindorph and asked him to help retrieve the woman, since they feared that the woman's kin in Krobo would seek revenge on Okue's kin in Osu if they heard about the incident. According to Reindorph it was of utmost importance to the people in Osu that something be done, since they feared the people in Krobo more than Danes feared "the plague and the Germans."[54]

The longest version of the story about Jessen selling a free woman was given by assistant Esau Christensen Quist, who had been in Guinea longer than any of the others, spoke several African languages, was cassaret, and had at least three children in Osu. Reindorph must have expected Quist to know more than the other witnesses about the case since he addressed him specifically, and Quist's answer suggests that Reindorph's assumption was correct. Overall Quist's testimony is consistent with Reindorph's version, but his wording is different, and he is worth quoting at length:

the said slave-woman was bought by Okue and sent away with Captain Knie by Governor Jessen . . . Okue was sent to Crobbe [Krobo] . . . where he took this woman as his wife against paying the costume [bridewealth] . . . and afterward upon his return to Christiansborg sold her to Governor Jessen against Okue's friends' will or knowledge, why they requested Chamber Councilor Reindorph, to relieve *it*. As *it* was already brought on board, Chamber Councilor Reindorph demanded *it* released again by the Captain, but the Governor refused and threatened to shoot her dead, when she got on the beach, about which several disputes were raised, and the mentioned slave-woman went away, whereupon all her friends immediately wanted revenge, and sought to arrest me along the way. . . . This incident will surely in time cause trouble.[55]

Quist was the only one of the former employees in Copenhagen who called the woman a slave, and there is an interesting ambivalence in his choice of words that offers an entry into the social world of the slave trade in Osu. Though Quist calls the woman a "slave-woman" throughout, he alternates between referring to the woman as it (*den*) and her (*hende*). In contemporary Danish documents from the slave trade, slaves were most often called *slaven* (the slave), which led to the neuter *it*, whereas referring to the woman as *her* suggests that she was a free woman. Interestingly, Quist referred to the woman as *it* (the slave) only when she was brought on board the slave ship. At other times—while she was getting married to Okue in Krobo, and when he, against the will of his kin, sold her to Jessen, and again when her kin objected to her sale to the Europeans—she was *her*. Whether Quist's choice of pronouns for the woman in question was conscious or not, it seems to suggest that Quist operated with two different social contexts; one, on the slave ship, in which she was a slave, and another, in Africa, in which she was not.

In Gold Coast society, as Quist knew, it is unlikely that the woman would have been considered a slave, because she had kin who were in a position to protest her sale. If she had been a slave, on the other hand, she would not have been protected against being sold in the transatlantic trade. The question therefore remains why Quist referred to the woman from Krobo as a slave when he knew that she belonged to a kinship group that protested her sale in the transatlantic slave trade. As mentioned earlier, his inconsistent use of pronouns for the woman suggests that he was shifting uneasily between two different social contexts. When on the Gold Coast, experienced traders like Quist knew that not all Africans were for sale. And given that he had both wife and children in Osu, he was probably also personally invested in policing the border between those who were and those who were not for sale in the Atlantic trade.

The explanation for why he called her a slave should be sought in the second of the two social contexts: in Copenhagen, where he wrote his answer to Reindorph's questions. Quist presumably called her a slave because the scribe and the other Danes around him thought of her as a slave, or perhaps his memory of the incident was colored by the knowledge that, in the end, she *did* end up on a slave ship. From the time she was brought on board that ship Europeans would have paid little attention to whether she was born a slave or of high status, whether she had been pawned, panyarred, or caught in war. In the context of the wider Atlantic system the woman was simply a slave.

Quist's shifting pronouns and the free woman's enslavement represent a battle of meanings. In 1764, when Quist was writing, the transatlantic slave trade had grown in size and importance, as had the slavery-based plantation colonies in the West Indies. In other parts of the Atlantic system, all Africans were likely to be associated with plantation slavery. In the Atlantic world European versions of who was enslavable won over local West African understanding. It is therefore not surprising that West African women who married European men in Osu would be hesitant to travel with them to Europe, nor that their families would resist letting them go.[56]

When the men returned to Copenhagen they left their African wives and children in Osu. For some of them, this probably meant feeling split between two worlds, similar to the way Edward Carstensen described it in the nineteenth century. The distance between Osu and Copenhagen was great, and traveling to Osu was like coming to "another world," as Rømer put it.[57] Just as Danes settling in Osu went through a cultural transition, so the same men had to resettle in Copenhagen when they returned with their histories and memories.

In this transition back to Europe, some old "coast men" made an attempt to keep their lives in Osu and in Copenhagen separate, creating a distance between the two worlds. Such attempts at separation depended on keeping knowledge about what was going on in Africa from circulating too freely in Denmark. A most powerful expression of this desire for discretion is a poem by the now familiar Carl Engman in his introduction to Rømer's 1760 travel account. Stylistically it is not the best poem, and one might wonder why

Rømer chose to include it in his book, since it clearly revealed that he had broken a promise to his friends in Africa. Yet, as historians we should be thankful that he did, since it offers a unique point of entry into the otherwise rather obscure world of former Africa employees in Copenhagen.

"Remember, my beloved friend, what in Guinea you promised me," Engman's poem begins. Apparently Rømer had promised Engman not to reveal everything that went on in Africa, but then, after he returned to Copenhagen and while Engman still lived in Osu, Rømer was urged by his friends in the city to tell more about Africa than he originally intended. Most notably Bishop Erik Pontoppidan encouraged Rømer to write and publish a longer account about Africa, and, well knowing that his friends in and from Africa would get upset about it, he revealed numerous details about the Euro-African slave trade and the social world in Africa. Engman's poem—though not so transparent—gives the impression of a long distance between the world in Africa, which Engman and Rømer had shared, and in Copenhagen, where Rømer now lived and Engman would soon resettle.

Remember, my beloved friend,
what in Guinea
you promised me. Now
take care to recall
the resolution made by you
at that time.
I believed you then,
And held you in high esteem.

Therefore I congratulated
you and myself,
And expected so certainly
to see the finest fruits.
You promised never more
to think on such madness.
But, alas! I see myself
forced to quench my hopes.

On the urging
of your friends, you wrote
Of things which—unintentionally—

Were most blameworthy,
for even if one should never
forget the truth
yet one should, at times,
conceal it.

I know that many [things] exist in
a mad world,
more than you or I can
describe in words.
Yet, who knows, perhaps the same is so
In even the finest of lands?
Indeed, much, much more so than
we could believe to be true.[58]

What were these "truths" about Africa that needed to be concealed? What was it Engman did not want people in Copenhagen to know? Perhaps Carl Engman was referring to what Rømer's narrative revealed about the Danish men's African families and how at home they felt in Africa, as in this quote: "When the White's Negress has borne him a couple of Mulatto children he cares as much for her and his children as a man does who has his true wife and children in Europe. Some among the Europeans do not wish to leave their family on the Coast even if they know they could live better in Europe."[59] For "old coast men" who were resettling in Denmark after a stay in Africa, public exposure of their intimate feelings for African families could presumably cause problems with family and friends. This was undoubtedly true for men who were already married in Denmark when they took positions in Africa, such as Christian Jessen, but it was also the case for men who returned and started new families, like Carl Engman, Ludewig Rømer, and many of the other returned employees from Christiansborg. Africa was far away, and it must have been hard to explain to Danes who had not been on the Gold Coast how crucial it was to cassare a woman if one wanted to survive and do well as a slave trader. Guessing at the specific information that Engman did not want included in Rømer's account is speculative though; it may also have consisted of any number of grim details about the slave trade, or political or personal intrigues among the personnel at Christiansborg.

    What the poem does more immediately tell us about is the distance—or lack of distance—between Osu and Copenhagen, and how Osu remained

present in the lives of Danish employees from Christiansborg after they returned to Copenhagen. Ludewig Rømer for one seems to have been acutely
aware of Osu, and to have wondered how his travel account would be received there. At the end of his account he addressed Engman's concerns directly by declaring that he was aware that he had promised "never [to] think
of the Coast" again.[60] And to make up for his broken promise he offered to
send several copies of the book on the first ship leaving for the coast, to let
the men there judge the issues for themselves. If they were to find things
missing or misrepresented, Rømer suggested, then he would be happy to in-
corporate them in the next edition of the text. He made communication between Copenhagen and Osu sound easy and smooth.

Traveling and communication between the two worlds was not always as
easy as that though, and by the time Rømer's account was printed in 1760,
Carl Engman was already back in Copenhagen. He came back in 1758 and
settled on Nørregade 53, and within the same year he married a Danish
woman, Ellen Lorentze Luno, in the same Church of Our Lady Cathedral, a
little way down the street, where their daughters would be christened a few
years later. His wife was the daughter of a brewer in Vimmelskaftet, and by
1762, when Engman witnessed Johan Reindorph's wedding, the former slave
trader was also listed as "brewer." Perhaps he had entered into his father-in-
law's business. In 1765, by the time Engman's daughter was christened, both
Carl Engman and Johan Reindorph had advanced to chamber councilors in
the royal administration. Ludewig Rømer was one of the godfathers at that
same christening; they had apparently remained friends despite the broken
promise. The knowledge and the secrets they still shared bound the "coast
men" to one another just as the rituals of their cassare marriages had once
bound them to Osu.[61]

CHAPTER 4

"Danish Christian Mulatresses"

In 1769, Lene Kühberg's husband died in his rooms at Christiansborg, not in the house he shared with Lene in Osu. Yet his death reverberated in both worlds. Interim governor Frantz Joachim Kühberg was well known in Osu, having lived in Africa longer than most European men. He was first hired as sergeant at Christiansborg in 1756 but soon advanced to trader and was stationed at the Danish trading post at Keta further east down the coast for a number of years. In 1768 he returned to Christiansborg to serve as governor. By then he was accustomed to a high level of comfort—he had five slaves just to wait on him personally at the fort. His death was marked there with the full ceremony he had requested: an honorable funeral with cannon salutes and the flag at half-mast. He saw to his affairs in Osu with equal attention to detail, requesting that the Secret Council make sure that Lene, all those people who worked for him, and people in Osu generally had what they needed to perform a proper service in his memory: money for mourning costumes, food, and drinks. His two favorite slaves, he told the council, should go to his daughter Anna Barbara.[1]

In the years following Frantz Kühberg's death, Lene continued to live in the house she had shared with her Danish husband. There were very few stone houses in Osu, and they signaled both wealth and power. Around the time Lene was born, Friderich Svane had begun building one close to Christiansborg, just beyond the small clay huts that housed the surplus population of fort slaves. Svane had bought Governor Boris's summerhouse for an anchor of brandy and had it dismantled, stone by stone; he collected other stones from near and far and had them all carried to the building site, but the work was never finished. By the time Lene lived in her own house, it was both a base of operations for her life as a trader and a mark of her status. Unlike many West African women who made their living through trade, she probably did not sit in the market herself. We can imagine her helping her slaves set up a stall with goods and meals to sell, and at home she would have overseen the management of her large household, directing slaves as they cooked and prepared goods. She provided important services to the traders at the fort, where her daughter Anna Barbara went to school. Sometimes she advanced the traders money or goods; at other times she let them stay in her house.[2]

These relationships brought her wealth, but they also kept her within the reach of Danish power on the coast. One trader, Engelhardt Kramer, who was stationed at Fort Kongensteen at Ada, stayed with her whenever he was in Osu. She let him keep a few private belongings in a bureau in her house—clothes, a small towel, and a hymnbook—an arrangement she may have come to regret when he died unexpectedly. When the news of his death arrived from Ada, two assistants came down from Christiansborg and sealed up the bureau as part of the assessment of his estate. But first they carefully went through his belongings and wrote everything down and made Kühberg formally declare that she had no more items belonging to Engelhardt Kramer in her house. A woman of her status may not have liked strangers going through her drawers.[3]

*   *   *

Euro-African women like Lene Kühberg were particularly well situated to take advantage of the Atlantic slave trade. Danish men never completely stopped cassaring women with African names, but in the last decades of the eighteenth century higher-ranking Danish assistants—who are the ones we encounter most often in the sources—were usually cassaret to Euro-African women with Danish names. As Euro-Africans with connections to Christiansborg, these women acquired a disproportionate amount of European trade, material goods, and employment. Indeed, as the generations passed, it became increasingly clear that Euro-African women in Osu could take advantage of their marriages to European traders. When women like Lene Kühberg settled in houses with Danish husbands prone to long absences and early deaths, they could establish households that were less influenced by the Ga patriarchal kinship groups to which they belonged and expand their market trading in their own right. Marking their difference with European material culture and, also quite important, with Christianity, they could position themselves as "the Christian Mulatresses, whom Europeans cassare," as chaplain H. C. Monrad later called them.[4]

However, the story of how Euro-African women took advantage of the opportunities opened to them during the slave trade is not only about industrious individuals expanding their opportunities. It is also a story of people responding to pressures from a social world they themselves helped create. The slave trade had social costs: not just the well-known dire costs of enslavement and displacement for the millions of Africans who were sold into slavery in the Atlantic world, but also a cost for the people at the center of this story, who lived in a social environment shaped by the slave trade. Once the slave trade had become a livelihood for many coastal families, everyone in Osu lived with its violence and with the risk of enslavement. Lines between traders and enslaved were never crystal clear, but as the trade intensified and European traders got more of a foothold in the trade—particularly through the practice of human pawning—those lines blurred even further. New groups of Africans were enslaved, and a growing number of pawns and other people who had not previously been considered enslaved on the Gold Coast were sold to European ships. Elite families with extended kinship networks, material goods, and weapons were better protected against the slave trade than many others, but even they lived in the shadow of violent conflicts and wars that the slave trade provoked and with the fear of seeing pawned family members being sold across the Atlantic.[5]

This put pressure on Euro-Africans to adopt elements of European Christianity and material culture that connoted prestige and wealth in order to distinguish themselves from enslavable Africans. Out there in the colonial system, in whose networks they were actively participating, there loomed a large, undifferentiated category of "the African." Out there, it was not at all clear that individual Africans' elite status in coastal society would keep them safe from enslavement. By signaling connections to Europeans and to coastal Euro-African culture they distinguished themselves from people from the north who had recently been enslaved, captured, or bought, at one of the northern slave markets or even further inland; people who, on the Gold Coast, were considered most enslavable.

By the 1760s there was a well-developed space for Euro-Africans in the social hierarchy at Christiansborg, and this position was at least nominally contingent on Christianity. Once Euro-Africans were Christians they could be integrated in a middle position at the fort. The cassare marriages—though they were still considered different than Christian marriages—were often blessed by the church. A 1765 church book from Christiansborg contained the same listings as other Danish church books: dates of deaths, christenings, and marriages; lists of adults and children attending confirmation classes with the chaplain; and a list of the members of the congregation who belonged to other Christian denominations. But unlike other Danish church books, this one recorded two different types of marriages, with "*calysarede*" couples listed in a separate column under the heading "After permission from the Governor and the Chaplain."[6]

This separate column of cassare marriages tells us at least two important things about the marriages in the 1760s (Figure 7). First, the cassare marriages could be performed only with permission from both secular and religious authorities, which in turn suggests that the cassare marriages were not solid enough an institution to pass without explanation back home in Copenhagen, where the church book was going to end up. Christian marriages did not normally require the permission of secular authorities. Second, the administration and the church did indeed accept and bless cassare marriages, which meant that these marriages were legitimate in the eyes of the chaplain and the governor, and the cassaret couple was therefore integrated in the fort hierarchy. When Euro-African families cassaret their daughters to employees from the fort, they willingly entered the social hierarchy at Christiansborg, and for some families this choice was common practice. They sent their daughters and sons to the school, worked as soldiers, married Danish employees, and were part of the Danish fort and congregation.[7]

Over the course of the eighteenth century the social hierarchy in which Euro-African families accepted inclusion became increasingly racialized. The group of soldiers at Christiansborg, for example, which earlier in the century had consisted of both European and Euro-African soldiers, became exclusively Euro-African by the end of the century. Long before then, the number of Euro-Africans working as soldiers at Christiansborg had exceeded the number of European soldiers. The administration never hired other Africans as soldiers, as the term "mulatto-soldiers" testifies, and they preferred Euro-Africans of Danish heritage. At the same time the growing number of fort slaves at Christiansborg—all of whom were of exclusively African ancestry— would have reminded everyone that racial heritage aligned with social status at the fort.[8]

African fort slaves were of a different status than the Euro-Africans at Christiansborg. Some of the fort slaves had the status of slaves, owned by the West India and Guinea Company or by people in Osu who rented them out. Others were free women and men who were pawned to the fort to work off

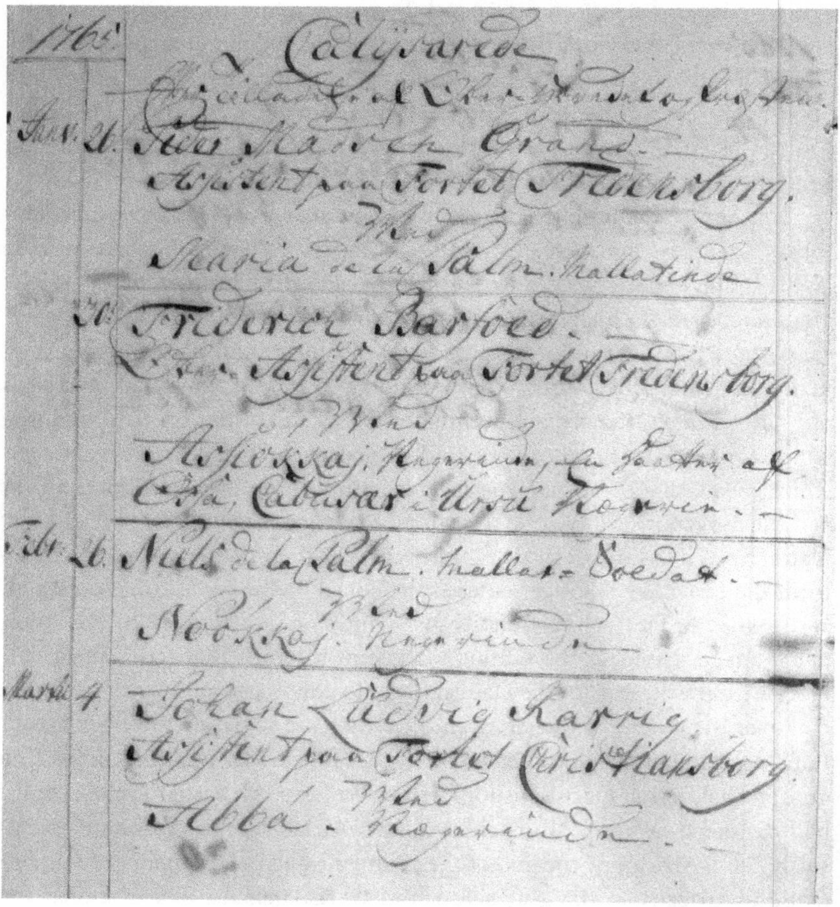

Figure 7. Chaplain Eyler Christian Hagerup's church book from 1765, listing "calysarede" (cassared) couples in a separate column from the other marriages in the church. Text reads: "1765. Calysarede. With permission from the Governor and the Chaplain. January 26: Peder Madsen Grand. Assistant on Fredensborg. With Maria de la Palm. Mulatresse," and further down, "February 26: Niels de la Palm. Mulatto soldier. With Nookkai. Negress." Rigsarkivet, Copenhagen.

debt. Fort slaves were not free to seek other employment, and though they did receive a minimal monthly payment, they could not have lived off this alone. Women were paid even less than men. As Paul Erdmann Isert, a German Danish doctor who had served at Christiansborg in the 1780s, wrote in 1786, "These wretched souls are most poorly paid for their work and if they were not able to supplement their pay by one means or another, they could not possibly manage."[9] How and whether they supplemented their minimal income at the fort is not clear. They may have been trading like so many other people in Osu, or they may have received material goods or cowries for services, sexual or otherwise, to men at the fort. We do know that some of the women who worked as fort slaves had sexual relations with European men, since they gave birth to Euro-African children.[10]

The growing number of fort slaves at Christiansborg changed the fort's racial makeup. Where the population of employees at Christiansborg earlier in the century had been a group of about thirty northern European men and a few Africans, the fort now became an important employer of African fort slaves and Euro-African soldiers and servants. The number of Europeans working at the fort remained about the same, while the number of fort slaves reached its maximum of 442 persons by the early 1790s. The number of Euro-African soldiers grew from a handful in the early eighteenth century to about thirty a century later.[11]

In the late eighteenth century chaplains at Christiansborg were clearly making social distinctions that linked freedom to European descent. In a case from 1770, for example, chaplain Feldtman told the administration that a Euro-African child born to the fort slave Akua[12] could not be forced into slavery, because he was son of a Danish man. Instead the chaplain requested that the boy be included in the Christian congregation, supported by the mulatto chest, and allowed to attend school at Christiansborg. Feldtman had linked freedom to the boy's Euro-African heritage—because the boy had a European father, he could not be a slave—and when the administration responded to the chaplain's request, it was also the boy's Euro-African origins that granted him the right to grow up as a free person and not a slave: "the said mulatto boy child, though he is born by a slave, will be free from being a company slave, since he, who is a mulatto and consequently should be incorporated in the Christian congregation, cannot be ordered to be a slave."[13]

This development toward a distinct social hierarchy following lines of European descent and race in the church congregation continued into the nineteenth century. When Monrad was chaplain at Christiansborg from 1805 to

1809, there was a noticeable racial hierarchy in his congregation, which now consisted of about two hundred members "of all colours."[14] This was a sizable congregation compared to the small number of Danish men and Euro-African wives and children that Chaplain Svane had served in the 1720s, or the hundred or so people that chaplain Eyler Christian Hagerup complained about not having room for in the 1760s. In the new church, built on the east wing of the fort while Governor Biørn was in charge in the early 1790s, the governor and his family sat in the first row, closest to the chaplain. The back of the church was assigned to the "soldiers and other mulattos," who now made up a large part of the congregation. As in contemporary churches in Denmark, the assigned seats in church showed the social hierarchy of the congregation. Apparently fort slaves did not attend church at all.[15]

A 1780 proposal from chaplain Hans Randers, in which he advocated making graded payments to the mulatto chest depending on the cassaret wife's race and religion, is a clear expression of the social hierarchy that the chaplains adhered to. Chaplain Randers's nine-item proposal for reorganizing the payments shows a distinction between Danish and foreign (*fremmede*) Euro-African women and a special position of "Danish Christian Mulatresses." The first item had six smaller parts:

   a. when one wants to calisare a Danish Christian Mulatresse, then he should pay four percent of his wages to the Mulatto Chest as soon as he has the permission.
   b. does he demand a Danish [yet] unbaptized Mulatresse then he shall give three percent of his wages.
   c. is it a Danish negress then he shall give six percent.
   d. is it a foreign Christian Mulatresse then he shall give six percent.
   e. is it a Mulatresse who is a heathen and not educated in the Christian Religion eight percent is to be paid.
   f. is it a foreign Negress ten percent is to be paid.[16]

Chaplain Randers's list suggests a varied and quite hierarchical table for inclusion at the fort, in which Danish Christian Euro-Africans had their own specific position. Not all Christian Africans, or all Christian Euro-Africans for that matter, were equally suited to be members of Randers's Christian congregation; according to Randers, the best marriage partner for a Danish man was clearly one of Danish descent. Like other chaplains, Randers evidently wanted the cassare marriages to have a missionary purpose. He imagined giving the Danish men an economic incentive to cassare "Danish [yet] unbaptized" Euro-African women by letting them pay the lower tax of 3 percent, presumably with the expectation that the husbands then would ensure their Euro-African wives' further education in and confirmation of the Christian faith. Euro-African women who had chosen to remain "heathen," on the other hand, were another matter: here Randers suggested that the men pay a high 8 percent to discourage such unions.[17]

In Randers's proposal, "Danish" meant belonging to the group of families who had Danish names and some Danish ancestry, the families "born under Christiansborg," as Rømer earlier put it. All others were, in Randers's terms, "foreign," and therefore less desirable as marriage partners for members of the Danish congregation, whether they were Euro-African or, worst of all, "Negresses." Here Randers was in line with the priorities of the administration at the fort, who also discouraged their employees from cassaring women from towns other than Osu. As discussed, Danish employees at Christiansborg had in fact periodically gained powerful positions on the coast by marrying into neighboring families, in Teshi or Aprag, for example, and risked putting the governor at Christiansborg in complicated political situations by claiming alliance to "foreign" African and European groups. When employees at Christiansborg were cassaret to "Danish" Euro-Africans from Osu, on the other hand, the marriages stayed within the extended fort network, where the Danes had at least some authority with caboceers and trading partners.[18]

Randers's ideal scenario was not cassare at all, but a regular Christian church wedding. In his last item Randers stated: "When someone marries[19] a Christian Mulatresse or Mastice, then all these obligations are annulled."[20] A few such Christian marriages between European men and African women had happened much earlier, in the 1720s, when Svane was chaplain. The only other Christian marriages involving Africans that are known from Christiansborg are the marriages between Friderich Pedersen Svane and his Danish wife, and Christian Protten and his West Indian wife, Rebecca (mentioned in Chapter 3), which both took place in Europe. In Elmina, on the other hand, at least seven such Christian marriages took place during the eighteenth century and were recorded in the Dutch books. Perhaps the official recognition of the cassare marriages at Christiansborg reduced the need for Christian marriages, whereas the Dutch and the English on the Gold Coast—who did not officially recognize the African-based cassare marriages—gave their employees no choice but to get married in a Christian ceremony if they wished to have their marriages recognized at the fort.[21]

At Christiansborg, inclusion in the fort community theoretically depended on Christian beliefs and Christian behaviors. It is not clear, though, that a Euro-African woman's extent and depth of knowledge about Christianity (in Danish) set any real limits on participation in the fort community. Some knowledge of Christianity appears to have been enough, combined with Christian behaviors such as attending church on Sundays, sending one's children to the school, and wearing European clothes. Initially, inclusion at a rank above fort slaves followed lines of race and heritage, but the position was also broadly cultural; it meant belonging to a hybrid cultural and religious group.

Church membership at Christiansborg meant more to the Euro-Africans who adopted it than simple religious affiliation. Claiming membership in the church was presumably a personal and family statement, emphasizing Euro-African status. When the Euro-African Nicolaas Van Bakergem in Elmina, for example, formally transferred his church membership from a church in Holland to the church in Elmina, it might be considered a mostly symbolic gesture, given that membership in the Elmina church did not offer its members social services as a church in Holland would. Yet Van Bakergem, who later had at least three children baptized in the church, might have needed membership of the Elmina church to be integrated in the local Euro-African community.[22]

Christian Euro-African women in Osu, with connections to both the European fort and the African community in Osu, were in a particularly good position to take advantage of their hybrid position. Euro-African men working at the fort had daily contact and encounters with European traders, but Euro-African women had direct access to European trading goods and contacts through their cassare marriages to European men. Even more interesting, women who were cassaret to European men appear to have had more autonomy in their daily lives, because their European husbands could not maintain the same authority over them that an African husband would have been able to. In the early nineteenth century chaplain Monrad gave the following impression of this dynamic: "From the moment a Negress is married she is her husband's property, and he can, on grounds of adultery or other crimes, sell, kill, or mistreat her with impunity. However, this is not the case with the [Christened Mulatresses], whom the Europeans cassare. These women, too, marry, as is the custom, in the Negro manner, but since they cannot easily be brought to account for their relationships, and, at least, cannot be harshly punished for their excesses, they indulge themselves greatly."[23]

Monrad, like most Danish chaplains at Christiansborg, was critical of behaviors and habits of both Europeans and Africans in Osu, and whether anyone but the chaplain believed that Euro-African women were particularly prone to indulgence cannot be determined from the evidence he provided. What Monrad's comment does suggest is that cassaring European men placed Euro-African women fully under neither European nor African patriarchal control, which allowed them to expand their room for maneuver.[24]

Within the Ga gender system women already lived separately from men and had a comparatively greater degree of economic autonomy than women living in the same house as their husbands in eighteenth-century Danish families. The stone houses built by European and Euro-African traders in Osu, like the one Lene Kühberg inhabited after the death of her Danish husband, could therefore play an important role in allowing Euro-African women to establish themselves as heads of successful trading households. When their European trader husbands left or died, Euro-African women slipped out from under European patriarchal authority but still, through their mothers and larger kinship group, remained connected to the West African community. When they married their daughters to European men, like Lene Kühberg did, they separated even further from the African men in their kinship group and community, while making their own direct connection to the Danish fort and expanding their opportunities as traders in their own right. The practice of women owning slaves enabled wives of European traders to have quite large households and trading businesses.[25]

The Ga houses had an importance well beyond their economic value. The distinct architecture of the stone houses alone must have signaled prestige and distinction, but establishing a new *shia* (house/household) typically also meant establishing a new lineage, which would take the name of the founder who built the house. Within these houses women like Lene presumably lived with their female relatives (mothers, sisters, aunts, cousins) and children, just as they would have in Ga kinship structure. Yet they no longer lived in the traditional Ga settlement pattern, with male and female compounds located in close proximity to each other or even connected to the same courtyard. Their marriages functioned as trading partnerships, just as if they had been married to Ga men: men supplied produce and trading goods for women to prepare and sell. When African wives traded with their European cassaret husbands, the latter probably did not have the same influence over their trading as more culturally adept African husbands would have had, which left the women in better control of the trade.[26]

Cassaring European men allowed some Euro-African women to accumulate goods and to trade independently around Christiansborg. For example, in the auction of the estate of assistant Christian Janssen, who died at Christiansborg in 1772, Christian Protten's widow, Rebecca, turned over some corals and a little silk, which she had been supposed to sell for Janssen. Interestingly, according to the auction book, both the silk and the corals were bought by other women, and this is not the only reference to women buying things at auctions. In another auction, for instance, several Euro-African women—among them Miss Linekensdorf, Miss Wikstrand, Miss Sødring, and Miss Nissen—bought cloth, clothes, and other goods, which suggests that Euro-African women were actively trading on their own at the Danish fort. Euro-African women also showed up at estate auctions as creditors, with claims on European men or the company.[27]

Euro-Africans became an ever more distinct minority population in Osu. By the later part of the eighteenth century, Euro-African families in Osu certainly employed enough markers of European material culture and practices to be viewed as different from other Africans. The slave trade with Europeans was central in bringing the European products that marked Euro-African difference to West Africa. The great majority of enslaved Africans were exchanged for textiles, iron rods, goods, weapons, and alcohol, whereas only a very small number of enslaved people were bought for currency (typically cowries or gold). Some of the important household or daily products exchanged for slaves included clothing, metal containers (pots, kettles, dishes, plates, bowls, cups), and other metalware (knives, swords, fishhooks, needles, locks, keys, scissors, nails, weights). These textiles and consumer goods did not alter the agricultural or fishing practices that most people on the Gold Coast lived off, but—particularly in the coastal trading communities—the wide range of new articles that became available with the trade generated new needs and consumption patterns among the different social groups on the Gold Coast.[28]

Given that neither profits nor products were evenly distributed, the slave trade also led to an increasing level of social stratification in Osu. The social disparities that had already been present before Europeans arrived became more and more obvious, particularly since the coastal communities were specifically organized around the Atlantic trade. European products, which had great value as status symbols on the Gold Coast before, during, and after the slave trade, became markers of this disparity. This did not mean that

African luxury items ceased to be important on the coast. Kente cloth, gold, jewelry, and other African products remained valuable markers of prestige and wealth, but African kings and rich traders increasingly also showed their privilege with silk scarves, hats, European flags, Turkish carpets, and many other imported goods. These became standard presents to be exchanged in trading or diplomatic deals.[29]

For Euro-African women in Osu, gold and silver jewelry, keys, and locks were common status symbols. From early on, Nhares in Senegambia and West African women all over the coast had worn such precious keys, bells, and other European jewels. In the 1780s, Isert noted that women in Osu wore bells and keys that jingled so loudly that one could hear them from a great distance. Rømer mentioned that though women in Osu often had only one chest with a lock, they would wear a large bunch of keys. In the early nineteenth century, Monrad found that women would wear keys of brass and iron as well as silver and gold that European men had ordered from Europe to give to their African lovers. Wearing such keys was ornamental in Osu, but it simultaneously signaled property ownership, participation in the Euro-African trade, and/or connection to a European man.[30]

Likewise, owning more common European clothes and material goods, and, in some rare case, stone houses, signaled prestige and privilege. When Euro-African women served coffee from a coffeepot, and when they dressed their daughters in cotton and silk textiles, they were signaling social distinctions between their families and other Africans, who did not have the same access to European products. Like Christianity, though, as much as these products bespoke connections to Europe, they were also integrated in Ga and Akan lives. Lene Kühberg and other Euro-African women in Osu lived with European furniture, silverware, and clothes, but their daily practices were likely much more African than European. When Euro-African women inhabited stone houses in Osu, they might have made these homes their own by mixing and matching African and European material culture and practices.[31]

Alcohol is one European product that exemplifies how West Africans integrated European goods in unexpected ways. Bottles and anchors of alcohol became an important element in many exchanges—both trading and otherwise—between Europeans and Africans on the coast. Alcohol was even more desirable because West Africans integrated it into a number of religious and social rituals and rites. Along with the Akan to the west and the Ewe to the east, the Ga believed in the spiritual potency of water, blood, and alcohol. In

Osu in the eighteenth century as in the twentieth, the Ga used alcohol to placate the supreme being, Nyonmo, and deities or ancestors, and Danes were asked to do the same, when and if they had offended a sacred animal or a spirit. Other European products were integrated into African religion and culture in similar ways.[32]

It is not surprising that European products would become status symbols when the trading encounter tied distant worlds together in ways that provided unequal benefits. European weapons exemplify how uneven the trading encounter was. European weapons were all produced in Europe in factories owned by investors in the colonial enterprise, who therefore profited from the sale of these weapons in more ways than one. In the Danish case, the Schimmelmann family is a telling example. In addition to their plantations in the West Indies and their sugar refinery in Copenhagen, they also owned a gun factory in Hellebæk, north of Copenhagen. They produced the so-called "negro-guns," of relatively low quality and specifically made for the slave trade in Africa—where the popular gun went by the name "Dane gun." The Schimmelmanns therefore profited both when the cheap guns were sold in Africa and when the slaves they got in return produced sugar for them in the West Indies.[33]

Likewise, the alcohol that Danes sold in West Africa was produced with profits accruing to Danes. Most of the alcohol was brandy and rum made from sugarcane in the West Indies, which also helped tie the Danish colonial system together. A comparison of the wealth produced by colonial investors like the Schimmelmanns with the kinds of temporary merchant profits obtained by even the wealthiest families on the Gold Coast would show not only the advantage of investing profits in industrial production, but also the fundamental inequality of the slave-trading encounter. The prestige and cultural and social capital attached to European products had to do with this overall unequal power balance of the Atlantic world.[34]

One of the places where European material culture and religion was made available to Euro-African families was at the fort school. At the school Euro-African children were given Danish clothes to wear and followed a daily schedule that was structured around prayers, book learning (mostly reading and writing), and meals (Figure 8). Every morning at six and every evening at five-thirty exactly the children met in the church for prayers. From seven to ten-thirty in the morning and again from two to five in the afternoon the children were in school. The time in between was for eating and recreation, since it was too hot for teaching in the middle of the day. The curriculum at the school at Christiansborg was consistent with the preparation that Danish children received before their confirmation in Denmark, but in addition to instruction in Christendom and Danish, boys were given military training in preparation for employment as soldiers at the fort, while girls were trained in practical household skills.[35]

The education at the fort school was permeated by Danish gendered and racial distinctions between Euro-Africans and other Africans. In 1765 chaplain Hagerup described how the girls at the school at Christiansborg were educated according to "their gender's decent education" in sewing, washing, cleaning, and cooking.[36] The previous years the two oldest Euro-African girls at the school, Dorothea Christiansdatter and Charlotte Møllers, had learned such practical household skills while working as maids for Governor Resch's Danish wife, and they were now teaching the present oldest girl in the school, Dorothea Sophia Røbe, the skills they had learned. Dorothea was then employed by the administration to teach the girls at the school what "the older mulattresses have learnt by years of service and education and daily experience."[37] By the time they were confirmed and graduated from the fort school, they would have been fully aware that they were different from other Africans living in Osu. They stood apart from the rest of the community, and the ways in which they stood apart were specifically and recognizably European.

When Euro-Africans in Osu marked their difference with European culture, it might seem—especially from a European perspective—that it involved some level of acculturation. Yet the European sewing and cooking practices, along with the pots, silverware, and other material products, were not signs of acculturation or of the abandonment of Ga practices. Over the century the chaplains continually complained that Euro-Africans "forgot" what they had learned at the fort as soon as they got home to their families in Osu. Even the most basic Danish language skills and Christianity were difficult to teach the children. According to one chaplain, most of the children learned to repeat "their catechism" before they were confirmed, but they forgot it immediately after, because they were speaking a language that they did not understand.[38] Chaplain Hyltoft reported that he had continued teaching some of the soldiers who had already been confirmed by his predecessor, Kop, since they were still not very strong in their "learning." This was not Kop's fault, Hyltoft added, but a result of the fact that the children were used to speaking only their mothers' language, and that they were

Peter Ditlev
Friedrich Hakkenborg
Christian Hakkenborg

Numer	Pigernes Navne	Fremgang		
		Forklaring	Catechismus	A: b: C.
1.	Dorothea Sophia Köbe		gandske	gandske
2.	Lena Heissing		Ditto	Ditto
3.	Anna Barbra			begynder
4.	Maria Langhausen			har ligt begyndt
5.	Ana Lovisa			Kiender A. b. c.
6.	Lena Abrahams			Ditto
7.	Catharina Küntze			Ditto

Specification

Dette for fattige smaae Börns Klæder

Drengenes Navne	Buxer	Skiorter
Carl Sonne	1	1
Jörges Sonne	1	1
Knud Sonne	1	1
Joran Magnus	1	1
Anthonile	1	1
Friderich August	1	1
Carl Benjamin	1	1
	7	7

Figure 8. School list from the Danish church school at Christiansborg, 1765. The list specifies the children's progress in learning the alphabet and the clothes they received at the school. Note Anna Barbara (Lene Kühberg's daughter) among the girls at the school. Rigsarkivet, Copenhagen.

surrounded by Africans, which made the Danish language even more difficult.[39]

The chaplains' complaints about the difficulties of teaching Euro-African children Danish language and religion speak to these religious officials' general lack of influence in the trading encounter. It was not only the children in their school who would not follow their precepts. Randers described how on Sundays, right after receiving the Lord's Supper, the European congregation would get so drunk that they ended up lying senseless on the battery outside the fort, and how they, in their drunkenness, yelled curses at the chaplain and told him to go to hell. Some even publicly said that they wished that the company would stop sending chaplains to the fort. What distressed Randers the most was that the Europeans' bad example spoiled the "good that perhaps with time could be awoken among the Mulattos." How could he possibly talk Euro-Africans out of sacrificing to "heathen idols," when they did not understand Danish well enough, and the Europeans at the fort set such a bad example? "They mix so little with the Danes that they can get no taste of our language and customs," Randers complained, and he concluded that there was no other way to "help this evil" than to take the children away from their mothers at an early age and place them among Danes in a reformatory.[40]

By isolating Euro-African children from their families, the chaplains hoped to expand the distinction between Christian Euro-Africans and other Africans to the extent that they would become a fully separate population group—"a people in themselves" (et Folk for sig selv), as chaplain Feldtman put it in 1769. Feldtman further suggested that the Danes teach Euro-Africans to farm (in a Danish manner) to make it easier for them to live separately from other Africans and "provide for themselves" rather than being dependent on other Africans.[41] This proposal speaks directly to the core of the matter: as it was, Euro-Africans were not at all "a people in themselves." They were fully integrated in the Ga and Akan communities on the coast, and the only way the chaplains could hope to have any control over Euro-Africans' religious and cultural lives would be to fully isolate them from childhood.

The chaplains' repeated suggestions to isolate Euro-African children indicate that they were either ignorant of, or chose to ignore, what it took for Euro-Africans or others to be successful in the slave trade. Isolation from Osu was the last thing a trader needed, and the idea of isolating children from their families in Osu would have worked no better in the later eighteenth century than it did earlier. When Euro-Africans sought Christianity and education from the Danish fort, their purpose was not at all to isolate

themselves from Osu. It was rather to place themselves strategically in relation to both the European cultural group at the fort and to the African cultural milieus in which their non-European relatives continued to live.

Euro-African women remained embedded in Ga culture and did not
adopt the full package of "decent education" that Hagerup wistfully described. When Euro-African women learned to sew, wash, and cook in European ways, or when they lived under the same roof as European men, they
did not simply take on identities of Christian European women. Such an
identity would have required giving up Ga religious practices, and it would
have required deferring to their husbands in economic matters, including
how to run their trading businesses. In the second half of the eighteenth century, a Danish husband would have been legally and practically owner and
guardian of the families' property and business, but this was not the case in
Ga families. When the Ga and the Danish gender systems encountered each
other in the Euro-African families, the Ga gender system prevailed—quite
the contrary of what Hagerup had hoped for.[42]

Throughout the century Euro-Africans as well as Europeans at the fort
continued to use Ga and Akan religious ceremonies and oaths. They clearly
did not adopt Christian religion or behavior to the extent or with the exclu-
sivity that the Danish chaplains would have liked. As always, the powerful
position Euro-Africans could obtain in the trading encounter depended on
their intermediary position, and successful Euro-African families were
grounded in African networks and African culture and religion. As the Atlantic slave trade intensified it was more important than ever to form and
maintain strong and durable ties to both Africans and Europeans participating in the trade.[43]

When Lene Kühberg made her choices about how to make a living and
provide for her family, she was not only taking advantage of the opportunities that came with the Atlantic slave trade, but also responding to the social
pressures that the slave trade produced. She lived at the height of the trade.
As sugar production expanded in the Danish West Indies and in Copenhagen, West Indian planters' demand for slaves became insatiable, and like the
English and Dutch slave trade, the Danish slave trade flourished in the last
decades of the eighteenth century. In 1786 Paul Isert described how a slave
ship that earlier would have carried 200 slaves now had to carry 452 slaves
crammed on board. An important turning point in the Danish slave trade
came in 1781, when both the English and the Dutch were engaged in the

major international conflict triggered by the American Revolution. Danish traders and investors saw an opening and asked the king to issue a new charter for a trading company, the Baltic and Guinea Company, with the explicit purpose of taking advantage of the good trading conditions for a neutral state during wartime.[44]

The Atlantic slave trade provoked a violent social climate on the coast. One of the most troubling examples from the trade out of Osu came in 1747. Just before a Portuguese ship carrying slaves reached Brazil, a group of slaves successfully rebelled and forced the captain to sail them back to Africa. By the time they made it back across the Atlantic they were starving, and many were ill, when they laid anchor off the Gold Coast they sent in a canoe with twenty-nine people who were nearly dead. The Danes at Christiansborg, who had noticed the ship and wondered why it sent no messenger to the coast, now considered sending an expedition out to the ship to negotiate for the freedom of the white officers. In the meantime, however, the Dutch factor at Fort Crevecoeur (Ussher Fort) claimed that the slaves onboard the ship should be considered his property—or that the Danes should at least split them with him—and as rumors of the ship spread on the coast, people from the local towns began to gather on the beach. By the time the canoes arrived with the starving slaves from the Portuguese ship, different groups of heavily armed people were waiting on the beach to panyarre[45] them and take them away.[46]

As the heavily armed people waiting on the beach at Osu suggest, the violence provoked by the Atlantic slave trade has to be viewed in light of the large numbers of weapons brought to the Gold Coast during the eighteenth century. All European nations buying slaves on the Gold Coast had firearms and powder among their trading goods, and there was an almost insatiable market for firearms in Africa. In 1705 Willem Bosman commented that if the Dutch did not sell firearms to Africans then they would just trade with other Europeans. It has been estimated that between 283,000 and 394,000 firearms were imported to West Africa annually by the British alone in the period 1750–1807. Firearms were particularly sought after by slave sellers. Though there were many other products exchanged for enslaved people, and textiles were more common than weapons, there seems to be little doubt that many weapons were brought to West Africa during the slave trade and that these contributed to the condition of more or less permanent conflict, which not infrequently grew into outright warfare.[47]

Living with the risks and violence of the Atlantic slave trade must have made for an uncertain social climate. Whether a person was kidnapped, caught in war, or unable to repay a debt, once he or she ended up in the slave dungeon under one of the European forts, Monrad wrote "his destiny is determined."[48] A person enslaved on a European ship leaving for America had an even smaller chance of escape. This meant that Atlantic enslavement had greater consequences than enslavement in Osu; "To be a slave in this country is not considered a great evil," Monrad accounted, "but to be exported [udføres] is synonymous with being killed."[49] Cases of Africans returning from being shipped as slaves on a European vessel were rare.[50]

Sale to European ships was surrounded by terrifying rumors and stories of cannibalism and what Europeans would do to Africans who were sold, which must have intensified the fear of the slave ships even further. As early as the late seventeenth century, Jean Barbot reported back to his readers in Europe that slaves sold across the Atlantic were so afraid of being eaten that many of them died from sorrow and despair on the passage. In 1709 chaplain Johannes Rask wrote that people on the coast believed Europeans bought Africans to use them as bait for fishing "bossies" (cowry shells) in the ocean. In 1760 Ludewig Rømer described how enslaved people from the north believed that they were going to be "fattened like swine" to be eaten by Europeans, and later in the century Isert related how an African man had asked him if his black shoes were made out of human skin, and how other people on the coast were convinced that Europeans would eat the slaves they bought and make gunpowder from their bones. Monrad wrote about slaves who imagined that Europeans would drink their blood like wine and make shoes out of their skin. These and other rumors about the destiny of people who were sold to the European ships presumably circulated in Osu, and the insecurity and fear created by the slave trade must have shaped how people made choices and negotiated their daily practices.[51]

By the latter part of the eighteenth century, the pressure on Africans to avoid enslavement in the intensified Atlantic slave trade gave Europeans—the only ones who were never for sale to the European ships—a power that they would not otherwise have had. The Danish presence on the Gold Coast had certainly changed since the earliest decades of the century, when Governor von Groenestein wrote his desperate plea from Frederiksborg that the Europeans had no means to protect themselves against African attacks.[52] In 1760 Ludewig Rømer depicted the Danish establishment on the Gold Coast quite differently: "As long as we have food and provisions for war, 30 cannons, and 300 Negroes as manpower, these fortifications . . . are invincible and impregnable against all the forces of Africans so far known on the Gold Coast—even if the Africans are united."[53] By then Danes had gained another level of experience in Africa and, like other Europeans on the coast, had developed systematic practices that gave them better control over their participation in the slave trade.

The most powerful means by which European slave traders gained control over and secured their success in the Atlantic slave trade was the practice of human pawning, which put an intense pressure on Africans who participated in the slave trade. With pawned family members at potential risk of being sold to European slave ships, African families became directly dependent on the goodwill and trust of their European trading partners, and the Danish company became an ever more important creditor in Osu, loaning out goods, cowries, and iron rods to African traders. To ensure that the debts were paid, the administration routinely pawned members of African families as security, and other Africans pawned themselves to the company and worked at the fort to pay off debts. The pay lists at Christiansborg included both pawns who had been taken on as workers according to their families' wishes and people who were held as hostages because their families had unpaid dues or unresolved disagreements with the company.[54]

From the perspective of African families participating in the slave trade, human pawning was not just any credit arrangement, since it put free Africans at risk of being sold across the Atlantic. As Monrad noted, pawning family members and kin to make up for unpaid dues, at the risk of having them sold as slaves, was a terrible risk to take: "who cannot see" Monrad asked, that this is "an abominable seed of misery in thousands upon thousands of families?"[55] Monrad was writing as the Danish slave trade was ending, when the number of pawns and panyarred people sold to European slave ships had escalated in the last decades of the eighteenth century. By the end of the century, sale to the European ships was a constant risk; both Africans and Europeans used sale as punishment in disputes over adultery, theft, and other offenses, and when a family was in conflict or dispute with other families, in Osu or in one of the nearby towns, there was a risk of being kidnapped and held for ransom, or simply of being abducted when traveling without enough protection.[56]

But human pawning as a credit system was fundamental to the slave trade, and without it the trade could not have been as systematized as it was. To Europeans, human pawns represented an almost immediate monetary value, since they could be sold to a European slave ship if they were not redeemed in time. If pawns could be sold without their families protesting too much, European slave traders apparently preferred pawns to slaves from the inland, since pawns, who most often came from coastal families, were stronger and had a better chance of surviving the middle passage than slaves who had endured an arduous passage from the interior and a lengthy imprisonment in a slave dungeon.[57]

Many pawned people sold across the Atlantic came from important trading families on the coast, which tells us that even the elite lived with the risk of enslavement. This should not be surprising given that most debtors in the slave trade were brokers, caboceers, or other persons of property and high social status. People who could participate in the slave trade were people who had the wealth (in gold, iron rods, or other goods) to buy slaves in inland markets and sell them on the coast for a profit. They were the families who could profit from the slave trade, but they often had to put their kin at risk of enslavement to do so, as in 1746 when Oku, the factor in Osu, was in such debt to the Danish company that he ended up pawning two men, two women, and three boys—including himself and several of his brother's children. Among the Asante there was apparently a set order in which a man chose to pawn his family members, beginning with his married sister and married niece, and ending with his slaves, the rationale being that there was a greater risk that a person with slave status—who had no kinship ties to the person in debt—would run away while pawned to another household.[58]

European slave traders generally sought to avoid selling pawns or family members from influential families, so as to maintain good relations with their trading partners. In the case of factor Oku's pawning to the company, the governor noted, "since this was Adovi's [the broker in Osu] brother and sole heir to his stool, it is almost an impossible matter to send such Negroes from the Coast."[59] He decided instead to make the group serve as fort slaves, meant to stay and work at Christiansborg. In that role, Adovi's kin were in theory safe from being exported. The Danes' understanding of fort slaves was exactly that they were not to be send out of the country, and the fort slaves protested strongly if another fort slave was sold to a European ship. But the fact that such protests do appear in the documents indicate that some fort slaves were indeed sold, and unlike free people from Osu—like Oku's relations—some did not have kinship groups to protect them against being sold to a European ship. When people in Osu were rented out or pawned as fort slaves at Christiansborg, they were therefore at risk when the European slave ships came in.

It was therefore always important that Africans participating in the slave trade protect themselves from enslavement, and choosing the right trading partners and allies was an essential element in this protection. When caboceers or other important people failed to protect people in their community, it could provoke fear and uncertainty. In 1760, for example, Rømer related a story from Anamabo, where the influential slave trader Eno Basie Kurentsi had not protected free people in town well enough from the European slave ships but, instead, over a number of years had sent men to abduct people and sell them in secret to European ships. People now lived in fear of being abducted and sold because "people had gone missing every week, just as in other places, and no one had known what had become of them."[60] When it was discovered that Kurentsi had abducted two men and sold them to a European captain who was going to leave the same night, the men's kin sent a canoe out to the ship with four slaves in exchange for the two men, who thereby escaped. But "everyone" on the coast thereafter thought it would be the end of Kurentsi, because his crimes had been revealed. Instead he made it through the scandal and stayed in power by promising to "cut the throat of his dearest son" to prove his innocence.[61] Though Rømer was in the habit of dramatizing such incidents, the story is indicative of the kind of terror produced by living in a slave-trading community.

Since pawns, fort slaves, and other members of the coastal community who were not supposed to be sold to European slave ships were indeed sold at times, sale could function as a powerful threat, as in 1747, when Ludewig Rømer tried to put force behind his demand that a debtor pay his dues to him. While a Danish slave ship lay at anchor by Osu, Rømer asked its captain, Bojesen, to take the debtor's pawn on board to put pressure on the debtor to quickly come up with the dues. The idea was that as soon as the debtor had paid up, Rømer would send a different enslaved person out to the ship and Bojesen would release the pawn. However, when the debtor had actually paid his dues to Rømer, Bojesen refused to exchange the pawned person for an enslaved person and demanded two persons instead. The incident showed up in a letter from Rømer to the company in which he complained about the conduct of Bojesen while in Africa; if Bojesen had followed Rømer's plan there would have been no reason to mention it. Such moments of threatened enslavement may have been common.[62]

The practice of human pawning often put European traders in a position to determine between enslavement and freedom. In 1787 Paul Isert recounted an emblematic anecdote: A man from Rio Volta living close to the Danish fort Kongensteen had fallen in debt to the Danish traders and could not pay his dues. He therefore proposed to his creditors that they could enslave him and sell him to the Europeans. They agreed and brought him from Kongensteen to Christiansborg, where he was imprisoned in the dungeons. However, when his son heard what had happened he arranged with the slave traders at Kongensteen to be brought to Christiansborg and exchanged for his father. "This kind of negotiation is often undertaken here, when the Europeans find it to their advantage," Isert wrote, explaining that he had been present in the warehouse when the traders arrived from Kongensteen and the son first saw his father in chains. "How deeply moved would even the most hardened trader of people have been by that scene." The son threw his arms around his father, and they cried, and the father was released from the chains that were instead placed on his son. But Isert, having witnessed the horrifying scene, told the governor at Christiansborg, Governor Kiøge, about the situation. The governor, "filled with love of mankind," decided to let the father have a little more time to pay his debts and released his son—"and they all went home happy."[63]

Isert dwelled lovingly on such stories, which emphasized Danes' innocence and benevolence—not their critical role in the coastal slave trade. Both Isert and later H. C. Monrad described how popular Governor Kiøge was among the Africans who traded with the Danes. One of the governor's personal servants took a bullet for him, Monrad recounted. Many years later, when news of Kiøge's death back in Copenhagen spread on the coast, people believed that he had in fact returned to Africa.[64] And though both travel writers were strongly critical of the slave trade and wrote about the harm and corruption Europeans had caused Africa, neither of them reflected on the fact that it was the threat of the slave sale that had placed Governor Kiøge and other European slave traders in a position where they, as almighty rulers, could choose to be benevolent.[65] Indeed, Isert's point in retelling the anecdote was not to question Danes' role in the slave trade; he was more interested in what the story told about Africans' great love for their children. "It is admittedly the case that a father has a right to sell his children," Isert begins his story, "but this happens so extremely rarely that it is difficult to imagine it." The slave dungeons were right in front of him, but what interested Isert was the question of Danish and African paternalism.

Isert's anecdote about the benevolent Danish governor exaggerates the level of control Danish traders had over who was for sale and who was not. Very often conflicts between African traders or smaller and larger wars on the coast or inland, not European traders, were the deciding factors in who was for sale. But from the perspective of both Europeans and Africans living close to the European slave forts, it must often have seemed that the Europeans could have the final word, and the last chance to save pawned or enslaved people from being exported. In particular, voluntary and involuntary pawning of Africans tied local African traders to the slave trade and made them directly dependent on their European trading partners not only for a profit, but for their families' survival

In a world where lines between free and enslaved were often blurry, Europeans were the only ones who were never for sale. On the Gold Coast, the clearest way to signal that one was free was wealth and physical power, but in the larger Atlantic world, connections to Europeans was a way to show that one was not enslavable. However, connections to Europeans did not at all guarantee safety from enslavement. Many Africans lost their freedom despite contacts with Europeans, or sometimes specifically because they associated with Europeans. Yet, when people negotiated their positions in the slave trade they must have sought, both consciously and unconsciously, to signal that they were not its commodities.

Even Africans from slave-trading families, like Lene Kühberg, were not completely safe at the height of the slave trade; only Europeans had that privilege, and Lene Kühberg and her family were always under pressure to be seen as belonging among the slave traders, not the slaves. Establishing oneself as an "insider" in relation to the European fort was a process of claiming a position as a Danish Christian Euro-African and signaling social distinction by appearance, practices, and family ties. In Osu one of the most powerful ways to demonstrate social distinction from enslavement and mark association with and connection to Europeans was to cassare and live with a Danish man in a European-style household. Claiming these powerful intermediary positions in relation to the Danes at Christiansborg was therefore both a way to take advantage of economic, educational, and social opportunities, and a strategy to protect one's family from sale across the Atlantic.[66]

When Euro-African women claimed their intermediate position in the social hierarchy at Christiansborg they incorporated Danish gendered and racial practices into their hybrid daily practices. Daily negotiations about how to live and reproduce, which names and cultural practices to pass on, which furniture and household equipment to have, and whether to accept Christianity and work at the fort in designated "mulatto" positions were all part of a larger production of meaning. When families such as Lene

Kühberg's accepted the higher bridewealth that European men could pay, sent their children to school at the fort, and settled in households with their Danish husbands, they made it possible for Danish men to settle in families that were more like the ones they would have known from home and to set the terms for the physical organization of their Euro-African families. Their families not only produced new generations; they also produced new meanings and hierarchies.

Over the course of the eighteenth century, Euro-African families became invested not only in the slave trade, but also in the hybrid Ga-Danish culture that it produced. They embodied a culture defined by their upbringing; by their Ga-Danish mothers and, in a more indirect way, their Danish fathers; and by the social and racial distinctions they met at the fort and in the community in Osu. Euro-African families were presumably quite aware of their special position in the social hierarchy in Osu, but since they were already distinct from others in Osu, it may have felt like an obvious choice to adopt and reproduce the Euro-African culture of their kin. When Lene Kühberg's daughter Anna Barbara married the Danish governor and slave trader Johan Emanuel Richter and settled with him in a stone house called "Barbara house," her cultural practices were family tradition. Her mother had sent her to school at Christiansborg and thereby placed her in a specific social network. Anna Barbara's own son, Henrich Richter, born in 1785, would grow up to become one of the wealthiest men on the coast. Anna Barbara may have taken for granted that her marriage to a Danish man would give her greater opportunities than those available to other African women.[67]

Consciously or not, though, Danish Christian mulatresses like Lene Kühberg and her daughter Anna Barbara were participating in a cultural production that went beyond the Gold Coast. As they employed their European heritage to distinguish themselves from Africans who were for sale in the Atlantic slave trade, they helped tie prestige to markers of European culture. By employing this distinction to distance themselves from slavery they helped link slavery to blackness. At the same time they also participated in moving a gender frontier between them and their European husbands by importing a new gender practice to Osu. As they settled with European men instead of living in a compound just for women, they adopted a European household setup where they were, at least outwardly, under the authority of their European husbands. As long as their European husbands stayed in the house only for a short time—like Frantz Kühberg, who was stationed in Keta for much of his time in Africa, and then later as governor stayed at the fort—women like Lene Kühberg were not restricted by a husband's presence or expectations. Lene had adopted the practice of wife and husband living together, but she integrated it to her own purpose and benefit. Yet this new physical arrangement of Euro-African families, ironically, helped move the cassare marriages in the direction of a more European domestic arrangement.[68]

CHAPTER 5

Familiar Circles

In 1842, as his wife, Sara, was pregnant with their third child, Wulff Joseph Wulff waited impatiently to move into their new house in Osu. It had already been more than a year since he had asked his brother-in-law in Copenhagen to send him a stone plaque to hang over the front door. "Frederiksminde built 1840 by W. J. Wulff," he wanted it to say. The plaque had still not arrived when they finally moved in, but much else was done. The house had large, flat roofs and a beautiful external gallery. Seven rooms, three warehouses, a bathhouse, and quarters for servants were complete, and a carriage shed and stalls for horses and sheep were planned. Wulff had ordered new furniture from Denmark—a mahogany secretary and two large oval mahogany mirrors—and while he was at it also four good black neck scarves, forty-eight half bottles of cherry brandy, one felt hat for himself, one for their five-year-old son, a straw hat for their daughter, and toys for both of the children. On January 9 Joseph and Sara finally had their housewarming party, where they served ten different types of drinks.[1]

The Malms were a well-known family at Christiansborg, and it was almost a given that Sara would cassare a European man. She would be a great help for any European man settling in Osu. Not only had her family been associated with the Danish fort for generations, but she was also one of very few women in Osu who could read, write, and do math. Joseph, in contrast, had not been capable of much when he first arrived on the coast. His health was bad, and it took him time to settle in. He was the first Jewish Dane to be hired as assistant at Christiansborg, and he was highly aware of being different than the others.[2]

In the first months on the coast Joseph had suffered terribly and longed so violently for Denmark that he could think of nothing else. After he began living with Sara, however, he felt much more at home in Osu. He started to like the food, his health and mood improved, and when they had their first son, his terrible homesickness left as abruptly as it came. Theodor Ulysses Wulff was born within Joseph's first year in Africa, and Wilhelmine Josephine not long after. Now Joseph could not imagine leaving Osu. When his term was up he hoped to travel to Denmark to visit his family, but only on the condition that they would let him return to Africa, because, as he wrote to his parents, "it is now a fact that the Coast and I shall live together." But Wulff died soon after, in December 1842, less than a year after he and Sara had moved into Frederiksminde. He was buried in the house. This would have suited the authorities at Christiansborg: as a Jew, who specifically had requested that there be no cross on his coffin, Joseph did not belong in the Danish cemetery. But perhaps more important it would also have suited Sara and her kin, for whom a home burial was customary.[3]

On the night Joseph died, Governor Edward Carstensen, along with two witnesses, came down to Frederiksminde. When all the preparations for the funeral were complete, they sealed a room with Joseph's belongings and took the key with them back to the fort. It was not automatically assumed that Sara Malm would be inheriting from her cassare-husband. Fortunately, three days later, after Joseph had been buried, Governor Carstensen found Joseph's will while registering his effects. The will made Sara Malm a wealthy woman: Joseph left his house, the grounds it stood on, and all his slaves and pawns to her; the rest of his fortune he asked to have divided equally between his European heirs and the family he and Sara had made together. At the age of thirty, Sara became head of a prosperous household. In the following decades she carefully oversaw both the house and her trading business, and she sent at least two of her children to the Basel Mission's school at Christiansborg. The mission called her "the most respectable mulatto woman in the whole town."[4]

*   *   *

When Sara Malm, also known as Tim-Tam, and Wulff Joseph Wulff moved into Frederiksminde in 1842, cassare marriages had long since stopped being crucial bonds in slave-trading alliances. What was left of them was a domestic arrangement in which Euro-African women—most often of Ga-Danish descent—lived with and kept house for their Danish husbands. People in Osu remained traders, and their cassare marriages to European men were probably always part of their trading businesses, but in the nineteenth century, after the Atlantic slave trade was officially over, the marriages no longer played the central diplomatic and political role that they had. Instead, they had taken the shape of family "circles" like the one that Edward Carstensen expected to settle into with Severine Brock—the one that could "vaguely resemble a home."[5]

In the nineteenth century, Danish men like Edward Carstensen and Wulff Joseph Wulff outwardly seemed to set the terms for their households. Wulff paid for his house, decided on the drawings, oversaw the construction, and ordered furniture from Denmark. His letters do not mention whether Sara Malm also had a say in what the house or the furniture was going to look like. Yet, as the example of Malm and Wulff shows, the story is not so simple. She kept house for him while he was alive, but she was also an experienced and successful trader who was fully capable of running a large household after he passed away. He may have been alone in deciding what Frederiksminde was going to look like, but she lived in and owned the house long after he was gone. To get this secure position in her own house in Osu after Joseph passed, Sara depended on his recognition of her as a wife—as someone whom he would will his property to when he died. This recognition, in turn, was contingent on Sara Malm positioning herself as distinctly Euro-African. Like Edward Carstensen, Wulff Joseph Wulff was under pressure from an Atlantic world where interracial marriage was increasingly questioned, and, like Carstensen, Wulff therefore had to see Sara Malm as an exception, and her Euro-African cultural markers helped situate her as different.

As the slave trade ended, some Euro-African families found means to secure themselves and make the transition to other livelihoods, and a few families did very well. In the seventy-three years that had passed since Lene Kühberg's husband, Frantz, died, the Malms, along with a few other Euro-African families, successfully established themselves as members of a merchant class elite. Known as the Christiansborg Mulattos, they inhabited a profitable intermediate position in Osu. Women belonging to this Euro-African elite in Osu still showed their hybrid culture by their dress, their possessions, and their names and practices, but the cultural encounter they inhabited had changed. Without the slave trade's demand for deep and sophisticated cross-cultural knowledge, the intermediate Euro-African position was no longer as crucial, and Europeans could demand that the cultural frontier on the coast take on a much more colonial manifestation.[6]

In fact, the ending of the Atlantic slave trade in the early nineteenth century was followed by an increasing European interest in colonizing the Gold Coast. Beginning in the 1820s, long before the formal establishment of the Gold Coast colony in 1874, British colonial control of the area was becoming apparent. But European colonial interests had developed earlier than that. Danish interest in the Gold Coast was already starting to shift in the last decades of the slave trade as it became clear that the trade would not go on forever, and in the last half century the Danes were in Osu—from the time the Danish slave trade officially ended in 1803 until the Danes sold Christiansborg to the British in 1850—more Danes turned to ideas of outright colonization. Indeed, throughout the nineteenth century Danish and other European intentions and actions on the Gold Coast were clearly recognizable as colonial; the precolonial encounter on the Gold Coast had become protocolonial.[7]

In the last decade of the eighteenth century a group of private Danish slave traders settled in Osu with Euro-African cassare wives and families in

Figure 10. Christiansborg and Osu, ca. 1802. Peter Thonning's drawing of Christiansborg seen from north with a few of the houses in Osu in the foreground. Rigsarkivet, Copenhagen.

European-style houses, and they began to show a greater interest in the upbringing and prospects of their children. They made a good profit from slave
trading, since both slave prices and demand were high, and they invested a
significant amount of these profits in their households in Osu. Ironically, their
private trading in slaves was a side effect of the 1792 Danish edict in which
King Christian VII declared that the slave trade was to be abolished in ten
years. As a measure to ease the transition for the planters in the Danish West
Indies he simultaneously opened the Danish slave trade to "all nations, without exception" and to private traders. The purpose of opening the trade was to
boost the trade in the years leading up to abolition in the hope that West Indian planters could import enough enslaved Africans to continue depending
on slave labor. Yet when the time came for the slave trade to be abolished, the
private Danish traders were well grounded and established in Osu, and they
were not inclined to stop trading right away. The slave trade had forged many
tender ties, and when the trade ended these ties were threatened.[8]

We see the strength of these family ties in the way the private traders in
Osu responded to the abolition of the trade. First they tried to ignore it, when
the ban on slave trade was supposed to take effect from January 1, 1803. Then
in September 1804 four of the private Danish traders in Osu sent an official
request to the king of Denmark for permission to continue slave trading. Their
request, which argued that the slave traders would be "ruined" if the Danish
slave trade was abolished, was passed on to the Chamber of Customs in Copenhagen by the Secret Council. The Secret Council supported the private
traders and agreed that the king's "Declaration of March 16, 1792" would ruin
the private traders. The Secret Council acknowledged that it might be too
much to expect that the decree from 1792 would be overturned but suggested
that the king at least would allow the trade to continue for another ten years.[9]

The private traders' and the Secret Council's best argument for continuing the trade was that if it stopped, the Danes would have no reason to stay in
Africa, and perhaps no way to do so in safety, which in turn would mean the
end of any Danish colonial ambitions in Africa. "The forts either have to be
abandoned or the trade must be continued until the colonies are established,"
the council argued.[10] Establishing Danish plantations on the Gold Coast had
been part of the plan to abolish the slave trade since the earliest discussions.
In acknowledgment that the Danish population had become dependent on
colonial products like sugar, cocoa, and coffee, the Danish state wanted to
keep the production of these goods within their control, so as to avoid having

to import them from other nations. The reasoning was that if the Danish plantations in the West Indies were to suffer from the abolition of the slave trade, then the Danes could develop a new plantation colony in Africa. Now, as the Secret Council pointed out, this part of the plan was put at risk by ending the slave trade. If the Danes were to keep the forts, it could be done only through friendship with Africans. Friendship in turn was obtained only through trade, and hence the slave trade had to be allowed, if not forever, then at least until the plantations were well established.

Clearly the private traders—and presumably most of the members of the Secret Council—had other things than colonial aspirations at stake in continuing the slave trade. If and when the slave trade actually ended they would lose their purpose and even their right to be in Africa. They would, they argued, be put in an awkward and even dangerous position. "The trade is the most important reason for the Africans to tolerate the presence of Europeans on the coast," and if the Danes no longer had friends on the coast, then "every white man [is] in risk of losing property and life, the establishment would have been put on the line and the honor of the nation would be lost among both inhabitants and foreigners."[11] Perhaps as important to them as their nation's honor, their Euro-African wives and children and the kinship groups to which they belonged must have been on their minds. These families would be put in an unfortunate bind if the slave trade ended, married as they were to European men who then no longer were allowed to trade. As the private traders wrote in their request to continue the slave trade, "will the Chamber please consider how hard it is for so many people to lose their welfare."[12]

The Chamber of Customs did not overturn the Danish ban on slave trading. Instead, a year after the request from the private traders, the chamber responded with surprise to the admission that Danes were still trading slaves in Africa. They did not take the details of the request into consideration or acknowledge the difficulties traders on the coast confronted as a result of the decree to abolish the trade. Instead the chamber simply restated that "no Danish subject at the establishment is allowed to export negroes."[13] The chamber's opinion on the issue having been clearly made, Danish participation did not end, but it did slowly diminish over the next couple of decades. As the Danish ban was followed first by the English ban on slave trading in 1807 and then by the Dutch ban in 1814, and as the prices offered for slaves fell across the Atlantic world, there was no question that the Atlantic slave trade was drastically scaling back, which threatened the Euro-African families trading slaves in Osu and the particular niche they had carved out for themselves in the Atlantic world.[14]

Interestingly, at this moment of uncertainty as to whether the Atlantic slave trade would continue a few of the Danish private free traders in Osu wrote wills and officially declared paternity over their children, suggesting that they were securing their ties to their African families in a formal European manner. By formally recognizing their families, the Danish traders could pass their property on to their children and wives, and they were presumably doing so to protect them and their futures just at the moment when their families' livelihoods were threatened. In 1807, 1808, and 1812, private traders H. C. Truelsen, Johan Emanuel Richter, and Tønne Bloch Ramus all officially claimed paternity of their Euro-African children in Osu. H. C. Truelsen's sounds the following: "I hereby declare that my four children Johanne Kristine born August 17, 1796, Caroline born March 10, 1800, Sophia Charlotte Lovise born May 24, 1803, and Birthe Elisabeth born July 16, 1807, who I have bred together with Mulatresse Maria Elisabeth and Christened here in this place, shall henceforward have the same rights that the law gives natural children, who are recognized as kith and kin, both in the case that I should remain unmarried till I die, and if I enter into any marriage."[15] Both Richter's declaration from the year before and Tønne Bloch Ramus's declaration from 1812 have very similar wording. All three declarations mention the christening of the children, and in both Ramus's and Richter's case they also emphasized the Christian status of their Euro-African wives and their membership of the congregation at Christiansborg. They also all refer to the same place in Danske Lov (the Danish Law), which stated that all contracts voluntarily entered by a person of age should be respected. With these declarations the traders made their African families rightful heirs.[16]

Other Danish traders and assistants in Osu secured their children and cassare wives by naming them as heirs in written wills. This practice had been used by Dutch and English traders on the Gold Coast in the eighteenth century, but by few earlier Danish traders.[17] Now Danish men were leaving property (often slaves and pawns, and even few stone houses) to their Euro-African families. In 1815, for example, former governor and trader N. C. Holm wrote a will in which he stated that everything he owned in Africa after his death should be "brought to Christiansborg and divided between my children such that the young ones get as much as the older."[18] Further on in the will he explicitly stated which of his slaves should be given to which of his children, and he made sure to mention that he had quite a large sum—5,807 rdl. (in 1815 the governor at Christiansborg made 83⅓ rdl. a month) in trust with a merchant J. D. Vogel in Denmark.[19]

Yet other Danish men wrote deeds of gifts willing single items of property to African family or friends, as in 1812 when former governor Schiønning passed on land and buildings "in Allatu quarter" to his "cassaret Negress," Tolo. As if he was uncertain whether his will would be respected, he specified all the iron and woodwork (including doors, windows, hatches, hinges, nails, cramps, hooks) on the buildings in question. The deed of gift was given as "reward for her five years faithful service."[20] For wages he had not paid her and in repayment of money she had lent him, he also left her several slaves, a bed, a table, twelve chairs, and more. Tolo is one of very few women with African names known to have been cassaret to Danish men in the nineteenth century, and it is tempting to suggest that Schiønning might have doubted that the will would be respected because his cassaret wife did not come from one of the established Euro-African families in Osu.

Without such official wills and deeds of gifts, African families were not entitled to inherit, but they might still be "paid" from the estates. Tolo, remember, was paid "wages" that she was due. As mentioned in Chapter 1, it did happen that women cassaret to Danish men from Christiansborg were paid "for their services," and this became increasingly common in the late eighteenth and nineteenth centuries. In 1799, for example, when assistant Jørgen Mandix died, there was nothing left in his estate when all his debts were paid, and Governor Wrisberg sent in a list of different expenses that were to be paid to Mandix's "boys" and "mulatresse with child," to be covered by the administration at Christiansborg. Both Mandix's "boys" (slaves Sabba, Adabie, Tobbo, Jabua, They Badue) and his "mulatresse and daughter Olavia" received their outstanding "reward and wages [prœmie and gage]."[21] Interestingly Mandix's Euro-African wife also received a piece of gold from his estate, which she said he had promised to return to her, since it had once belonged to her mother. Her claim was confirmed by the surgeon at the fort, and the gold was returned to her.

This increasingly common practice, in which Danish men in Osu officially declared their paternity and mentioned their Euro-African families in wills, suggests that they took an interest in the well-being and future of their wives and children. But it might also suggest that the private traders in Osu were aware that the pressure on the slave trade coming from the larger Atlantic world would eventually lead to an erosion of the material foundation of not only their own marriages, but also the larger hybrid Euro-African subculture that the marriages had produced. Their campaign to protect this world took form simultaneously in the new language of family and inheritance, and in an increasingly vocal defense of the slave trade itself.[22]

Perhaps the defense of the slave trade in Europe in the late eighteenth century was rooted in the intimate and personal investments some European men had in the trade. In Copenhagen, for example, one of the most vocal supporters of the Atlantic slave trade, Andreas Riegelsen Biørn, had family to secure and protect in Osu. Biørn was a very young son of a chaplain from Norway, who came out as assistant at Christiansborg in 1761; he became head merchant at Fredensborg in 1764, when he was still less than twenty years old, and according to a later list from Christiansborg, he must have had at least two children around that time. Biørn left for Copenhagen in 1768 but came back to Christiansborg again twenty years later, now in the position of governor. He arrived at Christiansborg in November 1789, and the following year he helped document the fort's economy in preparation for the arrival of a new administration. The documents from this transaction included a long list of the fort's creditors and debtors in Osu, and among the creditors were two Euro-Africans, who we must assume to be Governor Biørn's children: Anne Sophie Biørn and Christian Biørn. Governor Biørn might very well have had a hand in making sure that his children wound up on the receiving end of the debit ledger from the fort.[23]

Biørn's personal and family investment in the slave trade might explain why he chose to take employment in Africa a second time, but it also might explain why he was such an ardent supporter of the slave trade. After he returned to Europe and settled in Copenhagen in 1793 he wrote several publications in defense of the slave trade, most extensively a self-published pamphlet from 1806, in which he argued that it was neither practical nor beneficial to abolish the trade. Like the private traders at Christiansborg, former governor Biørn seems to have thought that there was still a possibility that the ban on the trade could be overturned, but instead of bringing any new arguments to the debate he recycled the ones that slave-trade defenders had presented in the abolition debates for decades: abolishing the slave trade would hurt the plantations in the Danish West Indies; millions of Europeans around the world now depended on the trade, directly or through the products produced by slave labor; no Dane would want to see the profits from the slave trade go to the southern European nations; Africans were better off being enslaved in the West Indies than living in inland Africa with heathen cannibals; all enslaved Africans were criminals and war captives; and so on.[24]

We usually think of such arguments from the proslavery side of the abolition debate as presented by emotionally detached capitalists, men willing to ignore the dire descriptions of conditions onboard the cramped and deadly slave ships. But what about those whose intimate, familial worlds were built on the foundation of those ships and dungeons, and for whom the end of the trade meant the loss not just of profit but of their families' livelihood? What do these arguments in defense of the Atlantic slave trade sound like, when they are understood in the context of the personal and family investments Danish and other European slave traders had in Africa? Their Euro-African wives and children and their extended kinship networks were threatened by the abolition of the slave trade, and it is easy to imagine them—and their families in Africa—feeling insecure as the basis for encounters between Europeans and Africans on the Gold Coast was about to shift radically.

The private traders were right: the transformation of the structures put in place during the Atlantic slave trade would put them in an awkward and probably risky situation. Africans who had traded with the Danes were likely to find other trading partners, and those who used to work for the Danes would form other alliances. Euro-African soldiers at Christiansborg made it clear that their commitment to the fort stretched only as far as they thought they were getting enough in return. One early example of a labor conflict before the slave trade officially ended shows how even Euro-African soldiers (men with Danish names and generations of European men in their paternal line of heritage) would not remain loyal to the Danes under all conditions. The conflict began when the Chamber of Customs in 1796 communicated to the fort that they wanted to cut the number and wages of their Euro-African soldiers. In 1798 the Secret Council called all the soldiers and officers together and informed them of this decision, and in protest the soldiers and officers then submitted a memorandum signed "Corporal J. Sonne, Engman and all the mulatto soldiers." In the memorandum the Euro-African soldiers laid out how they had been told by Governor Wrisberg that "our wages will be cut to a level we can't possibly live off."[25] The Euro-African soldiers pointed out that on top of their living expenses they were also required to pay for uniforms that were much more expensive in Africa than in Europe. They therefore asked to have their outstanding wages paid immediately, threatening to leave and seek employment at one of the other European forts if their demands were not satisfied.

Governor Wrisberg asked the members of the Secret Council to comment on the memorandum from the Euro-African soldiers, and they all agreed that it would be dangerous and irresponsible to let the soldiers go. Christian Schiønning argued that if the fort fired as many soldiers as they had been requested to, the fort could not possibly be defended, nor could the fort protect the property of the private traders in Osu. He added that though some of the Euro-Africans theoretically could be replaced by Africans from Osu at a lower wage, this would not work in practice because Africans in Osu were all related to Euro-African soldiers, and the latter would put pressure on the former to refuse the jobs or "buy them to infidelity"—meaning that these new soldiers' loyalties would be with the fired Euro-African soldiers and that this could turn them against the Danish fort.[26] Governor Johan Wrisberg concluded that even though the complaint from the Euro-African soldiers was a "disobedience," the fort could not do without them, since there were no other soldiers to fill their position. He resolved that all the soldiers should remain in their positions with their earlier wages until the Secret Council had heard further from Copenhagen and other military personnel had been sent out from Denmark to serve as soldiers at the forts.

When the slave trade officially ended, many of the Euro-African soldiers were in fact let go. In 1816 the Chamber of Customs suggested that the new economic situation after the slave trade had made several of the Euro-African soldiers as well as many fort slaves "superfluous."[27] The following year Governor Richter reported that all the reductions demanded by the chamber had gone through: "the superfluous soldiers have been dismissed and the bonus has been given them."[28] Three of the remaining four forts were closed, and if the Danes were to have any future on the Gold Coast it would be as plantation colonists and not as slave traders. In this new situation diplomacy was going to be just as important as before, but now Danes had very little to offer to African allies. Using the term "superfluous soldiers" would certainly have harmed the Danes' remaining connections among Euro-Africans, so it is improbable that Richter was using this language in direct communication with the Euro-African soldiers or their families.[29]

When Danish administrators and traders communicated with the king in Denmark, they used a different tone, which indicates the colonial mindset that shaped Danish action on the Gold Coast in the nineteenth century. In fact, the Danish king in Copenhagen seems to have assumed that Danes had a power over Africans that they did not have in reality. A telling example of this dynamic—of the Danish king acting as if he had authority in Africa, and Euro-Africans ignoring him—came up in regard to slave trading in the early 1820s. Probably responding to questions from Copenhagen about why slave trading was still going on in Osu, Governor Steffens reported in June 1821 on behalf of the Euro-African traders in Osu to the king of Denmark. According to Steffens they had not stopped slave trading because they had never been informed about the Danish ban. Almost two decades after the ban was supposed to have been in place, it is unlikely that the Euro-African slave traders in Osu were ignorant of it. The question then is why they did not just inform the king that he had no authority over them. Presumably they, or Governor Steffens, who was writing on their behalf, did not want to offend the Danish king, and perhaps they were hoping that the issue would stop there. Denmark was far away and correspondence slow.[30]

Perhaps they should have cut closer to the heart of the matter though, because King Frederik VI did press the issue further and demanded an explanation: it had been suggested to him by the Secret Council at Christiansborg that it was "doubtful" that he had the authority to stop Africans from slave trading, and he wanted to know if this also pertained to "Negroes who are under the Majesty's dominion [*herredømme*]."[31] If the Secret Council responded to this question from King Frederik, it did not do so quickly; there is no record of their answer in the years immediately following. It would have been difficult to respond politely to the absolute monarch to let him know that he had no authority in Africa. From the perspective of this story, however, the exchange is interesting because it suggests that the Euro-African traders, for whom Steffens was speaking, were still slave trading in 1821 and were not about to stop doing so simply because the Danish king and other European rulers had ordered it.

Even so, the Atlantic slave trade had in fact slowed down dramatically by that point, and whether the Danish king understood it or not, the changing configuration of the Atlantic economy, which had rendered Euro-African soldiers at Christiansborg "superfluous," had real material consequences for families in Osu. The end of the trade eroded the material purpose of the Danish presence in Africa and, more specifically, the practical necessity of the cassare marriages. In an Atlantic world without the slave trade, European men might still depend on African women to survive in Africa, and they might even need them to help them trade privately in goods, but cassare marriages were no longer central to Danish diplomatic and political interactions on the coast. The family and kinship networks that had forced (or allowed) Danes and Ga to see past racial difference were no longer crucial. Once the slave traders were no longer there to stand up for the marriages, colonial racial discourse, which had been steadily growing stronger over the course of the eighteenth century, gained a kind of power on the Gold Coast that it could not have had during the Atlantic slave trade.

This strengthening of racial hierarchies meant that interracial marriage was becoming increasingly suspect, and Euro-African families in Osu came under not only material but also discursive pressure. No colonial order had been established by Danes on the Gold Coast, but those who imagined such a possibility left no doubt where they stood: in Osu, as in many other places, the criticism and questioning of interracial marriage primarily came from Europeans with interests in establishing plantation colonies. In the case of the Danes in Africa, Paul Isert was one of the first published voices to seriously question and ridicule the cassare marriages. Isert, who has been mentioned several times in this story already, was an archetypical Enlightenment scientist explorer—referring to Rousseau whenever he got the chance—who first wrote a well-known travel account from the coast and later was involved in an attempt to establish a plantation in the Akwapim mountains. In his account from 1788 (Figure 9) he called the cassare marriages "one of the most peculiar customs" and remarked that he often tried to talk newly arrived Danes at Christiansborg out of cassaring: "I give each one the well-meant advice not to enter into such an arrangement, at least for the first year, since I have often been struck by the harm that results."[32]

Isert also sowed uncertainty about how officially the cassare marriages were recognized. After describing the rights and privileges involved in the cassare marriages, Isert noted, "It is understood here, however, that neither an engagement nor a marriage ceremony has taken place here, and the new husband can send his wife packing the next day if he feels like it."[33] Considering that women had rights to complain and to regular monthly payments, it is questionable what exactly Isert meant when he wrote that. Given that the Danish administration, many chaplains at Christiansborg, and Ga and Akan families all accepted and encouraged the institution, it is hard to see how they could *not* have thought of the cassare relationships as a type of marriage. Isert was probably implying that the men at Christiansborg disrespected the cassare marriages; he was generally critical of the behaviors and attitudes of the men at the fort. But his comments come off as a more general misunderstanding of the cassare institution. Perhaps Isert's problem was that he was

Paul Erdmann Isert's,
ehemahl. königl. dänisch. Oberarzte an den Besizzungen
in Afrika,

Reise nach Guinea

und den
Caribäischen Inseln in Columbien,
in Briefen an seine Freunde beschrieben.

Akraisches Frauenzimmer. S. 188.

Kopenhagen, 1788.
Gedruckt bey J. F. Morthorst, wohnhaft in der Pilestraß
No. 11. Litr. B.

Figure 9. "Akraisches Frauenzimmer." Frontispiece of Paul Erdmann Isert, *Reise nach Guinea und den Caribaischen Inseln in Columbien in Briefen an seine Freunde beschrieben* (Copenhagen, 1788). Isert was born in Brandenburg in 1755 and died on the Gold Coast in 1789. Isert, *Letters*, 16.

not a slave trader, and so could not see the deeper purpose and the binding agreement behind the marriages. Standing outside the trade that had given rise to the marriages, all Isert could see was a peculiar custom.[34]

Not only was Isert not a slave trader, he was a colonialist, and a stern Enlightenment critic of the Atlantic slave trade. On his way back to Denmark after his first stay in Africa, he sailed to the Danish West Indies on a slave ship and witnessed slaves revolting on the way. This experience along with the observations he made visiting plantations in the Danish West Indies cemented his belief in the inhumanity of the Atlantic slave trade and a need to reform the plantation system. From that point on, his view of both the trade and the cassare marriages in Osu flowed from his critique of the slave trade and his wish to replace the slave-trading posts on the Gold Coast with a plantation colony. This idea had been part of the discussions about abolishing the slave trade from the beginning, but Isert was a driving force in turning it into practice. In 1788, shortly before the edict of 1792 and as the plan to abolish the Danish slave trade was being developed, Isert, together with finance minister and West Indian sugar-plantation owner Ernst Schimmelmann's private secretary, drafted a formal legislative proposal for a plantation colony in Africa.[35]

This plan proposed a much more rigid racial hierarchy, with firmer divisions between Europeans and Africans than was the practice in Osu during the slave trade. In Isert's colony white settlers would wear their military uniforms even on Sundays and holidays, and no Africans, free or enslaved, would appear in public naked or half-naked. Free Africans would be distinguished from slaves by the clothes they wore, but perhaps by much more than that: "If and under what conditions free-negroes shall be allowed to settle in the colony," Isert wrote, "will be determined later."[36] Most important for the present story, the instructions that Schimmelmann and Christian V. Brandt sent with Isert when he left to put the colonial plans into practice specifically requested that the borders between Africans and Europeans in the colony be policed in a way that had hitherto been unknown in the Danish settlements. They would have been quite familiar to Schimmelmann and the other planters on St. Croix: "Regarding Europeans who settle in the Colony, it is desired that these always make up one race, a people in themselves, and it must always be the law for the Colony that between Europeans and the country's black inhabitants lawful marriages or alliances do not take place."[37] Isert, and presumably also Schimmelmann and Brandt, knew what influence and importance cassare marriages had in determining political and social alliances in Osu, and perhaps they were trying to avoid a similar situation in the plantation colony. Like other colonists, they probably generally considered official intimate relationships between Europeans and Africans subversive of the racial order they wanted to maintain. In any case, they specifically hoped to outlaw the officially recognized cassare marriages. The colonial plans did not mention whether unofficial unions were to be tolerated, as they were in the West Indies at that time.

When Isert called the interracial marriage practice a "peculiar custom," he took part in a long-developing Enlightenment discourse that indirectly helped make all types of interracial sex suspect in the colonial Atlantic world. Indeed, more broadly, the discourse that helped abolish the slave trade also helped produce racial difference. In the intense and ever louder debate about the slave trade in the last decades of the eighteenth and in the early nineteenth centuries, both sides of the argument were grouping all Africans together in one large category. One side saw them as victims of the slave trade who should be redeemed by abolition; the other side argued that they were victims of African savagery and heathenism who would be improved by enslavement in the Americas. In that debate, racial difference between Africans and Europeans overpowered the social distinctions that had for more than a century allowed the Danish slave traders of Christiansborg to make much finer divisions among Africans. Isert's strong criticism of the slave trade had of course grown out of a humanitarian aspiration to prevent the awful conditions for enslaved Africans sold across the Atlantic, but in the process it erased human individuality by discursively strengthening the broad unspecified category "the African."[38]

In the 1780s, at the height of the Danish slave trade, Isert's vocal opposition to that trade made him very much an outsider at Christiansborg. The developing Enlightenment discourse he represented had still not had much influence on the practices of the Atlantic slave trade, nor on the importance of the cassare marriages in the cultural encounters on the coast. Indeed, despite his critique of the marriages, he also detailed how they had become a well-established social institution. He described how a man proceeded if he had found a woman he wanted to marry: "He then sends a humble memorandum to the High Council wherein he announces the name of his chosen future half and asks that he may be given permission to take her as his (quasi) wife."[39] As soon as the couple was announced, the man paid half a month's salary to the "mulatto chest" and also began paying 4 percent monthly to the chest, and so on. Overall he was painting a picture of a marriage practice that was at least as crucial in the cultural encounter as it had been earlier in the eighteenth century. At the same time though, his belittling of the institution indicated the discursive currents brewing in the Atlantic world that would lead to a growing criticism of not only the slave trade, but also of interracial marriage and intimacy.[40]

Danish slave traders standing up for their wives and children in Osu in the decades around the early nineteenth century should be placed in the context of both material and discursive pressures. When they wrote wills and declared their paternity officially, they might very well have been responding to the insecurities produced by the oncoming abolition of the slave trade. Along similar lines and in the same year as the wills were written, bookkeeper Mathias Thonning stood up for his cassaret wife to defend her reputation. Thonning complained to the Secret Council, claiming that assistant Ernst Schrøder had offended him by accusing his cassaret wife, Cathrine Sonne, of adultery: "Last night Assistant Schrøder greatly offended me. In the presence of Commandant Krog, Chaplain Monrad, Merchant Ramus, the gentlemen Assistants Svanekiær and Reiersen, and several negroes in Merchant Ramus's house, he accused my wife of having lain with him in a disgraceful [*skammelig*] manner. He has even announced the scene of the crime: namely behind the church."[41] A commission consisting of the interim governor, a commandant, the chaplain, and an assistant investigated the case, heard several witnesses, and obtained a confession from assistant Schrøder, in which he declared that what he had said about Cathrine Sonne was untrue and that he had always known her to be "a proper wife, whose reputation is unblemished." The case was closed, Mathias Thonning's honor was rectified, and Cathrine Sonne's name was cleared: "today in public with proclamation and drummer Thonning's Mulatresse Cathrine Sonne's conduct as cassaret wife will be justified."[42]

It is not surprising that Mathias Thonning felt his honor offended by the accusation that his wife had slept with another man. What is interesting is that he brought the case to the Secret Council, and that both he and the accused assistant Schrøder referred to "a proper wife" whose reputation was to be protected. Why was it so important for Thonning to clear his wife's name? His concern makes good sense if we place it in light of the pressure on the cassare institution and the Euro-African families it had produced. In the following decades, the changes that the private traders had been protesting *did* unfold: the Atlantic slave trade waned, and the cultural encounter it had produced shifted from trade to colonialism.

The colony that Paul Isert had planned was never established. He arrived with his wife and a group of prospective settlers at Christiansborg in November 1788 and died two months later, followed soon after first by his wife and then by their newborn child. More successful Danish plantations did take root in the Akwapim mountains, some of them established by Danish slave traders who were cassaret in Africa and therefore would not have shared Isert's interest in maintaining a ban on marriages between Danes and Africans or Euro-Africans. The end of the slave trade had not meant the end of the cassare institution; it did continue. But the marriages now took place in a quite different and explicitly colonial encounter.[43]

The Danes' growing colonial ambitions had an impact on the relationship between Osu and Christiansborg, both symbolically and in how the Danish envisioned their role in Africa. The tree-lined alley, Kings High Road (leading from the fort to the Bibease plantation from 1803 and, starting in 1826, to the royal plantation Frederiksgave as well), was laid out with mathematical precision, and Danes established a growing number of decorative gardens; the Danish presence appeared more and more like that of a colonial power. This was not a coincidence. Danes at Christiansborg were sent out by a king who believed that he did in fact have authority over land and people in relation to his forts, and since well before the slave trade had officially ended, high-ranking people in the West Indian and Guinean office of the Chamber of Customs had been directly involved in the plans to establish a colony in Africa. The most important of these was Peter Thonning, who had personally traveled to and stayed at Christiansborg.[44]

Peter Thonning was sent out by the Chamber of Customs in 1799 to survey the possibilities of establishing a colony. Like Isert, he was an ardent supporter of the idea. Thonning was an Enlightenment scientist, and like his more famous contemporaries Alexander von Humboldt and Carl Linnaeus, he drew maps and catalogued natural and cultural phenomena. After three years in Africa, he wrote a long report about the marvelous possibilities of establishing a colony in Africa. After returning to Copenhagen, he was a tutor for the royal family for a number of years, and in 1811 he got a position in the Chamber of Customs. In 1815, he was put in charge of the colonial office, which supervised both the West Indian sugar colony and the former trading posts in Africa, and from 1816 he was also in charge of the Danish trading post in India. He was in charge, for example, when, after the Napoleonic Wars, the newly cost-conscious Danish state dismissed the now "superfluous" soldiers from the fort. To him there was no question about what the Danish king should do with his "possessions" on the Gold Coast: "Only through colonies will the Europeans be able to spread culture and milder customs, as well as win influence among the natives."[45] Even though the Danish colonial ambitions largely failed on the Gold Coast, such colonial attitudes had an impact on interactions between Europeans and Africans on the coast throughout the nineteenth century.

When European presence on the coast transitioned from mercantile to colonial, Euro-Africans in Osu found themselves negotiating a diminishing intermediate space between Europeans and Africans on the Gold Coast. As in many other parts of the Atlantic world in the nineteenth century, acceptance and encouragement of intercultural positions was shrinking. Colonial thoughts and practices—both the Danish plans and the British colonization of the Gold Coast—changed interactions between Europeans and Africans, and in the same process the Euro-African hybrid culture in Osu became ever more distinct. Euro-African positions on the coast were always varied and often had connections in both cultures, but over the course of the nineteenth century the cultural frontier between Europeans and Africans solidified, and it was no longer a given that Euro-African intermediaries would have grounding in both cultural groups simultaneously.[46]

Nineteenth century Euro-Africans in Osu still negotiated positions in both European and African communities, but they were now compelled to switch between two distinct cultural groups rather than assuming a flexible belonging in both. A case at Christiansborg in 1808 illustrates this shifting between two distinct statuses particularly well. When a Euro-African woman named Cathrine Schalz[47] came into conflict with Esau Quist, a Euro-African soldier from Christiansborg, she sought Danish protection by invoking her position as "child of a white."[48] What exactly the case was about is not clear from the minute books, but it had to do with Esau Quist's rights to seek retribution for his wife's infidelity, with a debt he owed to people in Ada, east of Accra, and with Cathrine Schalz's fear of being kidnapped and having her "people taken from her" if she traveled from Ningo, east of Accra, back to Osu. Schalz was, according to the minutes, willing to travel to Ada to settle the conflict with Esau Quist if the Danes would ensure her protection on the way, but what she really wanted was for the case to be settled at Christiansborg or at the Danish fort in Ningo, because, as "child of a white," this was where she had to "do her palaver."[49]

The Danes at Christiansborg were not sure what to think of Cathrine

Schalz's request for protection on the grounds of being Euro-African. When she first addressed Governor Schiønning and told him about the conflict with Quist, Schiønning thought that since Quist was in service as a soldier at the fort and Cathrine "live[d] under the fort" it was his duty to hear the case from both parties. He therefore called Esau Quist to the fort to hear his version of the story, but Quist protested and said that "he and she were not white but negroes, who did not belong under the fort's jurisdiction but under the fetish [Ga priest]." Even after several requests he insisted that "he did not owe the fort anything," and at that point Schiønning agreed that the conflict should be solved by the Ga priest in Ada.[50]

What is interesting here is that Cathrine Schalz invoked the difference between herself and other Africans to get help in the conflict, and that, to some extent, this invocation made sense to the governor. The case also suggests that Esau Quist's and Cathrine Schalz's positions in the coastal community were sufficiently ambiguous that they could claim to belong to both the European and the African communities. Esau Quist claimed they were "negroes," while Cathrine Schalz claimed they were children of Europeans. Belonging to one or the other group would have given them different opportunities. Esau Quist was certainly well connected to the Danes over generations, and so was Cathrine Schalz. From the letters in the case it is clear that both Flindt and Schiønning had conversations with her where they had heard her opinion about the conflict with Quist and were basing their assessment of the case on what she told them.[51]

Cathrine Schalz's connections to the fort were clear—but what of her connections to other Africans? In her request to have the conflict with Esau Quist settled at the fort because she was the "child of a white," she claimed that at Ada she would be a "total stranger [*vild fremmed*]."[52] If we follow this line of argument and see her as an individual seeking protection from the fort out of fear of being kidnapped, then she appears to have been fairly vulnerable. Yet according to Esau Quist she had bribed commandant Flindt to bribe the priest in Accra to overrule Quist's claim; if there were any truth to this claim, then she must have been rather well connected in Accra as well. In that case it seems likely that she, like Esau Quist, could sometimes be in alliance with the fort, but at other times be more closely attached to kin in the coastal community. She was traveling from Ningo with a number of people whom she claimed to fear would be taken from her. It may have been in Schalz's interest to portray herself as a fearful daughter of a white man, but a Euro-African traveling between slave-trading forts with a group of people she called "hers" was hardly the helpless innocent suggested by her appeal.

Euro-Africans occupied a variety of positions in the nineteenth-century coastal community. Their positions could change depending on the context, but they also varied from individual to individual. Some descendants of European men or Euro-African parents were not connected to the fort or to Europeans at all, while others were connected to varying degrees. Some were successful traders; others were poor. Important factors deciding the opportunities and positions of Euro-Africans included the status of their mothers and their fathers and the amount of attention and material support their parents could contribute to their upbringing. But in the constant positioning in the coastal community, claiming a belonging to the fort "as child of a white" was, at least by Cathrine Schalz, considered helpful.[53]

Being "child of a white" was also beneficial when inheriting property or attending school at the fort, but there were clearly limits to how far Euro-Africans could rise in the European social hierarchies of their fathers' worlds. Euro-Africans were not "white." This became clear when Johan Emanuel Richter tried to hire his Euro-African son as assistant at the fort. Richter became interim governor in 1817 and immediately hired his son, Henrich Richter, as assistant at the fort at a salary of 400 rdl. a year. After four months, the Chamber of Customs informed Governor Richter that his son would have to be dismissed. No "colored person" or any other than persons born in "His Majesty's European countries" could be hired as assistant at the fort. A few years later the Chamber again stressed that no "mulatto" could be hired as assistant. Exceptions to this could be made only under the conditions of a dire lack of people to employ, and then Euro-Africans should only be hired as "helpmates" and at a maximum of 15 rdl. a month.[54]

Henrich Richter's father did not believe his son's opportunities for employment on the Gold Coast should be limited by his race. The senior Richter's view on his son's race was expressed in a conflict a few years earlier between Governor Schiønning at Christiansborg and Johan Emanuel Richter, then commandant at Fort Fredensborg by Ningo. Governor Schiønning had called the young Henrich Richter a "dishonest mulatto," to which Richter responded to the governor that whatever else might be said about his son, and whatever mistakes he might have made in his youth, his race should not be brought into the question. His son, who had been educated in England, was "neither a mulatto nor a mestizo," Richter argued. Material wealth and education should, according to his father, make him equal to a European man: "I have given him for my money an education such as to enable him to match many a European." Unquestionably, Lene Kühberg's grandson (with his parentage and his later fortune) could have matched any of the other traders on the coast in these terms. But he was not a European.[55]

Johan Emanuel Richter's conflict with Governor Schiønning and his attempt to hire Henrich Richter at Christiansborg reflected broader disagreements about what constituted "white" and what race meant. Even as the slave trade was winding down, in Osu some old coast men still tried to argue that race was cultural. From Richter's perspective, the education and the Christian upbringing he had provided for his son made Henrich Richter equal to any man regardless of color; racial difference defined by color and descent could be erased by Christianity and education. The response of the administration in Copenhagen to the case about Richter showed that, to them, racial difference was not a malleable distinction. Richter was not alone in thinking that the small group of privileged Euro-Africans on the Gold Coast were equal to Europeans and should have the same opportunities, but however influential this view might have been in some circles on the coast, it was not the last word: the Richters and people like them lived in an Atlantic world where race, defined in increasingly rigid and biological terms, certainly mattered.[56]

Henrich Richter for one, never stopped believing that he was as capable as any European to serve the Danish king at Christiansborg, or perhaps even more capable. In 1840, when the post of governor of Christiansborg sat vacant, he wrote an application to the king in Copenhagen. He acknowledged that having been "born in Africa" would be an obstacle to his application, but he hoped his many other advantages would make up for this. Not only had his father sent him to England for his education, he had also participated in two wars in Africa along with the Danes, during the second of which he had received the important Knight of Dannebrog medal; he knew all the languages that were spoken in "the lands possessed by the King," was familiar with the customs of Africans, and was on good terms with all the chiefs in the area. All in all, he was a highly qualified candidate for the post as governor, but the administration in Copenhagen held to their policy of hiring men only from "His Majesty's European countries."[57] Though "child of a white," Henrich Richter did not have the same opportunities as his father.

In Osu, on the other hand, Henrich Richter was the wealthiest and most influential of a small group of Euro-Africans with Danish names and ancestors—soon known as "the Christiansborg Mulattos." This group over-lapped with the group of privileged families who have been called a "merchant class" or a "modern" social elite in Accra, though none of the others were as wealthy as Richter and many were just slightly better off than most people in Osu.[58] Such distinct Euro-African elites existed in several nineteenth-century Gold Coast trading towns and indeed all over the Atlantic world. Though Euro-Africans in Osu may never have constituted a separate social class in the same way that Euro-Africans did in the larger town Elmina, they were begin-ning to live separately from other Africans in the nineteenth century.[59]

One development that suggests Euro-Africans in Osu lived and thought of themselves as separate from other people in Osu was the distinct Euro-African asafo company that sources refer to in the early nineteenth century. In 1812 Governor Schiønning suggested dissolving a "mulatto asafo" after a conflict with soldiers from this asafo who had participated in the military force sent out from Osu in a battle against Akwapim, which is a rare reference to a distinct Euro-African asafo in Osu. In nearby Elmina, Euro-African de-scendants of Dutch employees, known as *tapoeyers* or *vrijburgers*, lived in a separate quarter of town and had their own asafo company. Like Elmina and Cape Coast, Osu was also divided into separate quarters with concentrations of a specific ethnic group, and it is possible that one of these was inhabited primarily by Euro-Africans.[60]

That Euro-Africans in Elmina had their own quarter and asafo company shows not only that they were a separate group in the community, but also that they were recognized and integrated in the larger Akan community, where asafo companies were important in the social organization of the com-munity. As much as Euro-Africans became distinct from other Africans in Gold Coast towns in the nineteenth century, this is not the whole story of their social positions. In both Elmina and Osu, Euro-African families always remained closely linked through marriage and blood ties. One indication of how Euro-Africans in Osu were thoroughly connected to other Africans in town was that when Euro-African soldiers at Christiansborg were buried, most of the kin who attended their funerals were not of European descent. Particularly as traders, but also more generally as community members, Euro-Africans were always at least as dependent on connections and relations with the larger Gold Coast communities they lived in as with Europeans. Their po-sition was intermediary, just like their hybrid identities were always a constant negotiation between European and African cultural elements.[61]

Plate 1. Wulff Joseph Wulff painted this watercolor of his cassare wife, Sara Malm, in a letter to his brother-in-law in Copenhagen in the early 1840s (his text encircling the image). Euro-African women in Osu in the nineteenth century most likely dressed much like Sara Malm—or Tim-Tam as she was also called—in this image (see Chapter 5). Museum Østjylland, Randers.

Plate 2. The prince of Joinville painted this watercolor of his lunch with
Governor Edward Carstensen and his men at Christiansborg in January 1843.
His accompanying text does not identify the women (see Epilogue).
M/S Museet for Søfart, Helsingør.

At the same time, Euro-Africans *did* increasingly present as different from other people in Osu. Education—particularly Christian education—was one of the most important signs of privilege and importance in the nineteenth-century Gold Coast. Education in Europe was only for the very few, and only for boys, but a slightly larger group of Euro-Africans (including girls) were educated at the fort school, and both literacy and Christianity became closely related with a Euro-African identity and affluence in the nineteenth century. Wealth became even more associated with European heritage and Western education in ways that advantaged Euro-Africans, and made them more likely to be considered members of the elite.[62]

As the group of Euro-Africans became wealthier and more distinct by religion, Western education, and clothing, there are indications that their position was both envied and criticized by other people in Osu. Chaplain H. C. Monrad—who, as we have seen several times already, considered Euro-Africans particularly suspect and "debaucherous"—believed that Euro-Africans were trapped between Europeans and Africans and did not fully belong in either group. According to Monrad, Africans felt animosity and envy toward the Euro-African subgroup, while Euro-Africans themselves felt proud of their special status. "It is common," wrote Monrad, "for the Mulattos to participate in both the Negroes' and the Europeans' customs, although they are held in disdain about equally by both: by the former because they elevate themselves proudly over them; and by the latter because they want to elevate themselves to their level."[63] Wulff, writing in 1837, saw even more enmity among the different groups—now more or less well understood as "races"—on the Gold Coast: Euro-Africans hated the Europeans but "stayed with" them because the Africans hated the Euro-Africans even more than they hated the Europeans.[64] Whether or not Euro-Africans were despised to the extent that Monrad and Wulff suggested, the pride that Monrad claimed Euro-Africans felt in their special status in Osu sounds similar to the way that Euro-Africans in Cape Coast were said to prize their position as Christian Euro-Africans. The overall image of the nineteenth century is one of a Euro-African community solidifying as a distinct group in the coastal town—but one whose status and primary affiliation remained contested.[65]

When Euro-African women settled with their European cassare husbands and helped them create familiar circles that could remind them of home, they were doing so by embodying a Euro-African culture. When Sara Malm inherited Wulff's house in 1842 and brought her children up among European furniture, sent them to school at the European fort, and dressed them in European clothes, she distinguished herself from the small community in Osu by marking herself as different with material culture that was recognizably European. Like Lene Kühberg seven decades before, Sara Malm benefited from and participated in the broader process of tying prestige and social value to these markers of European culture. Her daily decisions were structured choices. Living as she did in a community where European material culture connoted wealth and social prestige, and in a kinship group where generations of intermarriage with European men had created a Euro-African hybrid culture whose embodied practices revolved in part around this material culture, she probably did not think much about it.

Besides living in a stone house, one of the most important ways Euro-African women signaled their position as "Christian Mulatresses" was by their clothing, and luckily we have a good sense of how Sara Malm was dressed. Around 1840 Wulff painted a watercolor of her, included with a letter to his brother-in-law in Denmark (see Plate 1). This image clearly shows how women like Sara Malm represented a Euro-African hybridity, signaling the long history of cultural mixing with European slave traders, as well as wealth, and social prestige. Her European-style shirt and skirt was combined with an African headdress, which was and still is typical for Ga and Akan women. The characteristic bustle that Euro-African women in Osu were known to wear later in the nineteenth century was part of the same outfit as a European umbrella. She wore gold ornaments that Monrad described as characteristic for Euro-African women in this period—especially at festive occasions like weddings.[66] In a letter accompanying the watercolor Wulff described Sara Malm's dress in detail:

> The part drawn in ink shows gold [ornaments] or doubloons; marks on the face are painted on with chalk or white coloring. Around the neck they wear a so-called over-panties [cover cloth], that is, a type of scarf, not drawn here. Besides gold, beads are also worn around the neck, wrists and ankles. A yellow silk sash, bound in a knot [around the waist], serves as a place for keeping all their favorite ornaments. The lower panties [cloth] are of calico for daily wear, damask for formal use. I have seen Mulatinder [Mulatresses] wearing gold to a value of 100 *lod* [about 15 grams]. Bare feet. They often go without shirts,

thus, fully exposed, they usually paint their [upper] bodies with white colouring, drawing all manner of figures on their necks, shoulders, arms, breasts and backs. For formal attire they hang a silver ring, holding 30 silver keys and suchlike ornaments, on the silk sash around their hips. When they do not have gold ornaments in their hair they cover it with a yellow or black silk kerchief.[67]

The watercolor of Sara Malm is unique in that it gives an impression of the particular Euro-African hybrid way of dressing in Osu in the nineteenth century. But both Wulff's image and the text accompanying it also bear witness to the colonial discourse that put pressure on Edward Carstensen at this same historical moment—and that made him insecure and ambivalent about his relationship with Severine Brock. Like Edward Carstensen's account of his wedding day, Wulff's description of Sara Malm is oddly detached. It sounds much more like a descriptive ethnographic account than a personal description of the mother of one's children. The watercolor also is an impersonal portrait. The flatness and lack of perspective was perhaps mostly a result of Wulff's lack of drawing skills, but why did he choose to paint her in full figure? He seems to have been more interested in conveying the peculiarity and exotic otherness of her way of dressing—and her bare feet—than in showing the personality expressed on her face. And this was not because he did not like traditional portraits. Before he left for Africa he had his own portrait painted by a

Figure 11. Wulff Joseph Wulff, aged twenty-seven. Photograph of painting in Frederiksminde, Osu, painted by David Monies in 1836. Wulff, *A Danish Jew in West Africa*, cover.

professional painter in Copenhagen as a birthday present for his father; this
was probably closer to what a portrait looked like to him (Figure 11).

Yet for some reason he did not mimic his own portrait when he painted
Sara Malm for his brother-in-law in Copenhagen. He also did not mention
her as his wife, but as his "mulatresse," and nowhere in his letters to his parents or to his brother-in-law did he mention that he had three children in
Africa. He had not asked his parents' permission to marry, and given that
they were Jewish, a Christian marriage at Christiansborg might not have
been to their liking. He did not exactly hide that he was living with Sara
Malm, and his family in Denmark may have wondered about the two children for whom he was ordering hats and toys, but his letters did not address
their presence further. It is perhaps not surprising that he wrote so little
about them, given that he was writing to his parents and family, unlike Edward Carstensen, who was writing to himself, in his diary, when he described Severine. But why did Wulff Joseph Wulff bring Sara Malm up at all?
Why did he go through the trouble of painting a watercolor of her? Perhaps
he was as ambivalent about his relationship with Sara Malm as Edward
Carstensen was about his with Severine Brock. She made him feel at home
on the coast, but he was well aware that in the wider Atlantic world—and in
his family in Denmark—she was not considered an appropriate marriage
partner.

But then what did it take for Wulff to be able to recognize his marriage to
Sara Malm as real, as binding, as a promise for which he should take responsibility? Probably the most important factor was that he was able to recognize
his cassare wife and children as a family, just as Edward Carstensen in 1842
had recognized his union with Severine as a "circle that can vaguely resemble
a home."[68] Wulff and Sara's cohabitation lasted longer than Edward lived with
Severine, and Wulff clearly felt at home in Frederiksminde. Right after moving into the house he wrote to his brother-in-law that he wished his (Danish)
family could look through the door and see how beautiful it all was—"a pure
paradise"—and he no longer could imagine living anywhere else.[69] How
would he have felt about his family "circle" if Sara Malm had used only her
nickname Tim-Tam and had kept living in a gender-segregated compound
with her mother and all her female kin? Would he still have built Frederiksminde and made her the heir to the house and all his slaves? This is of course
a hypothetical scenario, because she did not. Her kin determined that she
would live with her European husband, as he wished.

To Wulff it must have been crucial that Sara presented herself as Euro-African and therefore as different from other Africans. Indeed, Wulff was not particularly fond of Africans in general. In his letters home he sometimes sounds like a typical white planter of his day: "The Negro must be treated strictly, he must have respect for the White Man, and fear must be instilled in him. . . . A White Man must be able to tame several hundred Negroes, or else he might as well pack up and leave. By good treatment he gets absolutely no-where with these devilish black animals."[70] Elsewhere he referred to Africans as "stupid animals," adding, "and this applies to all of them."[71] Presumably he would not have left house and property to someone he thought belonged to the broad category of "negroes" that he was referring to here. Indeed, he did not consider Euro-Africans like Sara Malm to belong to that category; he systematically made distinctions between Euro-Africans and other Africans and made a point to stress how his "mulatresse" could both read and write, how she could run his business for him, if he were to leave the coast to visit Denmark, and how thoughtful and considerate she was.[72]

Perhaps Wulff did not need to make Sara an exception to his generally derogatory perception of Africans to want to live with her. There were plenty of women living with European men all over the world of the European ex-pansion as "concubines" or "housekeepers," who were not made exceptions to racialist discourse. But for him to consider her a wife and legitimate heir to his property, he *did* have to think of her as an exception to his general im-pression of Africans. In a letter to his parents in 1839, before he and Sara had moved into Frederiksminde, he explained to them how he planned to leave her two of his slaves "as a gift" when he left the coast: "You should know, dear Parents, that these people count their wealth mostly in slaves, and when these two that I own have grown up she (the Mulatinde) can get a great deal of work out of them, indeed so much so that their work can sustain her."[73] When he died, he in fact left her several slaves and pawns beyond the ones men-tioned in his letter, and Sara was able to continue the household at Frederiksminde.

Given the material advantages, it is quite obvious why Sara's kin wanted her to be cassaret to Wulff. We don't know what she thought of the situation, but we can follow how she managed to do well in the decades after his death. The opportunities she gained from cassaring a European man were not di-minished by her living with him on a daily basis, as was the case for some women living under such direct patriarchal control in Europe or Africa.

European men in Africa lacked a steady patriarchal presence until they settled more permanently in the later Gold Coast colony. Even the private slave
traders, who had typically only stayed a few years in Africa, were never as
culturally adept or supported in their patriarchal authority as an African husband could have been. They had no real legal or legislative authority on the
coast to back them up. The fort was often supportive—as when the Secret
Council backed up the private traders in their complaint about the abolition
of the slave trade—but they mostly depended on understanding and negotiating the spoken and unspoken rules of a community that their Euro-African
wives must have been better at negotiating.

On top of the complications of living in a foreign culture, newly arrived
European men also still suffered from "climate fever" and all the other tropical diseases and hence still depended to a considerable extent on their Euro-
African wives for their survival in Africa. Wulff, for one, was in great need of
someone who would take care of him during illness, and Sara's cassare marriage to Wulff is a good example of both how dependent European men could
be on their Euro-African wives, and how successfully Euro-African women
could negotiate their position with connections to both European and African groups in Osu. Wulff depended on Sara, but she in turn could establish
herself as "one of the Christened mulatresses that Europeans marry." After
Wulff died, Sara kept living in Frederiksminde with her three children (see
Figures 12 and 13). She sent two of them to school at Christiansborg, which
was now run by the Basel mission, and was herself a member of the congregation there. In the eyes of the missionaries Sara Malm was "the most respectable mulatto woman in the whole town."[74] She was also materially
secure. Late in the 1840s, for example, she was among five Euro-African
women who rented slaves and pawns to the Danish fort administration as
soldiers, against receiving half of their salary from the fort. But her success
was dependent on her cassare marriage to Wulff, or, more precisely, on him
recognizing their marriage as a marriage—as a heartfelt union—so that he
would write her into his will, thereby placing her ahead of his family in Denmark in the distribution of his African wealth.[75]

This moment during which Danish men sought to secure the futures of
their "mulatresses" and children soon passed. As the nineteenth century progressed and British colonial rule was established, European men stopped
passing their property and slaves on to cassare wives. It seems that things had
already changed when Sara and Wulff's daughter, Wilhelmine Wulff, was cassaret. In 1859, nine years after the Danes had left the coast and the British had

Figure 12. Wilhelmine Josephine Wulff (born ca. 1840), daughter of Sara Malm
and Wulff Joseph Wulff. Notice the difference between the headdress Wilhelmine
Wulff is wearing in this photograph and Sara Malm's headdress in the watercolor
her husband painted (see Plate 1). Hilary Jones has noted a similar transition in the
dress of Euro-African women in Senegal in this period, as Euro-African daughters
"abandoned the conical head ties worn by their signare [high-status, property-
owning] foremothers in favor of uncovered, European-style coiffures with ribbons
or hairnet" (*Metis*, 91). Museum Østjylland, Randers.

taken over at Christiansborg, Wilhelmine Wulff (Figure 12) was courted by
the British commanding officer Cochrane at Christiansborg. Cochrane had
apparently encountered Wilhelmine Wulff at the fort, where she was a teacher
at the girls' mission school, and contacted Sara Wulff, proposing to marry
Wilhelmine "according to the country's custom."[76] Cochrane had not been on
the coast long and was reputed to already having had four to six concubines,

so Sara went to one of the missionaries to ask him to decline Cochrane's offer on her behalf. The missionaries, who agreed that Cochrane would not be a proper husband for Wilhelmine, tried to persuade him that it would be a sin for a Christian young woman to enter into a "marriage according to the custom." Cochrane disagreed. He thought it would be an honor for any girl on the Gold Coast to cassare him and that it would not be shameful, as it would have been in England.[77]

Meanwhile a "non-Christian" section of Sara Malm's kin had been "working on them," as the missionaries stated it, and Sara Malm finally accepted Cochrane's offer on behalf of her daughter. A deputation of Wilhelmine's kin went to the fort to inform Cochrane of the decision, and he then sent Wilhelmine the bridewealth, consisting of money and some pieces of cloth. On her wedding day, just like Severine ten years earlier, Wilhelmine was accompanied to the fort by a group of Euro-African girls. Perhaps this public display of the match upset the missionaries even further, or perhaps they were offended at being excluded from the festivities, like Elias Svane almost a century and a half before. In any case, the missionaries were disappointed enough that they expelled Wilhelmine, her mother, and all the Euro-African women who had participated in the procession from the congregation. That the mission readmitted them shortly after, upon "due signs of contrition," suggests either that the offense was not so grave after all or that the missionaries had expelled more congregants than they could afford to lose.[78]

There is also significance in the decision of Sara Malm—and her "non-Christian" kin—to let Wilhelmine marry the English colonial officer. Twenty years earlier, when Sara Malm herself was cassaret to Wulff, it seems to have been a strategic marriage alliance with material benefits to each party. But there is something in the dismissive comment that Major Cochrane made to the missionaries that suggests that he was not going to consider Wilhelmine Wulff, or any other woman from Osu, a "proper" wife. He said that it would be an honor for any girl from Osu to marry him, and then implied that such a marriage would have been shameful in England. Whether or not he was planning to stay with Wilhelmine longer than he had stayed with his reputed four to six "concubines," those comments suggest that he was not inclined to mention her in his will or declare his official paternity over children, even if he was to stay on the coast, build a house, and invest in his life there.

From a broader perspective, by 1859 there were also a number of other factors looming on the horizon that made Wilhelmine's options and

Your afectionately
Frantz Wulff

Figure 13. Frantz Wulff (born 1842), son of Sara Malm and Wulff Joseph Wulff.
Museum Østjylland, Randers.

opportunities different than her mother's. As Accra transitioned to colonial rule, at least three important social changes diminished opportunities that Sara Malm and others before her had been able to take advantage of. First, the institution of interracial marriage, as well as concubinage, declined dramatically in the second half of the nineteenth century as the Gold Coast colony solidified. As in so many other European colonies around the world, interracial intimacy became an issue of intense concern for the British colonial administration on the Gold Coast, which much preferred that English colonists arrive with English wives and stay as far away from African women as possible. On the Gold Coast, the panic around interracial relationships led the English administration to issue a number of "anti-concubinage" circulars in the first decade of the twentieth century, which resulted in cases against colonial officers. As in other European colonies, the colonial administration on the Gold Coast began to view prostitution as preferable to concubinage or marriage. In this colonial climate the British slowly replaced the local African elite with British colonists, and the Euro-African elite found themselves in a new position—in between two racial groups, along a hardening frontier, rather than in their former role as an intermediate cultural group whose members were well integrated on both sides.[79]

Second, slavery—not just the trade, but the institution itself—was outlawed by the British colonial government, which meant that Sara Malm would have lost control over a large part of her household and a large part of her property. As British rule solidified on the Gold Coast, both the colonial administration and the Christian missions put pressure on the institution of slavery. Already in 1841, some Euro-African women who had much of their wealth and property invested in enslaved Africans protested this development. When they learned that the British administration in the Gold Coast was going to abolish slavery, seven Euro-African women from Cape Coast wrote a complaint to the British colonial secretary in London. The women were outraged that the British colonial government would simply take away their slaves and that they were "without the least of warning to be deprived of their rights and property."[80] At the same time it became particularly difficult to remain a slave owner if one also wanted to remain a part of the Christian community. While some Basel missionaries argued that slavery was not as harsh and bad in Africa as in the Americas, other missionaries argued that slavery could not be allowed within the Christian covenant, and this position became the official stand of the mission. Although the mission never took a very systematic approach to preventing their members from owning slaves, it did at times expel Euro-Africans from the Christiansborg congregation for owning slaves.[81]

Finally, the general ideal of Christian womanhood, promoted by the Basel Mission at the girls' school that Wilhelmine Wulff attended and where she later taught, discouraged Euro-African women from the cassare marriages that might have enabled them to become heads of large trading households. Though some of the missionaries admired the business skills and acumen of Euro-Africans in Osu and marriage to a missionary did not completely stop all Euro-African women from trading, Sara Malm's position as head of a large trading household was not exactly in line with the ideals of the Basel missionaries. The Basel missionaries took Hagerup's concern that the Euro-African children should obtain their "gender's decent education" one step further, establishing separate schools for girls and boys in 1843.[82] In 1860 the school was even moved out of Osu to the small Christian farming village of Abokobi and turned into a boarding school, which finally gave the missionaries the better influence on the overall education of Euro-African girls that the earlier Danish chaplains had fantasized about.[83]

Needless to say, when the missionaries gained control over the schooling of Euro-African girls they were not going to train them to establish large trading households with loosened ties to patriarchal authority. Instead, missionary educational emphasis on Christian Victorian practices for women worked to distance women from the market opportunities of the nineteenth-century Gold Coast. In the colonial historical situation of this place and time, it was much less likely that adopting Christianity or Danish gender practices of living in households with husbands would allow Euro-African women to expand their trading businesses or their autonomy over larger households. That gender practice—the European family—that had always been attached to European racial and gender hierarchies of power in the Atlantic world was now supported by a colonial cultural encounter and could no longer be adopted or employed to enhance the autonomy of women traders. Cassare had come to an end. The gender frontier had shifted further to the disadvantage of Euro-African women, and Sara Malm was possibly the last Euro-African woman to start a new shia in Osu.[84]

The entangled families forged by the Atlantic slave trade did not immediately disappear. In 1893 Sara and Wulff's youngest son, Carl Ulysses Wulff, wrote from his home in Osu to the postmaster general in Copenhagen, asking if the Gold Coast Wulffs had any living relatives in Denmark. The postmaster delivered the letter to the ministry of finance, who, after having obtained information from the Mosaic Religious Society, wrote back to Wulff the same year to inform him of his Danish family. Nearly a hundred years after the Atlantic slave trade's formal abolition, the descendants of Koko and Frantz, Anna Sophie and Cornelius, Wulff and Sara, continued to ponder the slave-trading families and the faraway kingdom that was part of their patrimony, even if it sometimes seemed to have forgotten them entirely.[85]

Edward Carstensen's Parenthesis

Let us return to the pressure that Edward Carstensen was under when he enclosed Severine Brock's death in that parenthesis. By the 1840s we do not have to look far to find representations of that modern racial hierarchy that made Wulff Joseph Wulff inclined to categorize all Africans as essentially the same, and that would have questioned or forbidden Edward's choice of Severine as his marriage partner. One of the more striking examples of how European racial ideology structured—put pressure on—Severine Brock's and Edward Carstensen's local history in Osu came when the French prince of Joinville, François d'Orléans, dined with Governor Carstensen at the fort in January 1843. The prince later depicted this lunch—to which Severine Brock was not invited—in a watercolor, and he described the event in a published travel diary from his trip. It is quite obvious why Severine might not have fit into that picture (see Plate 2).

Rather than reflecting messy or contested colonial categories, the prince's watercolor depicts a clear colonial order. The prince of Joinville painted himself centrally seated with his back to the sea, watching one of Governor Carstensen's men making a toast to the king of France. The image represents powerful, white, upper-class men in control of themselves and their subaltern subjects. Unbent and proper, the prince has his eyes focused on the toasting man while a naked woman bends over to serve him. Unlike the bearded lunch guest at the end of the table, the prince apparently resists a closer look at the women. At some point, though, he must have turned to inspect them. Indeed, these women seem to have been the most memorable attraction from his visit to Christiansborg.

In his published diary from his travels, the prince described their hair, skin, and smell in a way that reflects nineteenth-century ideas of biological race. Remarking how the women's skin was particularly soft—when did he touch them?—he leapt from the particular women who served him at Christiansborg to all Africans and "negroes" in general and claimed that Africans shared a peculiar and irreducible smell: "I have never been able myself to endure the odour of Negroes of either sex; but I have known people whom it quite intoxicated, and who were always trying to get reappointed to Senegal, so as to get back to it, in spite of having their health shattered by African fevers."[1] In the prince of Joinville's description, African women were passive servants with whom European men could become intoxicated, and all Africans were grouped together and shared the same odor. Their difference from Europeans was not merely cultural, in the sense that it could be transformed or erased. Bathing and rubbing could transform their skin to satin, but nothing could erase the smell of difference, and when white men and black women stood close as in the watercolor, the hierarchies of colonial order were revealed to be fixed and stark.

The women in the French watercolor are stereotypes; they look almost the same, and they should not be considered realistic renderings of African women, but rather an ethnopornographic fantasy. Not every detail is imagined: the French prince was in fact invited to Christiansborg for lunch, and it is not impossible that he was served by almost-naked women. Yet such a staged and colonially ordered European lunch was not representative of the social world at Christiansborg and would have been possible only if the women were considered inferior to the men not only racially, but also according to social class. In other parts of the Atlantic world, race and social class more and more overlapped, but in Osu, even in the mid-nineteenth century, status was not perfectly predicted by race. Not all African women would have been serving European men, let alone with so few clothes on; if he did meet almost-naked women at his lunch at Christiansborg, they were most likely either of very low social status and/or enslaved. Indeed, the French prince's leap from these specific women to a point about all Africans constituted a misunderstanding of the social reality at Christiansborg.

Yet, misunderstanding or not, the prince of Joinville's diary and watercolor circulated widely in the Atlantic world. After Africa, the prince went on to Brazil, and when he returned to Europe his impressions of Africa were printed and read; indeed, such texts helped create European colonial ideology and expectations of racial superiority. The prince was only the latest in a long line of European men who had taken notice of African women, and who had embedded African women's bodies in narratives of European possession of the newly discovered or colonized worlds. He would not be the last. In the realm of European travel writing and fantasy, African women had never been likely to be recognized as the wives, sisters, or daughters of European men. The interracial marriages in Osu and the European men's dependence on African women had existed outside the space of European travel writing. They had existed alongside the power hierarchies of the colonial Atlantic world. But when they were no longer central in the cross-cultural interactions between traders, the marriages came under pressure from strengthened nineteenth-century discourses rendering African women's bodies simultaneously inferior and corrupting.

The French prince's representation of the racial hierarchy at Christiansborg had a power of its own, and this power represented the discursive pressure that made Edward Carstensen ambivalent about his relationship with Severine. According to Edward's ideal of romantic love, Severine belonged to an entirely different category than the women in the French watercolor, but he must have been uncertain whether this perception would be shared by his peers in other parts of the Atlantic world. In any case, when the European upper class came to visit, in the person of the French prince, Edward did not ask Severine to attend. Not everyone made this decision; the residing officers in an English colonial town further up the Gold Coast invited the prince to a dinner party with a company of "three very dark Mulattoes, in evening dress."[2] But Carstensen seemed to feel he could not mix the two worlds of local practice and Atlantic ideology; one of the worlds had to give, and in a recognizable act of colonial erasure Severine was written out of the story.

By the time Edward Carstensen excluded Severine from the dinner party, by the time he contained her death in the parenthesis and avoided her funeral, the European colonial order of race had all but triumphed in the Atlantic world. The modern meaning of race had made their marriage—and maybe especially Edward's expression of romantic and heartfelt love—almost inconceivable. But this was the end of a story that began at least a century and a half earlier, a story in which African and European slave traders had shared the opportunities and profits of the slave trade, and in which generations of Euro-Africans had adopted and embodied more and more markers of European culture. Claiming their European heritage had allowed Severine's ancestors a powerful position in the ever-intensifying racial hierarchy on the Gold Coast. Severine and Edward's marriage carried with it a history of entangled worlds, a history created in the intersection between local slave-trading practices and larger colonial structures of the Atlantic world.

The story of the intimate family circles between African women and

European men officially left the scene right around the time when Edward placed Severine in the strange little parenthesis. But so many generations of intimate family relations can never really be erased from history. The intimate family connections across the Atlantic Ocean persevered, in that parenthesis and other subtle places. Even before the Danes left Osu, family connections across racial lines seem to have been troubling Danish discourses about race, as in Henrik Hertz's novel *De Frifarvede* (The Free Colored) from 1836. In this tale, the protagonist, George, a son of a planter in the Danish West Indies, has to make a choice between marrying a free black woman from the West Indies, with whom he is having a child, and a wealthy white merchant's daughter. He ends up making the right moral choice, honoring his promise to his pregnant girlfriend while the white woman, conveniently, falls in love with the pregnant girlfriend's brother. But before the play reaches this conclusion, George suffers doubts. He vacations in Norway, planning to run from his paternal responsibility and marry the wealthy white woman instead, but he is haunted by his choice. Even before his West Indian girlfriend shows up in Norway with her brother and George's baby son, the reader understands that it will not go well for George if he runs from his promise.[3]

The figure of the seductive, beautiful, and haunting Euro-African woman is a common one in nineteenth- and twentieth-century European literature, and perhaps she is more connected to intimate familiar connections across the color line than we know. Take Mrs. Clarkson in *L'Etrangère* (1876) by Alexandre Dumas fils, for example. She was torn out of her mother's arms in a slave market in the West Indies, and in that terrifying moment her mother whispered, "take revenge." She grew up to be, in the Danish literary critic Herman Bang's words, the most seductive of women, with complete power over European men.[4] In his review of Dumas's play, Bang was very interested in this powerful mulatto woman, noting "how peculiar [*besynderlig*] she is, this Mrs. Clarkson." Peculiar or not, perhaps the figure of the haunting Euro-African woman is not surprising in nineteenth-century Denmark. Thirty years after the Danes had left Africa, perhaps there was a well-established parenthesis in Danish collective memory that contained all the familiar obligations left behind.[5]

The stories of promises left unfulfilled remains part of the Danish-Ghanaian relationship today. The Quist family of Nukpesekope in Keta tell the story of one young man who traveled to Denmark to find his father. Two brothers of Danish descent, traders in Keta, left their wives and children to return to Denmark. One of their abandoned children, Elias Mensah Quist, grew up and encountered a Dane who had come to Keta to trade. The Dane told Elias of the trade and of a merchant's life, and Elias became so interested that he—against the advice of his mother and his adoptive father—followed the Dane back to Denmark, to see if he could find his biological father. He left aboard the next European ship, but because of some conflict he was thrown overboard and subsequently washed ashore somewhere between Cotonou and Lagos. The people who found him there thought he was a fetish, because a water snake was wrapped around his body and because his long hair, now covering his face, was also wet (straightened, the detail implies).[6] In this tale, Denmark and the Danes beckon but also betray.

The Keta Quists' family motto is "unity is strength," but for the most part these Euro-African families in Osu were not united with their Danish kinsmen. Mostly they have not been remembered at all. Like Liverpool merchant William Kemp in Barry Unsworth's novel *Sacred Hunger*, we would much rather forget about the slave trade. Kemp stayed at home in Liverpool and trained himself not to contemplate the horrors of the slave trade, thinking to himself, "picturing things is bad for business."[7] When we—Ghanaians, Danes, and others—*do* remember the slave trade, it is most often as a narrative of victims and perpetrators, and a story of intimate family ties forged around the violent trade in human beings does not fit in this dichotomy. There is no room for remembering that people could establish families and worry about their children while profiting from the misfortune and pain of others, and so the complicated intimate and family relations between slave traders have been left out of the painful history of Atlantic slave trading.[8]

In Denmark much work has been done on Danish colonial history, as the bibliography in this present work shows, and the history of the Danish slave trade has entered the history books. But the intimate family connections between Danes and Ghanaians during the slave trade are not yet part of the story. Family connections across the Atlantic were made very public in 2005 in Alex Frank Larsen's five-part documentary miniseries *Slavernes Slægt*, about Danish descendants of African and West Indian slaves, but, like much other remembrance of the Atlantic slave trade, Frank Larsen's series focused on descendants of people who had been enslaved and did not mention descendants of slave traders. Even the episode that took place in Ghana did not mention the many families in Accra with Danish names and Danish ancestors.[9] Slave-trading families are complicated to claim as ancestors. They helped create those power structures of colonialism and racial hierarchy that later generations would rather forget.

In Ghana remembering the slave trade is even more complicated than in Denmark. Not only was the Gold Coast naturally much more negatively affected by the slave trade, leaving later generations deeper scars to heal, but the harmful stigma attached to slavery and descent from slaves makes dealing with the history of the Atlantic slave trade even more difficult. Added to the complications are the needs for conflicting narratives about the slave trade. People of African descent in the diaspora travel to Ghana and visit the slave-trading forts along the coast searching for a connection with and healing from the history of the violent enslavement that brought their ancestors to America. People living in the coastal towns, meanwhile, descended from both slaves and slave traders—neither of which position is easy to claim. These complications have made the slave trade almost absent from public versions of coastal Ghanaian family and national histories, and classrooms. The slave trade is, in the words of historian Anne C. Bailey, surrounded by a "blanket of silence and shame."[10]

Forgetting is rarely an option, though, at least not without repercussions. Just like Edward Carstensen's parenthesis, a haunting presence of intimate family lives made possible by the slave trade is likely to have persisted for at least as long as these familiar circles lasted. Indeed, the physical presences of the historical connections persist to this day. Some of the European merchant houses still stand, and the stones in their entryways are laid out just like the cobblestones in front of the Royal Archive in Copenhagen, where the letters from Christiansborg tell the story of the slave trade. The familiar ties that bound Danes to Osu for almost two centuries are most obvious in "Joseph Wulff's house," which still houses direct descendants, who are periodically visited by Danish journalists, historians, and writers, who meet with and take pictures of Wulff's descendants and begin to write about the history of Danish connections with Osu. At such a visit in 1995 a Danish-Ga connection was made, and Fred Wulff—a descendant of Wulff Joseph and Sara Malm—was invited to Denmark. Afterward he compared his visit to Denmark to the many American visits to Ghana every year: "Americans come to Ghana and loudly proclaim that they have 'come home.' That is how I experienced it when I came to Denmark. It was the fulfillment of an old dream in my family that I should finally see the country that Joseph Wulff came from."[11] The next step is that we go even further back to the beginnings of the long history of entangled family circles that ended with Sara Malm and Wulff Joseph Wulff and admit that slave-trading families are part of our ancestry, complicated humans that they were.

The notes contain the following abbreviations to sources in the Archives in Rigsarkivet in Copenhagen. All archival sources used are registered online at Statens Arkiver: www.sa.dk.

EC   Governor Edward Carstensen's private archive Erindringer og dagbøger 1842–75

GK   Det Guineiske Kompagni, 1765–90

GtK   Generaltoldkammeret, Vestindisk-Guineisk Renteskriverkontor, 1760–1816

GtK2   Generaltoldkammer- og Kommercekollegiet, Indisk Kontor, 1816–41

KGG1   Det Kongelige Guvernement på Guineakysten, 1755–66

KGG2   Det Kongelige Guvernement på Guineakysten, 1778–1850

RtK   Rentekammeret Danske Afdeling, Vestindisk-Guineisk Renteskriverkontor, 1754–60

SSB   Sjællands Stifts Bispeembede, Indkomne Sager fra korrespondenter uden for stiftet, 1710–1820

VgK   Vestindisk-Guineisk Kompagni, 1671–1755

Introduction

1. *Cassare* comes from the Portuguese *casar*, to marry; it was used by Danes to describe marriages between European men and African women as well as marriages between two Africans. H. C. Truelsen's daughters are listed in a letter from Truelsen, January 2, 1808, in KGG2. Rådsprotokol, 1806–13, box (*kasse*) 50–54. Niels Brock's daughters in his will of May 30, 1836, in GtK2. Sager til Guineisk Journal, 1839–40, box 1023. Here Severine is mentioned to be eleven years old, which would make her around sixteen or seventeen in 1842, when she met Edward and was cassared to him. In his unpublished diary Edward Carstensen mentions that she was only fourteen when they met; see *Noter mit liv angaaende*. Unpublished manuscript of his diary in EC, p. 31. All translations from his diary are mine.

2. On "cultural frontiers" in early modern encounters, see Merrell, "The Customes," 117–56. For Merrell's concept adopted specifically to gendered encounters, see K. Brown, "Brave New Worlds," 311–28 (the concept "gender frontiers" is first mentioned on p. 313).

3. I have used the term "Euro-Africans" to refer to persons of mixed European and

African descent. I use this term whenever the sources refer to "mulattoes" or "mulatresses."

4. For printed travel accounts making distinctions between Euro-Africans and other Africans Rømer, *A Reliable*, 56–58 and 185; Monrad, *A Description*, 183. See also the many references to "mulattos" in the transcribed sources in Justesen, *Danish Sources*, 1051 (index). Throughout the book I quote and make references to English translations of sources where they exist. If no English translations are mentioned, the translations are my own.

5. As historians have argued, the European link between slavery and blackness emerged long before the eighteenth century and influenced early European participation in and defense of enslaving Africans. See Sweet, "The Iberian Roots." However, as other historians have shown, the period of Atlantic slavery was marked by an ever-deepening linkage of slavery and blackness. See Jennifer Morgan's article in the same issue of *WMQ* as Sweet's article, "Some Could Suckle." Or, as Morgan later put it, the process of making blackness "inextricable from brute labor" was also a process happening over centuries in travel accounts, as well as in wills, laws, and legislative acts; see J. Morgan, *Laboring Women*, 12. See discussions of early modern conceptions of race, and the transition to a more "modern" scientific understanding of race, in K. Hall, *Things of Darkness*; Wheeler, *The Complexion*. As Jennifer M. Spear has recently argued in her work on eighteenth-century New Orleans, it was "daily decisions made within structural constraints that produced the concrete historical circumstances that made race real"; see Spear, *Race, Sex*, 2. Marcus Rediker has described European slave ships as "vast machines" that produced not only enslaved labor for the plantations, but also, more abstractly, "race" in the Atlantic system. Rediker's important work offers insight into a specific moment of production of "racial categories and identities," but such moments happened in many corners of the Atlantic world. Rediker, *The Slave Ship*, 260, 10. Gunvor Simonsen has written about the production of race in the Danish West Indies; see "Skin Colour." The present book mostly takes place in West Africa and is not comparative per se, but the production of racial difference that it follows could be compared to similar historical processes in other parts of the Atlantic world. For the production of race in practice in Africa, see B. Hall, *A History*; Glassman, "Slower Than"; and Glassman, *War of Words*.

6. Referring to Michel Foucault's "especially dense transfer point for relations of power," *The History of Sexuality*, 103, in relation to intimate encounters in the colonial world is not my own idea, but one borrowed from Stoler, *Carnal Knowledge*, 16, 140, 145. Since Ann Laura Stoler famously argued that sexual matters were foundational to European colonial projects (ibid., 14), a host of studies have investigated intimate negotiations of colonial power. See a discussion of gender and family history in the Atlantic world in Premo et al., "Cluster." In focusing on both local practice and larger Atlantic structures, the present book is a "new cultural history" that seeks to combine social and cultural history, taking as its starting point the recognition that cultures consist simultaneously of meanings and practices, and that cultural production is a process shaped by

both systems of meaning (structures, discourses) and of social practice. In this approach I am in line with historian Sewell, "The Concept(s)." For a broader introduction to new cultural history, see Hunt and Bonnell, *Beyond the Cultural*, which ended an important series started ten years earlier by Hunt and Bonnell with their edited collection *The New Cultural*.

7. In the tradition of Fernand Braudel's "Mediterranean World," historians of the region surrounding the Atlantic Ocean have for decades referred to an "Atlantic world." See Bernard Bailyn's introduction to the field of Atlantic history, *Atlantic History*; Canny, "Writing Atlantic History." John Thornton has described the Atlantic as a region defined by transport by water in *Africa and Africans*, 14 and 1, where he also describes Atlantic historians finding inspiration in Fernand Braudel. Employing a concept of an Atlantic world, as opposed to the more mechanical economic term "the Atlantic system" (as in Immanuel Wallerstein's economic world system), signals a focus on the social or cultural history of the European expansion. A world is inhabited by people, a system is not.

8. Edward Carstensen's application for employment in Africa is quoted in Carstensen, *Closing the Books*, 10.

9. On friends ridiculing him for taking employment in Africa, see *Noter mit liv angaaende*, 10. Not only was the mortality rate high (even in the nineteenth century), but there was also a great risk of getting sick and having to leave the position early. About Carstensen's family history and his application, see Carstensen, *Closing the Books*, xxiii–xxv. *Friends* is from the Danish *venner, for* "kinship group" or "relatives."

10. Carstensen, *Noter*, 7. In nineteenth-century fashion he had even played Lottchen (the young Werther's beloved) in a comedy in the law students' association in Copenhagen in 1834.

11. Carstensen, *Noter*, 33–34.

12. Ibid., 31–32.

13. This book contributes to a growing field of literature on interracial marriage in the European expansion. When Sylvia Van Kirk published her work on the Canadian fur trade in 1980 she remarked that the French and English "marriage à la façon du pays" to Indian women in the fur trade in western Canada was a unique institution created by the specific conditions of the fur trade; see Kirk, *Many Tender Ties*, 4. More than three decades later, dissertations, articles, and monographs dealing with questions of interracial marriage during the European expansion have shown that the western Canadian case, though unique in its particulars, shared common features with interracial marriages throughout the world of European expansion. Interracial marriages were in many other places called "country marriages" or simply "marriage." Among other works that discuss the role of interracial marriage in trading encounters in the early modern European expansion are, for the Great Lakes: Sleeper-Smith, *Indian Women*; Sleeper-Smith, "An Unpleasant"; India: Ghosh, *Sex*; Batavia: Blussé, *Bitter Bonds*; Louisiana: Spear, "Colonial Intimacies"; and Spear, *Race, Sex*. For titles about West Africa, see notes 18–21 in this chapter. For an analysis of dress, material culture, and racialization surrounding interracial marriage and mixing in French North America, see S. White, *Wild*

Frenchmen. For a broader look at how the European expansion "reinforced familial mixing and family frontiers" and transformed family structures, see Manning, "Frontiers." The general awareness of the importance of interracial marriage in trading encounters has not always made it into histories of the slave trade. In their groundbreaking work on the intricate role of the institution of pawnship in creating binding trading agreements between Europeans and Africans in the slave trade, Paul E. Lovejoy and David Richardson, for example, emphasize the importance of personalized relationships between traders through social interaction and "fictive kinship," but do not address the role of the more real kinship connections that the cassare institution allowed for. It is possible that the Euro-African encounters in Old Calabar during the slave trade did not lead to intermarriage, unlike so many other places in West Africa, but if this were the case it would also be an interesting finding; see Lovejoy and Richardson, "Trust, Pawnship," 343. In case of the Gold Coast it is difficult to understand the nature of trading or credit networks without considering the cassare institution.

14. Rømer, *A Reliable,* 187.

15. For a clear formulation of the argument that European trading posts in West Africa were far from colonial societies, see Robin Law, " 'Here Is No Resisting.' " I will return to the integration of European men in Chapter 1.

16. Among the works that discuss interracial relationships in European colonies are, on French Senegal: H. Jones, "From Marriage"; H. Jones, *The Metis*; on the southern United States: Hodes, *White Women*; and Bardaglio, "Shamefull Matches"; on Virginia: Rothman, *Notorious*. For earlier histories of interracial relationships, see, on Virginia: Smits, "Abominable Mixture"; on Dutch Indonesia: Stoler, *Carnal Knowledge*; on India: Ghosh, *Sex and the Family*; on Italian Eritrea: Barrera, "Colonial Affairs." About the transition from trade to colony and the policing of interracial marriage that followed on the Gold Coast, see Ray, "Policing Sexual." The very clear difference between interracial marriage and intimacy in colonies and trading posts does not mean that European trading posts were separated from or unaffected by the European colonial system, and I agree with Sylvia Van Kirk that the literature on interracial marriage in trading encounters has paid too little attention to the "larger colonial context" that shaped them; see "From 'Marrying-In,' " 1. As the present book shows, interracial marriages outside actual colonies were very much shaped by Atlantic colonial structures.

17. Isert, *Letters,* 156.

18. The Dutch in Accra called Euro-African marriage *calisaren*, while the English used *consar*, derived from the Portuguese *consagrar*. In 1712 there were already three generations of Euro-Africans at Cape Coast according to Rask, *A Brief*, 104. Rask did not mention whether they were of English or, more likely, Portuguese descent, or whether their parents had been officially *cassaret* or not. Robin Law mentions that the English called marriage to a Gold Coast woman "consar" already in the seventeenth century; see Law, *The English*, glossary. About Euro-African marriage in Anamabo, see Priestley, *West African*; McCarthy, *Social Change*, 36–47. About Dutch men marrying into African families on the Gold Coast, see Everts, "A Motley Company"; Everts,

"Cherchez"; Everts, "Brought Up Well"; Doortmont, "The Dutch"; see Feinberg, "Africans and Europeans," 89, about African wives of Dutch men in wills.

19. On intermarriage between European and African traders in West Africa, see Brooks, *Eurafricans*, 122–60; Havik, *Silences and Soundbytes*; Miller, *Way of Death*, 290–95; Curtin, *Economic Change*, 120–21; Candido, "Marriage"; H. Jones, *The Metis*. For a closer study of a Luso-African woman who traded and was "one of the most influential persons living in the Guinea-Bissau region" in the nineteenth century, see Brooks, "A Nhara."

20. Brooks, *Eurafricans*, xxi–xxii.

21. In her studies of the Anlo-Ewe in Keta, Sandra Greene has found that families married only daughters of their slaves to European traders; see "Crossing Boundaries," 31, where she writes that the Anlo-Ewe considered marriages with European traders "appropriate" only "for enslaved women." Indeed Greene has found the Anlo-Ewe to primarily marry their daughters within their ethnic group in the precolonial period, whereas I have found that the Ga actively sought to expand their group through intermarriage of their free daughters to European traders. For Greene's argument that the Anlo-Ewe were systematically "marrying in," see also Greene, *Gender, Ethnicity*; and Greene, "Family Concerns," 22–24. I discuss the status of Ga women cassaring Danish men further in Chapter 1. Studying Elmina, Natalie Everts has found that the principally matrilinear Akan married both free and enslaved daughters to European traders; see Everts, "A Motley," 56. In her work on French West Africa, Hilary Jones has found that French men primarily married free women, but she also states, "Occasionally, slave women became the 'country wives' of habitant men through marriage a la mode du pays"; see H. Jones, *The Metis*, 49. For social stratification on the Gold Coast, see Kea, *Settlements*.

22. On Nicoline Brock teaching at the school at Christiansborg, see Carstensen, *Closing the Books*, 43, 69.

23. For laws requiring free Afro-Caribbeans to wear particular clothes, see Simonsen, "Skin Colour," 263. In general, underlying my interpretation of the cultural transformation that Euro-African families in Osu participated in is a specific understanding of relationships between individuals and social structures. I understand daily individual negotiations with social structures to take place according to patterns sketched out by Pierre Bourdieu in his development of the concept of habitus. That is, individuals respond to "structuring structures, predisposed to function as structuring structures"; social structures shape and limit individuals' room for maneuver, while individuals, simultaneously, participate in producing and reproducing the structures and hierarchies that they have embodied (the embodiment of culture happening through their upbringing and social context). See Bourdieu, *The Logic*, 53. I am not the only historian to have found help in Bourdieu's work to understand the developments of hybrid Euro-African cultures in West Africa in the early modern period. See H. Jones, *The Metis*, 13.

24. I agree with Sheperd and Richards, *Questioning Creole*, xii, that the concept of creolization seems to be a dominant "intellectual construct" in Caribbean history, but I

am not sure the same can be said for the wider field of Atlantic history. There have been a few references to West African coastal traders as "Atlantic creoles": Rebecca Shumway found that already in the gold-trading era the Euro-African interaction on the Gold Coast led to the development of an "Atlantic creole" culture; see *The Fante*, 35. Randy Sparks has called the two princes of Calabar, sons of an important Efik trader, Atlantic creoles, but Paul Lovejoy has disagreed with him; see Sparks, *The Two Princes*, 4; Lovejoy, "An Atlantic," 348. Given the differences between the local contexts in Africa and the Americas I do not find it useful to simply adopt the concept in African histories. Ira Berlin's work from the 1990s has been formative for subsequent historical thinking about creolization in the Atlantic world; see "From Creole" and *Many Thousands*.

25. About Luso-African identities, cultural transformation, and European material culture as markers of difference, see Brooks, *Eurafricans*; Miller, *Way of Death*, 246–51; Havik, *Silences*; Mark, *"Portuguese" Style*; Horta, "Evidence"; Green, "Building Creole." On Euro-Africans seeing themselves as a distinct social group on the Gold Coast in the nineteenth century, see Parker, "Mankraloi," 34; Yarak, "West African," 57; Reese, "Sheep," 355. Writing about the most famous of the "Christiansborg mulattoes" in the nineteenth century, John Parker notes: "The nature and boundaries of [Reindorf's] identity were so fluid, however, that the terms "Euro-African" and "mulatto" are of limited analytical value without individual contextualization." Parker, *Making the Town*, 158. I discuss the position of Euro-Africans in Osu in the nineteenth century in Chapter 5. There are a number of impediments to saying anything categorical about Euro-African identity in the precolonial period. Besides the European sources that leave us little from which to draw conclusions about how Euro-Africans identified themselves (especially when Europeans were not around), identity is always a slippery category. In this history I am less interested in how and when individuals identified as Euro-Africans than in how the practice of intermarrying was shaped by the local world of Osu's entanglement in the larger Atlantic world, and in the centrality of interracial cassare marriages to the development of a Euro-African culture. Green, "Building Creole," 108, similarly notes that "Creole power and identity was intimately connected to wider patterns of power in the Atlantic world."

26. For a strong voicing of the critique that Africa has too long been just an opening chapter to histories of the "black Atlantic," see Beswick and Spaulding, *African Systems*, 2.

27. Rediker, *The Slave Ship*, 12.

28. Some important works to mention here are Sparks, *The Two Princes*; Sensbach, *Rebecca's*; Sweet, *Domingos Alvares*; Christopher, *Slave Ship*; Rediker, *The Slave Ship*; Smallwood, *Saltwater Slavery*; V. Brown, *The Reapers'*; and a historical novel that has probably inspired more than one historian to achieve a more "human" or "people-oriented" history of the slave trade, Barry Unsworth, *Sacred Hunger*.

29. For a discussion of agency, humanity, and the requirement that we "re-immerse ourselves in the nightmare of History," see W. Johnson, "On Agency," 121. As Sparks, *The Two Princes*, shows, even Africans who had personally experienced the middle passage and been lucky enough to escape did not hesitate to continue slave trading once they

were back in Africa, and as Walter Hawthorne has argued, we cannot simply divide the Atlantic world into "victims" and "victimizers" or into enslaved and enslavers; see *Planting*, 12. In 1998 John Thornton asked whether Africans participated in the Atlantic trade as equal partners, or as victims of European power and greed; see Thornton, *Africa and Africans*, 6. With the growing and elaborated social history of West Africa during the slave trade, the question now becomes "Which Africans?" Africans were victims, equal trading partners, and everything in between.

30. This formulation is inspired by Bourdieu, *Distinction*, 467.

31. Carstensen, *Noter*, 34–35. This description of Ga weddings correlates well with other accounts from the nineteenth and twentieth centuries. See Kilson, *African*; Nukunya, *Tradition*; and Robertson, *Sharing*.

32. Carstensen, *Noter*, 52.

33. Ibid., 55.

Chapter 1. Setting Up

1. This account is adapted from the description of Osu in Rask, *A Brief*, 156–57, and of the marketplace in Cape Coast in de Marees, *Pieter*, 62–65 and 85. Koko—also spelled Kaakoe or Coco—is mentioned a few times in the Danish sources; see Justesen, *Danish Sources*, 217, 234, 337, 503. Both kenkey and fufu are doughy balls of pounded and boiled starchy root vegetables; kenkey is made from ground maize, fufu from yams. These are still staple foods in Ghana.

2. *Caboceer* comes from the Portuguese *cabeceire* for "head," "chief," or "king." The term was adopted by Europeans on the Gold Coast to address African chiefs and ranked local headmen, who were in charge of trade with Europeans. See Rask, *A Brief*, 167.

3. About the arrival of Frantz Boye, see Justesen, *Danish Sources*, 116. Ga naming practice is very particular; a child is given several different names according not only to what day he or she is born (which is a tradition the Ga have adopted from their Akan-speaking neighbors), but also in accordance with the order of birth in the family and generation. Koko is the name given to a second daughter. See Odotei, "What Is in a Name?"

4. David Frandtsøn was born around 1713 and attended the school at Christiansborg in 1724. See Justesen, *Danish Sources*, 309. The early reference to Koko and Frantz is in ibid., 217.

5. Parker, "Cultural Politics," 207. By the seventeenth century there was a large number of smaller and larger polities of peoples speaking different languages belonging to the Kwa language group on the Gold Coast, especially Ewe, Ga, and various Akan languages. For a general introduction to the different languages and ethnic groups in Ghana, see Buah, *A History*; Nukunya, *Tradition*. On the Ga in the seventeenth century, see Quaye [Odotei], "The Ga"; Kea, *Settlements*; Daaku, *Trade*. About the expansion of the Akwamu empire, see Wilks, *Akwamu*. About coastal traders going inland to buy slaves, see Barbot, *Barbot on Guinea*, 334–35.

6. Brooks, *Eurafricans*; Miller, *Way of Death*; Kea, *Settlements*; Daaku, *Trade*. More specifically about the Danes in Osu, see Hernæs, *Slaves* and Hernæs, "African Power."

7. In 1625 King Christian IV issued the first Danish monopoly on trading in the area, directed by the Dutch merchant Jan de Willum. This attempt was probably a counter-move to the Swedes sending out a Dutch merchant to Africa the year before, but be-cause of lack of capital and support from merchants in Copenhagen, the charter was never used; see Justesen, "Vestafrika," 302. In the period 1658–1754 the Danish officials at Christiansborg were subject to four different companies: 1658–59, Heinrich Carloff's or-ganization; 1659–73, the Danish African Company in Glückstadt; 1673–90, the West India and Guinea Company; 1690–97, Nikolaj Jansen Arf; 1658–1754, again the West India and Guinea Company. See Justesen, *Danish Sources*, viii. In 1755 the king's admin-istration dissolved the West India and Guinea Company and opened the trade to private traders. In 1765 a merchant from Copenhagen obtained a charter on the trade there with the company known as the Bargumske Handelssocietet but did not get a monopoly on the trade, and in 1775 they went bankrupt, at which point the king's administration took over again. In 1781 a charter was issued to the Østersøisk-guineisk (Baltic Guinean) Company, which had a monopoly on trading at the Danish forts for a few years. Juste-sen, "Vestafrika," 373–85. For more about the changing Danish trading companies, see ibid.; and Justesen, *Danish Sources*, xiv–xvii.

8. About the expansion of Christiansborg, see Lawrence, *Trade*, 199–217. For number of slaves, see Hernæs, *Slaves*, 225–26, and "European Fort," 171. For another English introduc-tion to the Danish slave trade, see Svalesen, *The Slave Ship*.

9. Instead of the later names for these towns, Nleshi and Kinka, I have chosen to use Soko and Aprag, which are the terms used in the early sources. For coherence, I have kept these names throughout the book, though the later sources mainly refer to the areas as Dutch Accra and English Accra. For an early use of these town names, see Til-leman, *A Short*, 25.

10. Some early social visits between Danes and English people on the Gold Coast are mentioned in Justesen, *Danish Sources*, 145, 153, and 164. About one of several con-flicts between Christiansborg and the Dutch, see Hernæs, *Slaves,* particularly 49–69, and "Den balstyrige," 17–25.

11. Isert, *Letters*, 158; Monrad, *A Description*, 215.

12. Letter from Governor von Groenestein, Frederiksborg, to the king of Denmark, December 10, 1672, in Justesen, *Danish Sources*, 19.

13. Ibid.

14. Letters from Jacob van Tetz to Governor Prange February 19, 1681, and Governor Prange to the directors of the West India and Guinea Company in Copenhagen April 7, 1681, in Justesen, *Danish Sources*, 54–58. Ole Justesen discusses Bolt's sale of Christians-borg in ibid. on 55 n. 7.

15. Undated [1681] Andreas Jacobsen, Frederiksborg, to the directors in Copenha-gen in Justesen, *Danish Sources*, 62.

16. Ibid., 62–63.

17. Undated [1681] Peter Falck, Fetu, to Johan Conrad Busch, Frederiksborg, in Justesen, *Danish Sources*, 58–59. Interestingly Barbot mentioned that the king of Fetu had helped the Danes build the fort at Frederiksborg, and not only that the Danes paid tribute to him, but that he had a vote when a new governor was chosen. Barbot, *Barbot on Guinea*, 400. To this the editors add (410) that Barbot is the only contemporary source that mentions an African having a vote in the election of a European governor.

18. *Pantje* is equivalent to the Dutch *paan*, and the Portuguese *pano*; the term refers to a cloth worn by Africans from the waist to the knees, like a kilt. See Justesen, *Danish Sources*, 1006.

19. *Millet, mille*, or *millie* (from the Portuguese *milho*) was used for corn, maize or millet, which was the typical grain in precolonial Ghana. See ibid.

20. After five years in Dutch employment Busch was briefly employed in Danish service as subfactor at Frederiksborg, after which he returned to Europe and showed up in Copenhagen in 1680 to apply for a position in Danish Guinea; see Justesen, *Danish Sources*, 39. The letters mentioning the story of Governor Busch are in Justesen, *Danish Sources*, 66–69. Quote from 67. Busch was not the only man stationed at Frederiksborg in the early decades who was cassaret in Africa. We know that Pieter Valck and Hans Lykke were cassaret, and probably, already then, many others were as well. Like Johan Conrad Busch, the two others are mentioned to have African wives in the early documents in ibid.; Valck's "former Negress" mentioned on 89 and Hans Lykke's "Negress, called Jamenie," on 90. Johannes Rask also mentioned a man in Osu who called himself Hans Lykke after the former governor. Perhaps this man was Lykke's son; see Rask, *A Brief*, 154.

21. The Secret Council, in Danish *sekretrådet*, was the judiciary board (Privy Council) at Christiansborg consisting of the presiding governor and five members chosen among the assistants and merchants at the fort.

22. General letter from the Secret Council at Christiansborg (Governor Wærøe et al.) to the directors in Copenhagen, in Justesen, *Danish Sources*, 466. For a history of Ga relations to the Akwamu and Akan, see Quaye [Odotei], "The Ga." More specifically about the Akwamu conquest of Osu, Aprag, and Soko from the kingdom of Accra, see Wilks, *Akwamu*, 8–14. For Akwamu's engagement in the slave trade, see Perbi, *A History*, 63. For a reference to the king of Akwamu's discontent with the amount of Danish gifting, see Justesen, *Danish Sources*, 199.

23. As Jean Barbot noted in the late seventeenth century, there were very few slaves for sale on the Gold Coast in peacetime; see Barbot, *Barbot on Guinea*, 518. About most slaves in West Africa being captured in war, see Law, "Slave-Raiders"; Thornton, *Africa*, 99. In 1774 former traders from Christiansborg noted how people sold to the fort were either war captives, criminals, or free people "stolen on the road"; see Aarestrup et al., "Nogle bidrag," 169. About the connection between warfare and slave trade in Africa, see Thornton, *Warfare*; Lovejoy, *Transformations*, 3; Feinberg, "Africans," 14–16; Law, "Slave-Raiders"; Feinberg has also noted that "despite periods of relative calm, turmoil was undeniably prevalent on the Gold Coast in the eighteenth century" and that "wars,

rumors of war, and kidnappings occurred with depressing frequency"; see "Africans," 14 and 16. See also Perbi, *A History*.

24. About human pawning on the Gold Coast, see Perbi, *A History*, 3; Austin, "Human." For examples of pawns listed in the debt books, see Justesen, *Danish Sources*, 384–85 and 501–4; Hernæs, *Slaves*, 119. About the threat of sale of human pawns, see Lovejoy and Richardson, "The Business," 83; Hernæs, *Slaves*, 119.

25. Governor Meyer to the directors in Copenhagen, October 28, 1703, in Justesen, *Danish Sources*, 173.

26. *Fetish* is from the Portuguese *feitiço*. The term was used by Europeans to describe African religion—particularly devotion to inanimate objects. The word is often used in connection with ritual oaths in the Danish sources. It meant variously "charm," "spell," or "witchcraft." Early Europeans applied the term as a description of both African religion and inanimate objects used in religious ceremonies. In the Danish sources "to do fetish" usually meant to go through a religious ceremony, to swear an oath, or to test whether a person was guilty of an offense. For Danish descriptions of "eating fetish," see Rask, *A Brief*, 136. See also Monrad, *A Description*, 55.

27. Rømer, *A Reliable*, 240.

28. Rask, *A Brief*, 153.

29. See Rømer, *A Reliable*, 187, quoted in the introduction.

30. "Andre virckelig Militair betienter udi hans Maytts tienneste i faderland." This letter is translated in Justesen, *Danish Sources*, 235–36. Unfortunately Ole Justesen has omitted this section of the letter, which is therefore my own translation. Original letter from Frantz Boye to the company in Copenhagen, November 27, 1711; see VgK. Breve og dokumenter fra Guinea, book (*kasse*) 121. Christian V's "war articles" (*krigsartikler*) from 1683, section 21, mentions punishment for soldiers who committed adultery or rape, see Christian V, *Des Aller-Durchlauchtigsten*. However, a 1696 supplement to the law excepted soldiers from punishment for first-time extramarital sexual relations.

31. The company's ban dated July 1, 1713, is found in a letter copy book in VgK. Direktionen. Amerikansk og afrikansk kopibog, 1703–17, box 54, p. 345. The restatement of the ban is in a letter copy book in VgK. Amerikansk og afrikansk kopibog, 1716–27, box 55, pp. 106–7; the Secret Council's response is in a general letter from the fort dated March 19, 1718, in Justesen, *Danish Sources*, 267.

32. Minutes from the Secret Council's interrogations and witness testimonies in the case against Frantz Boye in 1717 are kept in VgK. Direktionen. Forhørs og domsakter fra Guinea, 1717–46, box 285.

33. Isert, *Letters*, 157. In the beginning of the nineteenth century chaplain Monrad also referred to Danish men getting married "in the Negro manner"; see *A Description*, 270. For Danes using "cassare" to mean African marriage, see Justesen, *Danish Sources*, 93 and 388. Paul Isert also mentioned that Europeans called a wedding between two Africans on the coast "*cassaren*"; see *Letters*, 140.

34. Isert described a Ga wedding in some detail in 1788; see *Letters*, 140. For other

descriptions of Ga and Akan marriage in the precolonial period, see Müller, "Description," 213–19; Rømer, *A Reliable*, 183–84. For twentieth century descriptions of Ga marriages that are similar to Isert's, see Nukunya, *Tradition*; Kilson, *African*; Field, *Social*; Robertson, *Sharing*. About the Ga marriages being initiated by the parents of the groom, particularly the father, see Kilson, *African*, 25; Field, *Social*, 37. When Gunner Thomas Bentzen wanted to cassare Hans Lykke's former wife, Jamenie, in 1688 he asked the company for permission to spend "1 white say, 1 slaplagen, 1 tablecloth, 3 fathom gingham or Turkish stuff and one anker [barrel] of brandy" on his bridewealth; see Justesen, *Danish Sources*, 90.

35. This impression is consistent with many later ethnologists' and historians' descriptions of the Ga as showing a great interest in and tolerance for integrating foreigners and foreign cultures. See Field, *Social*, 32 (Field also says that "the first care of the Ga towns was to keep up its numbers," in *Religion*, 2); Odotei, "External," 61–71; Robertson, *Sharing*, 28; Dakubu, *Korle*. The fact that the Ga in Osu were not part of a centralized kingdom or state when the Danes settled at Christiansborg probably contributed to their willingness to integrate foreigners and suggests that they would not have had the same centralized authority to establish rules against intermarriage with foreign traders as strictly "stratified" societies in Senegambia; see Brooks, *Eurafricans*, 2003, xxi. Sandra Greene has also found that the Anlo-Ewe east of Accra had firm policies encouraging them to marry their free daughters within their ethnic group, whereas they married daughters of enslaved women to European men; see Greene, "Crossing," 31. Per Hernæs has noted how the Ga were not a "single political unit"; see *Slaves*, 109. About the central Ga kingdom in Ayawaso fragmenting into seven towns along the coast, see Parker, *Making*, 6–7.

36. For Ga family structure, see Robertson, *Sharing*, and specifically about living in gender-segregated compounds, 56–67, and "Ga Women," 116; Nukunya, *Tradition*; Kilson, *African*. In *Making* John Parker cites a report from the Town Planning Department in Accra from 1953 that says that unisexual households still predominated in the old quarters of Ussher town (42 n. 109). An early description of this gendered segregation is in de Marees, *Pieter*, 22. Another good precolonial description of men and women living separately and how a man's wives took turns cooking for and sleeping with their husbands is by three Danish men who had been stationed at Christiansborg; see Aarestrup et al., "Nogle bidrag," 174–78.

37. About married couples being the central unit of household production in early modern Scandinavia, see Erickson, "The Marital," 3. About families and economic production and ownership in Scandinavia in general, see Dübeck, *Kvinder*. About the importance of kinship in Ga society, see Nukunya, *Tradition*, 17, 40–41.

38. For references to precolonial naming ceremonies, see de Marees, *Pieter*, 23; Brun, "Voyages," 88; Isert, *Letters*, 131. About Ga naming practice in the twentieth century, see Buah, *A History*, 47; Perbi, *A History*, 114–15. About children being adopted by male relatives from the kinship group (fathers or brothers), see Field, *Social*, 23; Robertson, *Sharing*, 48. For a chaplain at Christiansborg expressing the view that Ga mothers

and their families had too much influence on Ga-Danish children, see Hans Jensen Flye to bishop, February 3, 1747, in SSB. This is discussed further in Chapter 2.

39. This is a point both travel accounts from the precolonial period and later ethnographic descriptions seem to agree on. See de Marees, *Pieter*, 20. About Fetu, see Müller, "Description," 215; Monrad, *A Description*, 69. For twentieth century accounts of inequality between the sexes, see Azu, *The Ga*, 28; Nukunya, *Tradition*, 47.

40. About women's inferior status in Ga traditional society, see also Kilson, *African*, 19 and 25; Azu, *The Ga*, 34–35. About women's double reproductive roles, see Grier, "Pawns," 307. About most slaves in Africa being women, see Robertson and Klein, Introduction, 3; about women owning and controlling property, see Robertson, *Sharing*, 10.

41. The Danish word *venner* ("friends") was used in the Danish sources to describe family in broad terms, or kinship group.

42. Memorandum from A. Wellemsen, Christiansborg, May 2, 1729, in Justesen, *Danish Sources*, 389.

43. Ibid., 388–92.

44. In his Twi dictionary from 1881 J. G. Christaller wrote: "o-dom, a kind of tree, the bark of which is used in performing an ordeal"; see Christaller, *A Dictionary*, 88. R. S. Rattray describes an ordeal to try a man's guilt after an adultery accusation, where the accused person was asked to chew pieces of bark from an *odom* tree and drink the water that the bark had been soaking in. If the accused vomited, he or she was innocent of the charges, but if not, the verdict was guilty; see Rattray, *Ashanti*, 392–95.

45. This and the previous quotes are from the Secret Council's resolution regarding the case; see Justesen, *Danish Sources*, 378–79.

46. Ibid., 379.

47. Justesen, *Danish Sources*, 388–92 and 383.

48. My understanding of the conflict with Akwamu is in part based on Hernæs, "African Power"; and Wilks, *Akwamu*, 77–98.

49. Memorandum from A. Wellemsen, Christiansborg, explaining "the palaver concerning Sergeant Franz Mingechen's Negress," in Justesen, *Danish Sources*, 388–89. Natalie Everts has described a situation in 1790s Elmina, where a grandmother and a mother likewise prefer that their daughter marry a European "warehouse master"; see Everts, "A Motley," 60.

50. Ole Justesen supports Hans Debrunner's suggestion that Friderich Svane's mother was "from a good family in Teshi," in *Danish Sources*, 727. Ole Justesen's documents mention Svane's father only on 309 and 725. Friderich was not, as a circulating misconception has it, a son of Elias Svane but took Svane's name later in life. The misconception might have been started by Nørregaard, *Danish*, 167, which is still the only general history of the subject in English, but unfortunately not always to be trusted. For more details on other mistakes of Nørregaard's, see Wilks's review of the book, "The Danes." Justesen, *Danish Sources*, mentions Jacob Protten, Christian Protten's father; see 294 and 310. See more about his story in Sensbach, *Rebecca's*.

51. Sensbach, *Rebecca's*, 213. The story of Christian Protten and Friderich Pedersen

Svane's stay in Denmark is fascinating. See more about them in Chapter 3 in the present book.

52. As a Danish chaplain noted in 1724, European men could pay a higher bride-wealth than African men; see Elias Svane, Christiansborg, March 15, 1724, in Justesen, *Danish Sources*, 302. Later in the century the fact that Euro-African women, who were sought after by European men, never married Euro-African men was explained by the European men's greater affluence than Euro-African men. In 1769 Chaplain Feldtman apparently asked some of the Euro-African soldiers why they never married Euro-African women, to which they replied that they could not provide for (*underholde*) them (Feldtman to bishop, October 24, 1769, in SSB). Isert also noted that Danish em-ployees who could afford the bridewealth were attractive marriage partners and, ac-cording to Isert, seldom had to fear being turned down; see *Letters*, 157.

53. Feinberg has also called the Dutch fort in Elmina "another ethnic group in a multi-ethnic community"; see "Africans," 136.

54. Rømer, *A Reliable*, 185. Bosman, *A New*, 346. Selena Winsnes agrees with me that the situation Rømer described cannot have been "more than very uncommon"; see Rømer, *A Reliable*, 185 n. 237.

55. About marriage as the official venue for sexual relations in eighteenth-century Denmark, see Koefoed, "Synd," 45–46; Thomsen, "Hor." There is of course the possibil-ity that the Danish men, like Edward Carstensen in the prologue, themselves wanted to get married, rather than have a casual relationship. Carstensen's nineteenth-century be-lief in monogamous romantic love was not a widespread or dominant discourse a cen-tury earlier, but eighteenth-century Danish men certainly knew what marriage was. In Denmark, marriages were performed and administrated by the church.

56. Fifty-four men on whom I have year of both birth and arrival in Guinea in the eighteenth century had an average age of twenty-seven. Men who worked at Christians-borg were most often, though not always, from Denmark. Out of a sample of 303 men employed at Christiansborg between 1658 and 1810, 61 percent came from Danish-speaking areas of the conglomerate state under the king of Denmark; 22 percent came from German speaking areas within and outside the conglomerate state; 10 percent from Norway, which was also ruled by the king of Denmark in the eighteenth century; and the rest from Sweden and other parts of the world. The majority of employees at Christiansborg therefore spoke Danish, which was the language used by the trading companies both in Copenhagen and in Africa. When nothing else is mentioned the European men working at Christiansborg are therefore presumably Danish. A few of the men, especially lower assistants and soldiers, had grown up in villages, but most came from merchant towns, and during the eighteenth century a still larger number of the men had grown up in Copenhagen. If they had not grown up in Copenhagen they had most likely been through the city on their way to Africa.

57. About a ban on European women in the English fur trade, see Van Kirk, *Many Tender*, 3; about the Vereenigde Oost-Indische Compagnie (Dutch East India Company) restricting European women in Dutch Indonesia, see Stoler, *Carnal Knowledge*, 47.

58. Rask, *A Brief*, 165. Of seventy men who went to Christiansborg before 1730, I have recorded thirty-nine deaths in Africa or on the way home. K. G. Davies has found that well over half of the Europeans who went to West Africa in the early part of the slave trade died within the first year; see "The Living," 97; see also Brown, *The Reaper's*, Chapter 1.

59. See a description of Christiansborg and its successive expansions in Lawrence, *Trade Castles*, 199–217.

60. This social climate appears to have been very similar to that at other European forts on the Gold Coast in the period; see Feinberg, "Africans," 86–88.

61. Rømer, *A Reliable*, 235. Barbot, *Barbot on Guinea*, 400. Monrad, who in 1822 was trying to convince his readers that life at Christiansborg was not quite as uncultured as its reputation suggested, excused the men's excessive drinking with the fact that the "enervating heat, the heavy perspiration and evaporation, make some cheering and strengthening drink necessary"; see *A Description*, 264.

62. Isert, *Letters*, 156.

63. Daybook kept by Governor Fensman, Christiansborg, September 21, 1688, in Justesen, *Danish Sources*, 90.

64. Isert, *Letters*, 147.

65. Rømer, *A Reliable*, 232.

66. This distinction was also later used by Paul Isert and H. C. Monrad in their accounts from Christiansborg; see Isert, *Letters*, 156; and Monrad, *A Description*, 230.

67. As mentioned on page 21, a creolized Portuguese was the lingua franca of Europeans and Africans on the Gold Coast during the slave trade.

68. Rømer, *A Reliable*, 234. Modern psychological work on the phenomenon of culture shock suggests that though people's reactions when encountering foreign cultures of course vary, there are certain typical patterns of responses that can be grouped under the concept. The psychological state of culture shock resembles a type of buzzing confusion. Some of the affective responses include confusion, anxiety, disorientation, suspicion, bewilderment, perplexity, and an intense desire to be elsewhere. The experience of cultural displacement is, to no surprise, enhanced by the size of the cultural gap between the groups encountering each other. For an introduction to the field, see Ward et al., *The Psychology*. Rømer's description of the European men's transition to living on the Gold Coast in the eighteenth century is, in my opinion, reminiscent of this modern understanding of culture shock.

69. Rømer, *A Reliable*, 234. Isert mentions that the council looked positively on such relationships because they eased the men's homesickness; see *Letters*, 157. That the company was in support of their employees marrying women in Osu fits with Ann Laura Stoler's findings in her research on the Dutch East India Company. Allegedly the company there encouraged its employees to take concubines until well into the nineteenth century; see *Carnal Knowledge*, exs. 47–48.

70. In 1724 chaplain Elias Svane, for instance, complained to the company about a group of sailors, who, after having received the Communion at his church, went brawling around town in the evening. See Justesen, *Danish Sources*, 305.

71. As Durba Ghosh has remarked in her study of English men with Indian wives in colonial India, "going native" is not as straightforward a cultural conversion as it sometimes may seem; see *Sex and the Family*, 254.

72. Jan de Wit is mentioned in a letter from Governor Lygaard to the directors in Copenhagen, February 23, 1708, in Justesen, *Danish Sources*, 213. Wellemsen's letter to von Suhm, November 18, 1727, is in ibid., 371. Again forty-three years later, in 1770, another Danish chaplain demanded a resolution in the case about the fort slave Aquva's "mulatto boy child." See the case about Aquva's child, January 12, 1771, in GK. Guvernementet på Guineakysten. Justitsprotokol, 1770–71, box 177, pp. 37–38.

73. Governor Schielderup et al.'s accusation against Wærøe appears in Justesen, *Danish Sources*, 509. The case against Jessen, July 6, 1764, is in GtK. Europæiske journalsager, 1760–68, box 31 (1764) and is further discussed in Chapter 4.

74. About keys from Europe, see Monrad, *A Description*, 182. About the meaning of keys and locks in West Africa, see Blier, *African Vodun*, 107, 287–92. I want to thank Jim Sweet for helping me think about these keys and amulets. About men at Christiansborg wearing amulets (fetishes) under their clothes and Danish men loving their African wives, see Rømer, *A Reliable*, 104 and 234.

75. As Claude Lévi-Strauss noted in 1949, marriage is the archetype of exchange, and a system of exchange always lies behind rules of marriage; see *The Elementary Structures of Kinship*, 483 and 478. Joseph C. Miller's term "commercial marriages" speaks well to the trading-alliance element of the Euro-African marriages in West Africa; see *Way of Death*, 290–91.

76. In most societies a marriage contract also entails a more direct transfer of goods and/or services. In precolonial West Africa the economic transaction when entering a marriage contract was a payment of bridewealth, wherein the groom paid the bride's family in goods for the right to marry her. Alice Schlegel discusses different patterns of marriage transactions in "Marriage Transactions." She mentions the predominance of bridewealth in marriage transactions in large parts of Africa on pp. 295 and 300. But apart from the direct payments involved in entering a marriage contract, the unions had broader economic functions as the primary institutions for wealth and property distribution between generations and the basis for the division of labor between the sexes. Moreover, in the case of Osu and the rest of West Africa, trade was organized through conjugal relationships. Ideologically, marriage was one of the social institutions endlessly compared and discussed in European travel accounts, and it became a point of contention for missionaries as well as colonial authorities. As Gunlög Für has explained, this interest in gaining control over indigenous marriages was linked to "at least two centuries of concerted colonial efforts to organize the world's diverse peoples and societies into one hierarchy"; see Für, "The Struggle," 59.

77. For the French in Louisiana, see Spear, "They Need," 35. On the English in western Canada, Van Kirk cites a ruling from 1886 that decided that *marriage á la façon du pays* was not to be considered lawful marriage; see *Many Tender*, 241. For the growing literature on interracial marriage and cohabitation in trading posts and

colonies in the early modern period, see notes 12 and 15 in the Introduction to the present book.

78. Ghosh, *Sex and the Family*. William Dalrymple's account of English resident James Kirkpatrick's relationship with an aristocratic Indian woman, Khair un-Nissa, at the court in Hyderabad, is a more romanticized history of an interracial familial union in India; see Dalrymple, *White Mughals*. See also Ballhachet, *Race*.

79. This history asks what, if anything, racial difference meant in the encounter between Africans and Europeans in Osu, and what work racial difference did. What racial difference meant changed over the course of the eighteenth century, and the cassare marriages and the Euro-African families and children they produced were central in attaching meanings to racial difference. About the advantages of asking questions about difference rather than employing analytical categories that assumes its existence, see Boydston, "Gender." For asking about the "work" that race does, see Hall, *A History*, 14; here Hall also discusses the development of a "language of race," which was shared by both "colonizer and colonized," 16.

80. On a process of gender functioning as "communication tool" in a cultural encounter in North America, see Barr, *Peace Came*, for example 11, "A Diplomacy." About gendered cultural encounter in the early modern Atlantic world, see also Pearsal, "Gender." See also Brown, *Good Wives*, introduction. About Europeans understanding native American culture by "attaching" the "new" to familiar European culture (and often quite misunderstanding what they encountered), see Pagden, *European*.

81. Asafo companies were "town militias" that became increasingly important on the Gold Coast during the eighteenth and nineteenth centuries; see Hernæs, "Introduction"; J. Osei-Tutu, *The Asafoi*.

82. About social class on the Gold Coast in the seventeenth century, see Kea, *Settlements*. For further discussion of the role of wealth and European material culture in signaling prestige on the Gold Coast, see Chapter 4 of the present volume.

83. Ole Feldbæk writes about this provision, known as "stavnsbåndet" in *Den lange*, 154–57.

84. About the term *odonko*, see Rattray, *Ashanti*, 35–36; and Dumett, "The Work," 70–71. On the Ga adopting the word, see Parker, *Making*, xiv.

85. Perbi, *A History*. In a study of the western Sudan in the precolonial era, Martin A. Klein mentions that enslaved people's positions in the family they worked for was additionally weak, precisely because they had no kinship group of their own to turn to if there were disputes in the family they lived in, whereas wives or pawns could still turn to their own lineage for help; see Robertson and Klein, Introduction, 78. Studies from the twentieth century show that knowledge of who descended from slaves still very much exists among Ghanaians today; see Bailey, *African*. Monrad noted how slavery was inheritable and that "a wealthy family in Accra who descended from a slave woman would never be considered free and independent"; see *A Description*, 97.

86. See Rømer, *A Reliable*, 28: "the farther up in the land the slaves come from, the more stupid they are. Among these slaves, we have seen those of nations whom one

could hardly call human." Rømer also suggests that one could tell from a face if a slave had come from the north, 224.

87. For the differences between the status of pawns and slaves more specifically at Christiansborg in the eighteenth century, see Hernæs, "Fort Slaves," 201. See also Law, "On Pawning," 59; Lovejoy and Richardson, "The Business." For a more general introduction to pawning, see Toyin Falola and Paul E. Lovejoy's Introduction to *Pawnship in Africa*.

88. In *Trade*, 96, Kwame Yeboa Daaku argued that it was the acquisition of a common trading language that "threw up a new class of middlemen who acted as a liaison between African and European traders." I suggest that this common language was shaped by the racializing discourse of the Atlantic world, and was powerfully reproduced through the cassare marriages.

89. For early Portuguese racialist thinking, see Sweet, "The Iberian."

90. See a few early references to this practice of referring to nonenslaved Africans as "free" in Rask, *A Brief*, 103 ("free Negro"), 152 ("free Negro"); Justesen, *Danish Sources*, 467 ("free Mulatta").

91. In "Fort Slaves," 219–20, Per Hernæs describes the ideological connections (and shared ideas about what slavery meant and was) between the different parts of "the Danish Empire": "The Danes at Christiansborg must have had certain models of slavery in mind when they classified a person as a slave. Their way of thinking must, *inter alia*, have been influenced by plantation slavery in the West Indies and by certain prevailing perceptions in Europe and Copenhagen from where they received instructions" (215).

92. Jean Barbot originally wrote in French, but he later settled in England, where his travel account from West Africa was published in English. Quote from Barbot, *Barbot on Guinea*, 496.

93. Rask, *A Brief*, 103.

94. Ibid., 104. For comparison, in seventeenth-century accounts, authors have expressed themselves more authoritatively about skin color; see Müller's "Description of the Fetu Country, 1662–69," 153: "Who would not conclude from this that the black complexion of the Moors must be caused by the great heat of the sun."

95. Indeed, just as Rask had trouble believing that babies had black skin before they were born, he was uncertain whether black skin would persist after death. His predecessor at the fort, Andreas Vinter, had told him of an episode where some Africans had been killed by Akwamu. The dead bodies had been lying on the beach close to the fort for a few days, and "being washed as the surf went in and out, their skin had become pale white." Just as black skin color could perhaps be enhanced by the sun, so too could it be washed off by water after death; see Rask, *A Brief*, 105.

96. Rask, *A Brief*, 104–5.

97. For an example of Rask's derogatory descriptions of Africans, see ibid., 77: "They are usually well-trained and expert in thievery and swindling. . . . [They are] very lazy and indolent, absolutely content in such ignorance and coarseness." In *Central Africans*, 299, Linda Heywood and John K. Thornton "address the contention that Europeans

held uniformly negatively attitudes about Africans." This impression that European derogatory racial discourse was less solidified or uniform before the eighteenth century is consistent with historical works on English literature and discourses about race that follow the development of racial discourse over the course of the early modern period; see Wheeler, *The Complexion*; K. Hall, *Things of Darkness*.

98. I will return to this question in Chapter 3.

99. When Johannes Rask stopped in London on his way back to Copenhagen, he stayed with Frantz Boye's English family and brought "greetings to his virtuous wife." Boye's new brother-in-law, Edward Smith, apparently liked him so well that he shipped him more than six hunting dogs from London; see *A Brief*, 202 and 169.

100. *Rigsdaler* (rdl.) was the currency in Denmark in the eighteenth century.

101. About inland kings claiming war captives as their property, see Daaku, *Trade*, 32. Koko's father developed a large debt to the Danish company. In 1729, when Governor Wærøe took over the administration, the debt book at Christiansborg listed Caboceer Tette Osu as owing 128 rdl. for "himself and all in the town for which no pawn," Justesen, *Danish Sources*, 384. See the case against Frantz Boye starting June 9, 1717, in VgK. Direktionen. Forhørs og domsakter fra Guinea 1717–46. The last reference to Koko I have found is from 1735 (a debt of 8 rdl. owed to Governor Wærøe and assistant Sparre) in Justesen, *Danish Sources*, 503 ("Noyte Akon's sister, Kaakoe, who was Frantz Boye's Negress"). Koko remained a common name in the sources from Christiansborg, as in Osu, but Frantz also became a common name. While the first Frantz Boye died in Ouidah a little further down the coast in 1727, there was a Frantz Boye, with a son named Fredrick, living on the coast in 1806 (mentioned in a letter to commandant Holm, January 16, 1808; see KGG2. Brevkopibog ført på Christiansborg, 1807–12, boxes 57–58). About Frantz Boye's death at Ouidah, see Law, *Correspondence*, 9.

Chapter 2. A Hybrid Position

1. I am assuming that Anna Sophie attended school at the fort in 1724. In 1727 she was both christened and married to Elias Svane's assistant teacher Ole Larsen Grue. Justesen, *Danish Sources*, 365. For Anna Sophie, see also ibid., 365 and 467. Ole Larsen and Anna Sophie are described as having been married in "Suhm's time," which means that it must have happened after Governor von Suhm came out in 1724. There were only three small windows in the church room at the fort, and two of them faced out to the slave yard. Several chaplains mentioned the smell: Elias Svane mentioned that the smell was caused by "the gutters and the uncleanness of the slaves"; see Justesen, *Danish Sources*, 308; Hagerup to bishop, June 1, 1765, in SSB, mentions that the schoolchildren at Christiansborg were sent to collect anise leaves and twigs to use against the "poisonous stench" from the slave yard that came through the windows; see also chaplain Trane to bishop March 28, 1734, in SSB.

2. In a letter to the company Elias Svane vividly described the crumbling school-

room and the lack of respect accorded it by both Europeans and Africans; see Justesen, *Danish Sources*, 306.

3. Anna Sophie's father's name suggests that he was son of the Danish assistant Peter Witt, who had spent fifteen years on the coast when he became interim governor at Frederiksborg in 1678. Peter Witt would have named his children in Africa according to traditional Danish naming practices—in this case, as Peter's son (Petersen) followed by his family name, Witt. Peter Witt had at least one son in Africa according to *Danish Sources*, 89, and I am here assuming that this son is Christian Petersen Witt. Peter Witt may also have had a son with one of the fort slaves at Christiansborg; a letter from 1708 mentions a Jan de Witt, who was son of a fort slave and a Danish man; see ibid., 213. In 1710 Rask mentioned the fort's "drum major, Christian Whit, who is a native heathen on his mother's side, and was 30 years old before he was christened"; see *A Brief*, 136. Both Ole Larsen Grue and Jørgen Bendixen Warberg are listed as coming from Norway in the wage lists from Christiansborg. Ole Grue was from Christiania, Norway; he arrived in Africa in 1723 and died at Christiansborg September 28, 1728. Jørgen Warberg is listed as born in Bergen, Norway. See VgK. Mandtal og gagebøger, 1703–54, box (*kasse*) 942. The case of Warberg, Anna Sophie, and her father wanting them to be married by a chaplain is mentioned in chaplain Niels Lange to bishop, December 24, 1730, in SSB. The administration's attempt to convince Warberg is mentioned in a letter from Governor Wærøe et al., Christiansborg, February 19, 1733, in *Danish Sources*, 467.

4. Governor von Suhm et al., letter from Christiansborg, August 15, 1724, in Justesen, *Danish Sources*, 326.

5. The adoption and integration of elements of Christianity in a different cultural system happened everywhere in the world that Europeans settled, and Christianity became an important part of processes of "creolization" in many parts of the Atlantic world. In the case of West Africa, local African traders who made their living trading with Portuguese traders were at times known as "Christians of the land." See *Silences*, 14. Horta, "Evidence," 99, argues that Christianity constituted a "common Luso-African language."

6. Hagerup to bishop, June 1, 1765, in SSB. Quote translated from the Danish: "nyttige Lemmer af vor nærværende Republique."

7. Daybook kept at Christiansborg, August 9, 1688, in Justesen, *Danish Sources*, 89 (brackets are Justesen's). The son of Peter Witt mentioned here was presumably Anna Sophie's father, Christian Petersen Witt.

8. Governor Lygaard, Christiansborg, February 23, 1708, to the directors in Copenhagen, in Justesen, *Danish Sources*, 213 (Justesen's emphasis).

9. Ibid.

10. Fort slaves were Africans enslaved at Christiansborg who received a very minimal payment for their labor. Their numbers grew during the eighteenth century. See Hernæs, "'Fort Slaves.'"

11. Governor Pahl et al., general letter from Christiansborg, September 10, 1727, in Justesen, *Danish Sources*, 365.

12. He compared the Danish case to the English fort in Accra, which he said often hired sons of Dutch men and African women; see Rømer, *A Reliable*, 58.

13. Governor Boye, Christiansborg August 18, 1711, to the directors in Copenhagen; see Justesen, *Danish Sources*, 236.

14. For references to both Dutch and English chaplains on the Gold Coast, see Debrunner, *A History*. According to Natalie Everts the presence of the chaplains in Elmina was "an ambivalent one, and their influence on the castle-community quite limited," in "Cherchez," 48. She notes that the school at Elmina most often lacked a teacher in ibid., 53. See also Daaku, *Trade*, chapter 5.

15. For the regulation and punishment of extramarital sexual relations in Denmark in the eighteenth century, see Koefoed, *Besovede*.

16. Erich Trane to bishop, March 28, 1734, in SSB.

17. See, for instance, S. Unger's request to be repatriated in 1782 or Johan Kiøbke Meyer's persistent requests to be sent home in 1793, 1794, and 1795. Perhaps the hardship of a posting in Guinea circulated in Copenhagen after that: a chaplain Randrup, who had already accepted a position at Christiansborg, wrote to the bishop, October 5, 1797, to ask if it was still possible to be sent instead to Ringsted (a town in Denmark), since he had heard from friends that one needed a very special constitution to make it on the coast. Perhaps the chaplains later in the century were more inclined to want to be sent home early because of a general dislike of working in a slave-trading post. In any case, several later chaplains speak of the slave trade as "horrible" and "distasteful," which correlates with the general change in the attitudes toward the slave trade in Europe in the late eighteenth century. Monrad described how he had to "stand in opposition to most of the Europeans I lived with in Guinea"; see Monrad, *A Description*, 275.

18. Unfortunately no payroll survives from 1724, but according to the payrolls from 1708 and 1727 there were respectively thirty-one and twenty-one employees at the fort in those years. The reason that more of the employees had not taken African wives was probably that they had just arrived or that they were soldiers, who could not always afford to cassare.

19. Elias Svane, Christiansborg March 15, 1724, to the directors in Copenhagen, in Justesen, *Danish Sources*, 301.

20. Ibid., 301–2. Among other examples Svane mentions the case of merchant Hans Christian Borch, who sailed for Europe in 1724 with no plans to return, leaving his African wife pregnant on the coast.

21. Ibid., 301.

22. Governor Herrn, Christiansborg April 20, 1722, to the directors in Copenhagen in ibid., 293–94. David Herrn was governor of Christiansborg from 1722 until his death in 1723.

23. H. C. Monrad mentions how the Danish chaplains were specifically not to be missionaries; see *A Description*, 271. See also the work by Hans Werner Debrunner on the role of the Danish chaplains at Christiansborg, in "Pioneers," 373–425; and *A History*.

24. Justesen, *Danish Sources*, 302. Svane suspected that Danish would be a hard language for people in Osu to learn and instead suggested that they learn Portuguese, which he believed to be easier for Africans. This was most likely not due to the nature of Portuguese, but because it was already the lingua franca on the coast and therefore familiar to many people in Osu. Apparently the church in Elmina, which never had as steady a presence as the church in Osu, did not have a missionary purpose either but was "exclusively to serve Europeans"; see Doortmont, "The Dutch," 105.

25. Elias Svane, Christiansborg, March 15, 1724, to the directors in Copenhagen, in Justesen, *Danish Sources*, 302.

26. This argument was made by Bishop Pontopiddan in his foreword to Ludewig Rømer's travel account; see *A Reliable*, 8. I will return to this foreword in Chapter 3.

27. Sandra Greene has found that families in Keta married daughters only of their slaves to European traders; see "Crossing," 31. Natalie Everts has found that Akan families in Elmina married both free and enslaved daughters to Dutch traders; see "A Motley," 56. As mentioned in Chapter 1, employees at Christiansborg had sexual relations with enslaved women at Christiansborg and possibly with enslaved women in Osu, potentially including long-term relationships.

28. About the letter being passed on to Weigaard, see VgK. Det Sekrete Råd på Guineakysten. Sekretprotokol, January 22, 1731, box 881.

29. Hans Jensen Flye to bishop, February 3, 1747, in SSB.

30. Ibid.

31. VgK. Det Sekrete Råd på Guineakysten. Sekretprotokol, January 22, 1731, box 881.

32. Ibid. It was not, as Hans W. Debrunner suggested, Erich Trane who first induced Bishop Worm to confront the question of the interracial marriages in Guinea. In fact, in a letter from Trane that Debrunner cites Trane specifically referred to a letter Worm had sent to Christiansborg "in Mr. Svane's time"; see Debrunner, "Pioneers," 385.

33. VgK. Det Sekrete Råd på Guineakysten. Sekretprotokol, January 22, 1731, box 881. According to the marriage statute of 1582 that was repeated in Danske Lov (1683) there were three reasons that justified a divorce: fornication, "*desertio*" (desertion), and impotence. See Anette Jensen, "Staten, kirken og stridbare ægtefolk," 111.

34. VgK. Det Sekrete Råd på Guineakysten. Sekretprotokol, January 22, 1731, box 881.

35. Justesen, *Danish Sources*, 346.

36. Governor Pahl et al., Christiansborg, September 10, 1727, to the directors in Copenhagen, in ibid., 365.

37. Ibid.

38. Ibid.

39. Chaplain Erich Trane to bishop, March 28, 1734, in SSB. In Rømer, *A Reliable*, 185, Selena Winsnes has translated in Rømer's first Danish sentence "Der har været på Christiansborg en dispensation af Bishop Worm" to "Bishop Worm has granted a dispensation." I think Rømer's use of the past tense "Der har været" is important, since it suggests that the written proof of such a dispensation was gone when Rømer was on the

coast in the 1740s. See the Danish text in Ludewig Ferdinand Rømer, *Tilforladelig Efter-*
retning om Kysten Guinea, 245–46.

40. Rømer, *A Reliable,* 185.

41. Feinberg, "Africans," 89.

42. For an essay on how such a colonial hybrid might come about, see Bhabha,
"Signs," 145–74.

43. Governor Herrn, Christiansborg, February 10, 1722, to the directors in Copenhagen, in Justesen, *Danish Sources,* 288.

44. Governor Suhm et al., Christiansborg, August 15, 1724, in ibid., 326.

45. Debrunner, *A History,* 55; Daaku, *Trade,* 101–2, describes Dutch and English
failed attempts to start fort schools on the Gold Coast. In the second half of the century,
an English missionary society also sent out missionaries to Cape Coast Castle, but they
were not very successful either; see Reese, "Sheep." For governors mentioning it being
harder to find employment for daughters of European men and African women, see
Governor von Suhm, September 28, 1726, and Governor Pahl et al., September 10, 1727,
in Justesen, *Danish Sources,* 346 and 365.

46. Hans Jensen Flye to bishop, February 3, 1747, in SSB.

47. Ibid.

48. Elias Svane to the directors in Copenhagen in Justesen, *Danish Sources,* 303.

49. Ibid. Later missionaries and chaplains at Christiansborg could, for example, use
Christian Protten's Danish introduction to Fante and Ga, *En nyttig.*

50. Elias Svane to the directors in Copenhagen, March 1, 1724, in Justesen, *Danish*
Sources, 303.

51. Ibid., 308.

52. Ibid., 307.

53. Ibid.

54. In "Africans and Europeans," 89–90, Feinberg notes that patrilinear families on
the Gold Coast were less ready to integrate Euro-African children than were the matrilinear Akan families. I have found no evidence that it was difficult for the patrilinear Ga
families in Osu to integrate Euro-African children, quite the contrary in fact, as discussed in Chapter 1. It would be fascinating to do a more systematic comparison of the
different Gold Coast cases of intermarriage with European men.

55. Quoted in Reese, "Sheep," 355.

56. Ibid.

57. Governor Wærøe et al., Christiansborg, May 28, 1729, in Justesen, *Danish*
Sources, 394. See Governor Suhm's suggestion in Governor von Suhm, Christiansborg
September 28, 1726, in Justesen, *Danish Sources,* 346. By 1700 in Elmina, Dutch administration had apparently already proposed that employees should be required to take
any children they had with African women back to Europe or, if the employee died
while in Africa, "to reserve, each for himself, according to his position, a proper sum for
honest maintenance and Christian education of such products"; quoted in Akyeampong, *Drink,* xix.

58. Isert, *Letters*, 157. By the late 1750s, monthly payments to the "mulatto children's chest" were formally recorded in the company's books. See salary books listing payments to the mulatto chest in KGG1. Gagebøger, 1755–60, box 37–40.

59. See fines paid to the chest in books from the Secret Council from 1768 and 1771 in GK. Guvernementet på Guineakysten. Justitsprotokol, box 177 and KGG2. Justistprotokol, 1794–1813, box 61, p. 46, 55, 69, 78, 79.

60. Monrad, *A Description*, 273. The payments to the "mulatto chest" also at some point in the later eighteenth or early in the nineteenth century changed into a more general payment that all employees, including the growing group of Euro-African soldiers, paid according to their salary. See salary books (gagebøger) from 1815, 1816, and 1817 in KGG2. Gagebog ved hovedfortet Christiansborg, 1815-17, box 66.

61. See estate after Johan Rodolph Muyol in VgK. Direktionen, Guineiske registrerings- og venditiebøger, 1699-1754, box 245. See more details about Auchue and her three Danish husbands in Chapter 1.

62. Isert, *Letters*, 157. See a few examples in estates from the 1790s in GtK. Skiftebreve indsendt af det kgl. Guvernement på Guineakysten, 1793–99, box 1051. Mulatress Anna had a "gagebook" that her cassaret husband, Adam Gerhardt Just, had given her. He died November 14, 1798. When Jørgen Mandix, commandant at Fredensborg, died in 1799, Governor Wrisberg saw to it that Mandix's "mulatresse" and "boys" were paid "their outstanding wages and reward." On August 31, 1812, Governor Schiønning wrote a deed of gift to his "cassarede Negress," Tolo, "as reward for her five years faithful service"; see KGG2. Rådsprotokol, book (*bog*) 50, p. 345.

63. Hans Jensen Flye to bishop, February 3, 1747, in SSB. Hagerup to bishop, June 1, 1765, in SSB, where Hagerup also described how the children had a "*spise-moder*" ("eating-mother"), who was paid by the company to cook for the children.

64. Hagerup to bishop, June 1, 1765, in SSB.

65. Hans Jensen Flye to bishop, February 3, 1747, in SSB.

66. Jacobus Capitein quoted in Everts, "Cherchez," 54; Philip Quaque in Reese, "Sheep," 362.

67. Niels Lange to Bishop Worm, December 24, 1730, in SSB. As the attentive reader might have noted chaplain Lange has been mentioned earlier in this chapter as the chaplain who refused to marry N. J. Bagge to "a free negress" by the name of Sachiva, the event that provoked chief assistant Reinholt Nielsen Kamp to order Bishop Worm's letter read aloud from the pulpit. It is therefore not surprising if in the same year, 1730, chaplain Lange also came into conflict with other employees.

68. Governor Wærøe et al., Christiansborg, February 19, 1733, in Justesen, *Danish Sources*, 467. The later wills mentioning Euro-African families in Osu are discussed in Chapter 5.

69. See more about these wills in Chapter 5.

70. About contemporary missionaries in the Danish West Indies, see Sensbach, *Rebecca's*. When the Basel missionaries arrived in Osu in the nineteenth century, they encountered a number of Euro-African people in Osu who had been christened and had

shown interest in Christian cultural and religious worldviews and practices. See microfilm of letters from the Basel missionaries on the Gold Coast, 1828–51, including some transcriptions by Hans W. Debrunner, available from Yale Divinity School (English transcriptions of documents in series D-1) and the mission's archive in Basel. See also Sill, *Encounters*; and Haenger, *Slaves*.

71. Hernæs, "Den balstyrige," 17–18.

72. Cowry shells were used as currency in several places in West Africa in the eighteenth century.

73. The soldiers' account of the mutiny at Christiansborg, October 22, 1744, is in Justesen, *Danish Sources*, 629.

74. Justesen, *Danish Sources*, 635 and 661. Christian Petersen Witt's escape with his son-in-law is mentioned in ibid., 661, 666, and 671. Anna Sophie and Cornelius Petersen met sometime around 1729, shortly after Cornelius arrived on the coast as a soldier, and they were still together in 1744. Like Jørgen Warberg, Cornelius Petersen was listed in the wage books as coming from Bergen, Norway. VgK. Bogholderen på Christiansborg. Mandtal- og gagebøger, 1703–54, box 942. Per Hernæs describes this conflict in "Den balstyrige," 17–25. Several documents from the case can be found in Justesen, *Danish Sources*, 618-67, in which it is mentioned that there had been other points of contention between Billsen and employees at Christiansborg. Assistant Ludewig Rømer had, for example, traveled to Popo against Billsen's orders, which led the governor to suspend both Rømer and assistant Klein from their positions. The suspension of Rømer and Klein is mentioned in Justesen, *Danish Sources*, 626.

75. In a Secret Council resolution from January 1745, after Cornelius Petersen had been captured and returned to Christiansborg, Governor Billsen expressed fear that people from Aprag would attack Osu again, as they had done recently; see Justesen, *Danish Sources*, 635.

76. Justesen, *Danish Sources*, 746. Ludewig Ferdinand Rømer also presented a story of Anna Sophie poisoning "several persons at our fort"; see *A Reliable*, 86.

77. Cited in Hernæs, "Den balstyrige," 25. Per Hernæs has also later suggested that it was fear of her threats that led Governor Hackenburg to release Cornelius and send him off to the West Indies; see ibid., 24.

78. Governor Platfues et al., Christiansborg to the directors in Copenhagen May 23, 1748, in Justesen, *Danish Sources*, 724.

79. Hackenburg is mentioned as having married the daughter of the broker Adoui (Adovi) in 1744, when Governor Billsen ordered him to give her up and "submit himself to the discipline of the chaplain," in Justesen, *Danish Sources*, 619. In his long declaration from 1748 Friderich Svane mentioned both Rømer and Platfues as being cassaret to Euro-African women; see *Danish Sources*, 748. Joost Platfues was also married in Copenhagen and may therefore not have referred to his African wife much in public; see *Danish Sources*, 787.

80. Marcus Svane was cassaret to a daughter of Odoi Kpoti, who was caboceer in the nearby town of Labadi, while Sonne was cassaret to a daughter of Soya, the

aforementioned important company messenger and broker from Osu; see Governor Hachsen et al., Christiansborg, January 5, 1752, in Justesen, *Danish Sources*, 844–45.

81. When cassare marriages were mentioned in wage books or in the one surviving church book from 1765 (see Chapter 4), the phrase "after permission from the Governor and the Chaplain" was used. In 1807 (July) Børgesen asked permission to cassare, after which Fredensborg account books debited the stipulated expence to the "fattig kasse"; see KGG2. Brevkopibog ført på Christiansborg, 1807–12, box 57–58, and two other examples from the same letter copybook. Lutterodt got permission to cassare mulatresse Cathrine Schmidt and paid to the "fattigkasse" May 14, 1807, and on August 21, 1808, soldier Carl Quist was permitted to cassare "Thessing Negress Manda," if he paid the stipulated to the "fattigkasse." Throughout the century there are also references to men cassaring without obtaining permission first, which suggests that permission was officially required; see a letter from merchant Schmidt to Governor Wrisberg, November 2, 1754, in RtK. Indkomne diverse ujournaliserede guineiske breve 1755–59, box 2249-26, or the earlier reference to Hackenburg cassaring without permission from Governor Billsen, who demanded that he retract the marriage, in Justesen, *Danish Sources*, 619.

82. Rømer, *A Reliable*, 86–87. Friderich Svane mentions that Anna Sophie (or Sophia) had moved to "the Dutch town" (meaning Aprag) by 1748; see Justesen, *Danish Sources*, 746.

83. In 1703 there were one or two African-born employees (the drummer, Christian Petersen Witt, and possibly a boy) out of thirty employees at the fort. In 1727 four mulatto soldiers were listed as well as fifty-two "fort-slaves" (men, women, and children); see VgK. Bogholderen på Christiansborg. Mandtal og gagebøger, 1703–54, box 942. The number of African workers at the fort grew substantially through the eighteenth century; see Hernæs, "European," 176. It was not uncommon for Euro-African employees who had worked at the fort for longer periods to receive a pension. Per Hernæs also mentions a "kind of social security system" for the fort slaves, who received half of their initial pay when they retired, in "Fort Slaves," 208. In 1725 Governor Suhm sent Christian Petersen Witt inland with a letter and brandy to the king of Akwamu; see Justesen, *Danish Sources*, 334. In 1728 he was present at Christiansborg and witnessed how Auchue's husband, Sergeant Franz Carl Minche, had her fidelity tested; see ibid., 378. Even after Witt had served the company a lifetime, Governor Wærøe still described him as "Christian Petersen Mulat" (400) and later in the same letter as simply "the Mulatto" (402). This might be ascribed to Wærøe's generally derogatory attitude toward Euro-Africans. On p. 415 Wærøe again called him "my Mulatto Christian Petersen Witt."

84. Here I am saying something similar to Walter Hawthorne's excellent introduction to *Planting*, 11: "Individuals themselves could not hope to alter the structural realities of the Atlantic system; they could only seek to make the best of the options presented to them at the most local of levels."

Chapter 3. "What in Guinea You Promised Me"

1. Carl Engman's first daughter, Christina Sophia, was christened in Vor Frue Kirke, October 31, 1765. Ludewig Rømer and chamber councilor Johan Reindorph were witnesses (godfathers) at the christening.

2. About Rømer living under the butcher shop in Gothersgade in 1745, see subpoena (*vidneindkaldelse*) in the case about Governor Boris's estate, December 23, 1745, in VgK. Direktionen, 1680–1754. Breve og dokumenter vedk. skifte og afregning efter afdøde kompagnitjenere i Guinea, box (kasse) 244. About the shipwreck and Rømer's story in general, see Selena Winsnes's introduction to Rømer, *A Reliable*, xiii–xv.

3. According to John Parker, Carl Engman, and Johan Reindorph, and Frederick Hackenburg had all been cassaret to the same woman, Ashiokai Wondo, daughter of Caboceer Adovi; see Parker, "Mankraloi," 37. Hackenburg is mentioned to have been cassaret to a daughter of Adovi in Justesen, *Danish Sources*, 619 and 748. Rømer described Adovi as one of the most powerful men in Osu in Rømer, *A Reliable*, 163 and 216. I have not found any references to Engman or Reindorph being cassaret to Adovi's daughter, and Engman was, according to Marcus Svane at least, supposed to have been on bad terms with Adovi; see Justesen, *Danish Sources*, 911. But it is not at all impossible. As mentioned in previous chapters, some women in Osu were cassaret to a succession of European men. I suspect, however, that Engman also had a different relationship in Africa. In a letter from 1754 Engman refers to "my mulatresse in Osu," and it is unlikely that he would here be referring to Ashiokai; see Engman to Rentekammeret, September 17, 1754, RtK. Indkomne diverse ujournaliserede guineiske breve, 1755–59, box 2249-26. According to the same Marcus Svane, Engman was also cassaret to a daughter of a caboceer trading with the Dutch, Tette Ahinnekwa (*Danish Sources*, 911). Engman and Hackenburg have a total of five sons listed on the school list in 1765, and they probably did not all have the same mother, which has led me to believe that Engman's sons—Erich, Carl, and Friderich—were sons of the said Euro-African woman. See the school lists in letters from Protten of March 27 and March 29, 1765, in SSB and GtK. Indkomne guineiske breve, 1760–68, box 70. Ashiokai Wondo may also be the "Assiokkay" who in January 1765 was cassaret to assistant Friderick Barfoed, according to a church book from Christiansborg. Barfoed had come out in 1764 and died shortly after the marriage in February 1765; see the church book in SSB. Per Hernæs also cites several cases from palaver books where a woman named "Aschiokay" had claims after deceased employees involving trade in pigs and other things in 1767; see Hernæs, *Slaves*, 118. The name was common, but if even a few of the references are to Ashiokai Wondo, then she must have been well known at Christiansborg at the time.

4. According to the company's letter copybook two of Carl Engman's and one of Hackenburg's sons sailed to Denmark in 1775; see GK. Guvernementet på Guineakysten. Brevbog, February 24, 1775, p. 38, box 172. Carl Engman had been in Africa thirteen years in 1756; see RtK. Amerikansk og afrikansk kopibog, 1755–60, p. 90, box 2249-10.

5. I agree with the common assertion in Africanist scholarship that from an African

perspective Europeans played only a minor role in the actual enslavement of Africans. However, we should not leave this comparison detached from its larger economic context. On the question of whether and how the slave trade affected West African societies I agree with Joseph E. Inikori and Stanley Engerman's very clearly stated position that it is "clear that western Europe and North America were gainers in the Atlantic slave trade. Tropical Africa was a loser"; see *The Atlantic*, 17. Though of course in individual cases and perhaps even in individual decades there are many exceptions to this general rule.

6. For a study of what Africans got in return for slaves, see Alpern, "What Africans." About the differences between merchant and industrial capital and the economic dynamics of the Euro-African encounters in Africa, see Cooper, "Africa," particularly p. 17, where he argues that to understand economic development in Africa we must shift our focus from trade to production, and p. 29, where he discusses how the temporary and vulnerable position of new traders in Africa (and Europe) "is indicative of the vulnerability of merchant capital." Since Eric Williams, *Capitalism and Slavery*, was first published in 1944 there has been much discussion about the relationship between the industrial revolution in England and the slave trade. In 1987 David Richardson argued that though Eric Williams was basically right that there *was* a marked relationship between the increase in slave trading and the growth of British industrial production, the relationship between the two was more complicated than Williams had indicated; see "The Slave," 741. About sugar's contribution to the economy of Copenhagen, see Sveistrup and Willerslev, *Den danske*.

7. Rømer, *A Reliable*, 30.

8. Ibid., 31.

9. During the first years the administration took place in the state's Chamber of Revenues, and after 1760, it took place in a separate office in the Chamber of Customs. See histories of the administration of the trading post and the colonies in Gøbel, *A Guide*; and Justesen, "Vestafrika," 373–75. According to Sv. E. Green-Pedersen the number of plantations on St. Croix increased from 264 in 1742 to 375 in 1755, while the number of enslaved Africans went from 1,906 to 8,897; see "The Scope," 150.

10. Justesen, "Vestafrika," 373.

11. The figure was seventy thousand people in 1711, when a third of the population died of the plague. For the sizes of the populations in Copenhagen and the other European cities (Paris, 547,000; Berlin 172,000), see Feldbæk, "Den lange," 25 and 85.

12. Sveistrup and Willerslev, ibid., 40–41, 353, and 126. For the effects of the Danish colonial enterprise on Copenhagen, see also Hopkins, *Peter Thonning*, 11–12.

13. See Rømer, *A Reliable*, xv, about Rømer and his wife, and xviii, about connections to Africa. Rømer's sugar refinery was established in 1754; see *Nationaløkonomisk tidsskrift* 17–18 (Copenhagen: Nationaløkonomisk forening, 1831), 161.

14. Most often, though not always, the men at Christiansborg had grown up in Denmark or Danish-speaking areas of the conglomerate state under the king of Denmark, but some came from German-speaking areas within and outside of the conglomerate

state, and from Norway, which was also ruled by the king of Denmark in the eighteenth century; and a few came from Sweden and other parts of the world. From very early on in the eighteenth century, the majority of employees at Christiansborg spoke Danish, which was the language used by the trading companies both in Copenhagen and in Africa. About settling in Copenhagen after returning from Africa, in a case from 1745, only one of the four men might have been born in Copenhagen, but they all settled in the city when they returned: Hans Hansen Blas, born on Funen, lived on Christianshavn in Copenhagen in 1745. Christian Glob Dorph, born somewhere on Zealand, also lived on Christianshavn. Ludewig Ferdinand Rømer, born in Oldenborg, lived on Gothersgade in Copenhagen in 1745. I cannot locate where tailor master Jørgen Rød was born, but in 1745 he lived in Copenhagen; see subpoena (*vidneindkaldelse*) in the case about Governor Boris's estate, dated December 23, 1745, in VgK. Direktionen. Breve og dokumenter vedk. skifte og afregning efter afdøde kompagnitjenere i Guinea, 1680–1754, box 244. Twenty years later, five witnesses in a different case in the Chamber of Customs also hailed from widespread parts of the Danish conglomerate state, and Engman in Sweden. Three of them settled in Copenhagen when they returned from Africa; of the others, one settled as chaplain in the Danish countryside, and Esau Quist went back to Africa. GtK. Europæiske journalsager, 1760–68, box 31. This case involving a conflict between former Merchant Reindorph and former governor Jessen is discussed in detail later in this chapter.

15. The history of Copenhagen in this period is described in Gamrath, *Residens*; and Sv. Cedergreen Bech, *Storhandelens*. For "flourishing [*florissante*] trading period," see Feldbæk, "Den lange," 98–99.

16. Rømer, *A Reliable*, 250.

17. Atkins, *A Voyage*, 94–95.

18. Ibid., 95.

19. Justesen, *Danish Sources*, 346.

20. Gøbel, "Den danske," 45; in the second half of the eighteenth century an average of fifty ships left Denmark for the colonies every year, and 96 percent of them went directly to the West Indies; see 37–69.

21. Justesen, *Danish Source*, 437.

22. Ibid.

23. Ibid., 467.

24. The letter of February 24, 1775, did not mention which two of Engman's three sons came to Copenhagen; see GK. Guvernementet på Guineakysten. Brevbog, box 167–72, p. 38.

25. It was common practice to hire African sailors on slave ships; see Christopher, *Slave Ship*.

26. In the 1801 census, one of the daughters, then thirty-five, also still lived with her mother. The census is available online at https://www.sa.dk/content/dk/ao-forside/find_folketallinger.

27. In his studies on Jamaica, Daniel Alan Livesay has shown how children of mixed

race from "unofficial" long-term relationships between free black women and white men were more or less officially accepted in the eighteenth century. They inherited from their fathers, and sometimes they followed them to England. In the nineteenth century, however, their status as heirs to white fathers became increasingly questioned; see Livesay, "Children," and "Extended"; see also Dresser, *Slavery*.

28. Justesen, *Danish Sources*, 749.

29. See the council's permission to Rømer to have a boy named Ludewig Ferdinand sent to Copenhagen in GtK. Amerikansk og Afrikansk brevkopibog, box 10, p. 521. Letter from Rømer, April 25, 1763, describing the boy as "forældreløs" (orphan), is in GtK. Indkomne europæiske (og guineiske) breve, 1760–68, box 30. Apparently the administration had ended up sending the wrong boy. Rømer wrote, "instead of sending me this Ludewig Ferdinand, you sent me another by the name of Peter." The Ludewig Rømer from the 1830s (died 1838) is mentioned in GtK2. Dokumenter vedr. Guinea, 1791–1838, Reglement for de Guineiske besiddelser, December 13, 1816, box 1050, p. 7. As Selena Winsnes has pointed out, in case he did have an African wife, the fourteen children he later had in Denmark with his Danish wife suggest that he would also have been capable of procreating in Africa; see introduction to Rømer, *A Reliable*, 18. Another example of a Euro-African son leaving Osu is the boy Governor Suhm brought with him to St. Thomas when he took employment there after leaving Africa in 1727; see *Danish Sources*, 357.

30. Friderich Pedersen Svane's family is mentioned in Chapter 1. His father is specifically mentioned in Ole Justesen's *Danish Sources*, on 309 and 725. As also mentioned in Chapter 1, Christian Protten's mother was daughter of the Ga king Ofori in Little Popo; see Sensbach, *Rebecca's*, 163. Ray Kea also mention that Christian Protten and Friderich Svane came from high status kin in "But I," 183.

31. In his Moravian "Lebenslauf," Christian Protten says he and Svane were baptized on November 17, 1727, which has been repeated by several historians, who also specify that the event was to have happened in the Garrison Church in Copenhagen; see Eriksholm, "En Degn," 32; Nedergaard, "En Sort," 374; Debrunner, "Pioneers," 382; and Debrunner, "Friedrich," 25, where Debrunner cites P. Steiner, *Ein Blatt aus der Geschichte der Brüdermission* (Basel, 1888). I have not been able to find this event in the church books from the Garrison Church or any of the other major churches in Copenhagen at that time. See an example of other ceremonial baptisms of people of African or Indian descent in Copenhagen in *Kiøbenhavns kongelig allene priviligerede Adresse-Contoirs Efterretninger* 6 (58), (1764); 7 (37), (1765); 7 (39), (1765); 14 (107), (1772)—in this last one a boy from Tranquebar "about a score years old" was baptized. The most famous of such baptisms was possibly the one taking place at the coronation of Christian VII, May 1, 1767. About Africans in Europe, see Debrunner, *Presence*; Earle and Lowe, *Black Africans*.

32. About their marriage and about Rebecca Protten in general, see Sensbach, *Rebecca's*, 185-96. Protten's plea to be rehired is in a letter to Frederik V dated October 30, 1762, in GtK. Europæiske journalsager, 1760–68, box 29.

33. Jon Sensbach describes how Christian Protten's "African and European selves" were at war with each other; see *Rebecca's*, 164. See Protten's application to be sent out a third time dated July 5, 1764, in GtK. Relationer og Resolutioner ang. VI og Guinea, box 1. His troubles with Governor Resch are mentioned in Fiscal Esau Quist's daybook (October 20 and December 15, 1766) in GK. Direktion og Hovedkontor. Kystdokumenter, 1767–78, box 12.

34. About Svane's arrest, see Justesen, *Danish Sources*, 727–37. About Friderich Svane's life in Denmark, see Debrunner, "Pioneers," 383; Eriksholm, "En Degn," 375; Debrunner, "Friedrich," 34; and Nedergaard, "En Sort," 378–79.

35. For Europeans linking slavery to blackness long before the Danes entered the slave trade, see Sweet, "The Iberian." See also note 5 in the Introduction.

36. Letter from Quau, September 12, 1760, in GtK. Europæiske journalsager, 1760–68, box 27.

37. Letter from Ludewig Rømer, March 6, 1761, in GtK. Europæiske journalsager, 1760–68, box 27; Ludewig Rømer to Frederik V, August 19, 1761, in GtK. Europæiske journalsager, 1760–68, box 28. Another Euro-African man, Peder Ludewig, also wrote to the Chamber of Revenues, February 1, 1764, asking for help to return to Guinea. Peder Ludewig had first been employed by West India and Guinea Company for twelve years and then another seven years in Frederik V's administration of the trade. He requested free passage on the next ship leaving Copenhagen for the Gold Coast; see GtK. Europæiske journalsager, 1760–68, box 30.

38. Portrait of Queen Anne of Denmark (1574–1619) with a black groom in painting by Paul van Somer is reproduced in K. Hall, *Things of Darkness*, 239, which also discusses the phenomenon more broadly. For a reading of a similar image see also Bellhouse, "Candide," 743–46.

39. Rømer, *A Reliable*, 7–8. Interestingly, Pontoppidan emphasized family bonds as the one social factor that would make him hesitant about selling enslaved Africans across the Atlantic: "I feel that the Negro who is transported to the West Indies, as long as he is not separated from his wife and children, will be far less miserable, as well as far more secure concerning his life and sustenance." Thirty years after a Danish bishop was supposed to have allowed Danish men to marry temporarily in Africa and leave their wives there, Bishop Pontoppidan apparently thought that separating husband and wife was the one harmful aspect of enslaving Africans and transporting them to work on plantations in the Americas and the Caribbean. See also Green-Pedersen, "Negro Slavery," 85–103.

40. VgK. Direktionen. Amerikansk og afrikansk kopibog, November 19, 1750, box 63.

41. The answer from Governor Hachsen, assistant Engman, and assistant Toyon is found in a long general letter from the fort. Most of this letter is transcribed in Justesen, *Danish Sources*, 837–48, but not the specific reference to the marital suit against Jessen, which is therefore my own translation; see Danish text in VgK. Direktionen. Breve og dokumenter fra Guinea, 1683–1754, January 5, 1752, box 125.

42. VgK. Det sekrete råd på Guineakysten. Sekretprotokol, 1723–54, January 8, 1753, box 883.

43. General letter, April 12, 1749, in VgK. Direktionen. Breve og dokumenter fra Guinea, box 124. Some of the letter is translated in *Danish Sources*, 765, though not this part, which is my translation. Chaplains on their way to or from Africa also complained about slave ship captains being rude and unconsidered. On March 23, 1734, chaplain Trane reported to the company that Captain Bagge had treated the African traders who came to the ship very badly, "which I know is not the meaning of the Directors." See also chaplain Hyltoft's complaints, December 23, 1760, and again November 7, 1761, in SSB.

44. Ole Erichsen's response to the accusations, signed October 13, 1749, in the same general letter cited above is in VgK. Direktionen. Breve og dokumenter fra Guinea, box 124.

45. "Videre bedes deres excellence og høje herrer underdanigst at intruere capitain-erne som farer her på kysten at de bedre omgåes Negerne, og tractere en Neger som en Neger," ibid.

46. For the present purpose, whether Ole Erichsen had in fact threatened Caboceer Qvansang is not as important as the ways in which the captain and the traders respec-tively describe the incident on the Danish slave ship.

47. Justesen, *Danish Sources*, 764.

48. Marcus Rediker's term "floating dungeon" appears in *The Slave Ship*, 156.

49. Rømer, *A Reliable*, 35

50. Governor Jessen accused Reindorph of having encouraged the residing broker Adoui (Adovi) to protest against a company messenger, Soya, calling himself a broker. Reindorph's answer to the accusations Jessen had brought against him and the detailed answers by the witnesses he called in the case are all in a letter from Reindorph to the Chamber of Customs dated July 6, 1764, in GtK. Europæiske journalsager, 1760–68, box 31.

51. Esau Christensen Quist's wife and children are mentioned in a letter from mer-chant Smith, June 2, 1762, where he sends his regards to Quist's family; see GtK. Eu-ropæiske journalsager, 1760–68, box 30. As mentioned in note 55, Esau Christensen Quist also had at least three sons in Osu. Reindorph mentioned his African wife and her family in his response to Jessen's accusations, September 9, 1761, in GtK. Europæiske journalsager, 1760–68, box 31. Friderich Svane implied that Rømer was first cassaret to a woman of African descent, but later replaced her with a Euro-African woman; see Just-esen, *Danish Sources*, 749; on 748, Svane also mentioned that Joost Platfues was cassaret to Svane's niece, the Euro-African woman Helena Svendsdatter. See note 3 above for discussion of Engman's different possible wives.

52. Reindorph to the Chamber of Customs dated July 6, 1764, in GtK. Europæiske journalsager, 1760–68, box 31.

53. Ibid.; "protected negress" is translated from the Danish "freden negerinde."

54. Reindorph in letter to the Chamber of Customs dated July 28, 1764, in GtK. Europæiske journalsager, 1760–68, box 31.

55. Esau Quist's testimony is dated July 19, 1764, and was received at the Chamber of Customs July 24, 1764; see GtK. Europæiske journalsager, 1760–68, box 31, my emphasis. Two of Quist's sons, Jacob Quist and Johan Albrecht Quist, were listed on a school list from Christiansborg March 29, 1765; see GtK. Indkomne guineiske breve, box 70. A third son of his, Emanuel Sebaldus Quist, is listed in a church book from 1764 as born in 1760 and passed in 1764; see GtK. Indkomne guineiske breve, box 70.

56. See literature about the strengthening link between slavery and blackness in the early modern period in note 5 in the Introduction. About Africans being associated with slavery in the Atlantic system more generally, see also Curtin, "The Atlantic," 303, where he remarks, "For the Europeans of the eighteenth century, Negro was synonymous with slave." See also Davis, *Inhuman*.

57. Rømer, *A Reliable*, 232.

58. Ibid., 3–4.

59. Ibid., 234. In 1756 Rømer had published a shorter version of his account, which primarily dealt with trade (it had fewer details about the specifics of the slave trade, but it also had many fewer descriptions of both African and European social life and practices in Osu). Apparently neither Engman nor other of Rømer's friends from Christiansborg complained about this version. Or maybe Engman actually complained back then too, in private, but later reverted to harsher measures by making his grievance public.

60. Rømer, *A Reliable*, 240–41.

61. Carl Engman and Ellen Luno got married on August 16, 1758. Ludewig Rømer was not witness/godfather at the christening of Carl Engman's second daughter, Paulina Gustava Maria Engman, on September 8, 1767, in the same church. Danish church books are available online at https://www.sa.dk/content/dk/ao-forside/find_kirkeboger. Vor Frue Kirke is located in Sokkelund Parish (herred).

Chapter 4. "Danish Christian Mulatresses"

1. Frantz Kühberg's last wishes are mentioned in Larsen, *Guvernører*, 84. I have not found any reference to him officially leaving his house to Lene, but in the years after his death, she lived in a house and went under the name "Lene, the mulatresse" or "Lene, salig [literally, blessed; figuratively, widow of] Kühberg."

2. Friderich Svane described how he planned and worked on his house in a long "declaration" about his life that he wrote Copenhagen in 1748; see Justesen, *Danish Sources*, 734-37. On the meaning of stone houses in West African trading communities and their centrality to Euro-African "identity" and culture, see Mark, "*Portuguese*," esp. introduction, 46 and 145. Anna Barbara is on a list of children attending the school in 1765; see Christian Protten's letter of March 29, 1765, in GtK. Indkomne guineiske breve, box (*kasse*) 70. When assistant Ole Aagaard died in 1774 he owed Lene Kühberg 16 rdl. in gold, and she had a written document to prove it; see Estate of Ole Aagaard (July 3,

1774) in GK. Direktion og hovedkontor. Skiftebreve efter kompagniets på Guineakysten afdøde betjente, 1770–77, box 27.

3. Estate of Engelhardt Kramer (April 22, 1771) in GK. Direktion og hovedkontor. Skiftebreve efter kompagniets på Guineakysten afdøde betjente, 1770–77, box 27, mentions that the men from Christiansborg found "a light blue dress, a vest, and a pair of pants with imitation silver buttons, other assorted clothes, some socks, a small towel and a hymnbook" in an "old brown bureau" of Kramer's in "Mulatresse Kühberg's house" and had her declare that there were no more of his belongings there. A "mulatresse" Marie Kuberg (Kühberg is spelled in a variety of ways in the sources) is mentioned in the "overleveringsforretning" when the new company took over in 1789 (as creditor) in GtK. Guineiske uafgjorte journalsager, 1775–1803, box 1037, but this is the only reference I have to this woman, who might be Anna Barbara's sister. For another reference to a "Mulatta Eva" to whom a European man owed gold, see Justesen, *Danish Sources*, 870.

4. In her translation of Monrad's account Selena A. Winsnes has omitted "døbte" (christened) from the text, but since this refers to the women having a special relationship to not only the Danish chaplain but also the fort school, it is important to the points that I want to make here; see Monrad, *A Description*, 62; and the Danish text in H. C. Monrad, *Bidrag til en Skildring af Guinea-kysten og dens Indbyggere* (Copenhagen, 1822), 48. I am not the first to notice how Euro-African women in West Africa could use their marriages to European men to enhance their opportunities; see Brooks, *Eurafricans*, 122–60; Havik, *Silences* and Havik, "Gendering"; Miller, *Way of Death*, 289–96; Curtin, *Economic*, 120–21; for the Gold Coast, see Everts, "A Motley," and "Cherchez."; and Reese, "Wives," 301. Cooper, "Africa," 13, has suggested that "external" trade gave young men an opportunity to set up their own households, thereby "undermining elders' control of reproduction." I suggest that marrying European men similarly allowed African women to expand their room for maneuver in the slave trade. Along the same lines as this, Emmanuel Akyempong has noted in passing that Gold Coast women's marriages to European men "offered them an opportunity to escape the control of elder kinsmen. Women who were fortunate could acquire enough wealth to remain independent after the departure of their European partners"; see Akyempong, *Drink*, xix. In a study of enslaved women among the Anlo-Ewe, Sandra Greene has followed how "those disadvantages because of their gender used the prevailing ethnic relations to ameliorate their own situations"; see "Family Concerns," 15. Euro-African women in Osu similarly used marital relations to ameliorate their positions as women.

5. In this analysis I have been inspired by Pierre Bourdieu, who has phrased a different interaction between individuals and structures as individuals responding to "the invitations or threats of a world whose meaning they had helped to produce," in *Distinction*, 467. As historians focus more on the social and cultural aspects of the slave trade, there is an increasing emphasis on how the terror and violence produced by the slave trade affected people living with the trade; see Shumway, *The Fante*, 14–16. Lovejoy and Richardson have described how slave traders in Old Calabar protected themselves from

sale in the export trade in a process of establishing themselves as "insiders" by adopting English cultural markers (clothes, furniture) and English (pidgin) language; see "Anglo-Efik," 105–6; see also Hawthorne, *Planting*.

6. Unfortunately, this is the only surviving church book from Christiansborg, as far as I know; see a copy (dated June 1765) among the letters from Chaplain Hagerup in SSB or a copy of the same in GtK. Indkomne guineiske breve, box 70. When chaplain Hagerup was on the coast in the 1760s, he claimed that chaplains preceding him had brought their books back to Denmark with them, and he could find no record of marriages or other church ceremonies at the fort. He therefore requested new books for the church, and perhaps it is no coincidence that the one church book that has survived from Christiansborg in the eighteenth century bears his signature. Hagerup to bishop, June 1, 1765, in SSB. As mentioned in Chapter 2, several other chaplains were also supposed to have entered the cassare unions in the church books.

7. The justifying heading about permission from both governor and chaplain was probably meant for readers in Copenhagen and would not have been necessary among people at the fort or in Osu, for whom the cassare marriage was well-established practice. One family in which cassare had become common practice was the de la Palms; both Maria and Niels of that family were among those who were listed as cassaret in the one surviving church book from 1765. Their family shows up again and again in the sources from Christiansborg. They may have been descendants of the Dutch director-general Willem de la Palma, who was governor in Elmina from 1702 to 1705, referred to as "de la Palm" in the Danish sources; see *Danish Sources*, 164, 194.

8. In 1767 the newly chartered slave-trading company Bargumske Handelssocietet decided that to save money they would replace all European soldiers with less expensive Euro-African soldiers; see Justesen, "Vestafrika," 381. In 1788 Isert mentioned that Euro-African soldiers were paid 2 rdl. less a month than whites; see *Letters*, 152. According to a payroll from 1753 the monthly pay for soldiers did not follow the soldiers' race. The distinction had apparently started sometime in the ensuing thirty-five years. Monrad mentions that all soldiers were Euro-Africans when he was on the coast from 1805 to 1809; see Monrad, *A Description*, 260. I am assuming that the fort slaves were of African and not Euro-African descent based on their African names in the pay lists (*mandskabsruller*) from Christiansborg. Euro-African soldiers on the same lists all have Danish or other European names.

9. *Letters*, 152, where Isert also mentions that women were paid less than men to work as fort slaves.

10. Monrad mentioned that the fort slaves had no local kinship group or family to turn to in Osu, which in Gold Coast society, as described in Chapter 1, implied that they had the status of slaves; see Monrad, *A Description*, 37. See case about Oku and other free Africans pawned to the fort because of debt in Justesen, *Danish Sources*, 675. In Chapter 1, I discuss a few cases of European men having sexual relations with female fort slaves. It is possible that the fort slaves at Christiansborg lived in a separate quarter

of Osu, as the slaves working for the English James Fort lived in a separate quarter (Alata); on Alata, see Parker, *Making*, 12. See also how the "slave hytter" (slaves' huts) are separate from Osu on Erick Tilleman's drawing of Christiansborg from 1697 in *A Short*, cover.

11. Per Hernæs has called this process a "numerical Africanisation"; see "European Fort," 175. The number of fort slaves decreased gradually during the early decades of the nineteenth century after the abolition of the slave trade in 1803. In 1817 the administration in Copenhagen decreed a drastic reduction. By the early 1830s the number of fort slaves was down to about eighty; see Hernæs, "Fort Slaves," 202–3.

12. Akua—the typical Akan female day name for Wednesday—is spelled "Aquva" in the Danish sources. Many Akan names had been adopted by Ga speakers in Osu, but it is also possible that the fort slave Akua at Christiansborg belonged to the growing Akan-speaking minority in the town; see Odotei, "What Is in a Name?" 44. Monrad mentioned that Akan day names (including Aeua [Akua]) were common in Accra around 1800, in *A Description*, 65.

13. See the administration's response in the case about Aquva's child, dated January 12, 1771, in GK. Guvernementet på Guineakysten. Justitsprotokol, 1770–71, box 177. According to a copy of a letter from chaplain Feldtman to the Secret Council among the letters sent to the bishop of Zealand, Feldtman conducted a paternity investigation at the fort after Akua named Esau Quist the father of her child. Quist refused to take responsibility for the pregnancy and sought to question Akua's testimony in several interesting ways; see letter from Feldtman to the Secret Council July 18, 1769, in SSB. This case was similar to when chaplain Anders Winter in 1708 requested permission to christen a drummer, Jan de Wit, who was a son of a fort slave and a Danish employee, mentioned in Chapter 1.

14. Monrad, *A Description*, 272.

15. Ibid. On chaplain Hagerup's complaint about the old church being too small, see Hagerup to bishop, January 28, 1765, in SSB.

16. GtK. Guineisk journal, 1776–81 mm, box 985–86, no. 94 (1780).

17. This proposal indicates a scenario where Danish Euro-African girls were cassaret before their confirmation and then presumably continued at the school and were confirmed when possible. In 1781 another chaplain from the fort, S. Unger, also mentioned that cassaret women were attending the fort school, in a letter to the bishop of Zealand (dated March 18), in SSB.

18. GtK. Guineisk journal, 1776–81 mm, box 985–86, no. 94 (1780). Later in his proposal he explicitly stated, "The council should be especially careful that nobody is calisaret with foreign Mulatresses, unless it for specific political reasons can be allowed. Even then it should be done with the greatest caution."

19. "Tager til ægte" instead of "calisare."

20. GtK. Guineisk journal, 1776–81 mm, ks 985–86, no. 94 (1780).

21. About the Christian marriages in Elmina, see Feinberg, "Africans," 89.

22. About Nicolaas Van Bakergem, see Doortmont, "The Dutch," 105, where Doortmont also calls the church at Elmina "an ailing institution in this period." About Van
Bakergem having three children baptized in the church, see ibid., p. 119.

23. Selena A. Winsnes has omitted "døbte" (christened) from the text—see n. 4 in
this chapter. Monrad *A, Description*, 62, and the Danish text in Monrad, *Bidrag*, 48.

24. Philip Havik has also used the expression "room for maneuver" to describe
these opportunities; see Havik, *Silences*, 350; and on 28, how "the evolution of these
relationships [Afro-Atlantic] and of trade settlements was directly associated with
women's quest for autonomy." For references to literature arguing that West African
women could gain materially from their marriages to European traders in this period,
see n. 4.

25. Lene Kühberg lived in a social context where it was not at all a given that women
would be powerful heads of households. In "Slaves," 295–96, J. D. Fage has argued that
"few, if any, women were 'free' in precolonial West Africa and in "African Societies," 112,
and that "almost all women in traditional African societies could be viewed as slaves to
the men." Though not all women were equally "for sale" on the Gold Coast in the eighteenth century, there is no doubt that women were subordinate to men in both the
patrilineal Ga families and in Akan matrilineal families. This is a point that both travel
accounts from the precolonial period and later ethnographic descriptions seem to agree
on; see de Marees, *Pieter*, 20; Müller, "Description," 215, about Fetu; Rask, *A Brief*, 103;
Isert, *Letters*, 134; Monrad, *A Description*, 69; Azu, *The Ga*, 28 and 34; Nukunya, *Tradition*, 47; Kilson, *African*, 19 and 25. In the patriarchal social structure of eighteenth-
century Ga society, slavery became an important way for women to acquire dependents
and to gain the free time to trade. Moreover, women enjoyed control over both their
slaves' labor and their slaves' children's labor.

26. As late as 1810 there were only eight stone houses in all of Accra; see Robertson,
Sharing, 29. About the establishment of a new *shia*, see Parker, *Making*, 27. In the case of
Lene Kühberg's daughter Anna Barbara, the house she shared with her Danish husband
Emanuel Richter was named after her, "Barbara House," but other houses were named
after the Danish traders who had lived there. About distinct European architecture of
stone houses farther up the West African coast being specifically linked to Luso-African
identity, see Mark, "The Evolution," and *"Portuguese."* For Ga marriages as work units,
where husbands supply produce and wives process and market it, see Field, *Social Organization*; Odotei, "Gender," 20; see also Chapter 1, n. 35.

27. See reference to Rebecca in estate of assistant Christian Janssen, copied in 1783,
in GK. Direktion og hovedkontor. Skiftebreve efter kompagniets på Guineakysten afdøde betjente, 1770–77, box 27. Since Linekensdorf and the other women went by "Ms"
(mademoiselle; in English, Miss) and not Madame in the auction lists, they were presumably not yet married and were using their mothers' or fathers' names; see estates
auctions after cooper Ole Olsen, carpenter Henrich Kuntze, assistant Christian Janssen,
and assistant Frantz Michael Prang, all copied under the year 1783, in ibid. In 1787 a
mulatresse Maria Cramer was paid back a debt from chaplain Hans Mortensen

Knudsen's estate. Mulatresse Anna Jessen is mentioned several times in estates in GK. Direktion og Hovedkontor. Skiftebreve efter kompagniets på Guineakysten afdøde betjente, 1770–77, box 27.

28. The population of interracial families in Osu was small; possibly there were fewer than a hundred families. In 1788, for example, former merchant and governor Andreas Riegelsen Biørn estimated that Osu could muster two hundred men "to which should be added the mulattos and the whites' wives"; see "Beretning," 196. In "West African," 57, Larry Yarak has argued that Euro-Africans in Elmina by the middle of the nineteenth century "saw themselves as constituting a distinct class with a distinct identity and role in Gold Coast society," and the same could be argued about Euro-Africans in Osu at that time; see Chapter 5 in this book. About European products brought to West Africa during the slave trade, see Alpern, "What Africans"; Metcalf, "A Microcosm." The most common trade goods used in the trade on the Gold Coast were European, American, and West and East Indian textiles; see Metcalf, "A Microcosm," 386.

29. Alpern, "What Africans," 29, describes these gifts as "Pompous trappings"—"these were the status symbols, the privileges of rank and wealth. They propped up the egos of African kings, chiefs, grandees, and rich merchants. The list world be long: from white satin robes, brocaded silk mantles, . . . hats, European flags . . . turkish carpets." About social stratification on the Gold Coast and European trade goods, see Kea, *Settlements*, 183; Reese, "'Eating,'" 862; Arhin, "Rank," 2. Since Walter Rodney, in *A History* (1970), presented the argument that the Atlantic export trade led to increasing social stratification in West African coast societies, there has been a long debate about the extent and the nature of this development. See Fage, "African," 108, for an entry into an early chapter of this debate, where Fage supports Rodney's overall claim, but probes at some of the specifics.

30. Isert, *Letters*, 117; Rømer, *A Reliable*, 99; Monrad, *A Description*, 182. About the meaning of such keys, see n. 73 in Chapter 1.

31. This is very similar to what Susan Neylan has described happening in cultural encounters in North America; see *The Heavens*, for example 237.

32. Among many other references to alcohol used in religious ceremonies, Rømer described a Ga oracle who could consume more alcohol than two hundred people; see *A Reliable*, 84–85. Field, *Religion*, 72, mentions that she has not encountered a Ga religious ceremony (in the twentieth century) that did not involve rum. About the meaning and use of alcohol in Ghana, see also Akyeampong, *Drink*, esp. 22–45.

33. Rostgaard and Schou, *Kulturmøder*, 89.

34. About the vulnerability of merchant capital for African slave traders, see Cooper, "Africa," 29. For the argument that wealth obtained from the slave trade did not contribute to economic growth in West Africa, but rather "that the transatlantic slave trade seriously retarded the developments of markets and the market economy in West Africa over the period 1650–1850," see Inikori, "Changing," 75. Here I do not agree with Metcalf, "A Microcosm," 393, where he suggests that because the Fante were such great traders, and because so many in the community were involved in the trade, "it was carried on in an orderly fashion and with strict rules . . . and appear to have caused little

disorder at the waterside" and that "it does not appear to have rendered the poor any poorer." Far from all people benefited from the slave trade, and it was not always carried out in "an orderly fashion." More recent work on the Fante also suggests otherwise; see Shumway, *The Fante*, introduction.

35. For the daily schedule at the school, see Hagerup to bishop, June 1, 1765, in SSB. In the same letter Hagerup wrote to the bishop that Governor Resch had decided to have the boys educated in "war exercises" to make them good soldiers while also allowing them to take up learning any skilled craft that they might want.

36. Hagerup to bishop, June 1, 1765, in SSB.

37. Ibid.

38. Randers to bishop, March 22, 1779, in SSB.

39. Hyltoft to bishop, July 11, 1761, in SSB. Given that there were only a very small number of Danish speakers in Osu, the children probably had little reason to practice the language. Apart from a few Danish words, the language does not seem to have been very useful in the trading encounter on the coast, where Portuguese and later English were much more useful lingua francas. It is interesting to consider why the chaplains still insisted on teaching the African children in Danish, even though the language appears to have been the greatest hurdle in their religious instruction. After 1764, when Christian Protten's introduction to the Ga language and translations of important passages from the Bible were printed in Denmark, they had an alternative. But even then chaplains still wrote about the problems of teaching the children Danish without considering that this problem could have been avoided if they instead carried on instruction in Ga. In comparison, later Basel missionaries on the coast wrote endlessly about the necessity (and difficulty) of learning African languages to run a successful mission on the Gold Coast. A microfilm of letters from the Basel missionaries on the Gold Coast, 1828–51, including some transcriptions by Hans W. Debrunner, is available from Yale Divinity School (English transcriptions of documents in series D-1) and otherwise accessible at the missions archive in Basel.

40. Hans Randers to bishop, March 22, 1779, in SSB. Randers mentioned that he had sent a drawing of a plan for a reformatory with an application for funds to build it to the Chamber of Customs in Copenhagen. Neither Svane nor Randers confronted the question of whether the children's mothers would have agreed to have them living in an isolated reformatory. Since it was already difficult to get the mothers to send their children to school, as both administrators and chaplains mentioned, it would probably have been even harder to convince them to let their children live at Christiansborg.

41. Feldtman to bishop, October 24, 1769, in SSB.

42. As mentioned in Chapter 1, the Ga in Osu appear to have been both interested in and able to adopt foreigners and foreign cultures very easily. This pattern also seems to have been the case for adaption of Christianity. In the early nineteenth century, for instance, Monrad also mentioned how the Ga were open toward Christianity; see *A Description*, 49. In *Making*, 19, John Parker similarly states, "Like Ga culture generally, religion and belief in Accra was characterized by a high degree of eclecticism."

43. About Europeans swearing African oaths, see Isert, *Letters*, 130; Monrad, *A Description*, 54; Aarestrup et al., "Nogle Bidrag," 190. About Euro-Africans visiting Ga oracles or priests, see the case of Anna Sophie in Chapter 2, or the case of Cathrine Schalz in Chapter 5.

44. Justesen, "Vestafrika," 385–89. The transition to a new trading company in Copenhagen did not make much difference in how the Danes administered the forts on the Gold Coast; see Justesen, "Danish," 28. About the Danish slave trade, see Hernæs, *Slaves*, 396; and Justesen, "Vestafrika," 396. Ole Justesen mentions that 2,500 slaves were brought from Africa on Danish ships in 1781. Per Hernæs has a number of 1,258 slaves being bought from Danish forts and factories that same year; the remaining half of the slaves who were brought over on Danish ships were probably bought at other European trading stations. For further description of the developments in the Danish slave trade, see Per Hernæs, *Slaves*, part 3. See Isert about overcrowded slave ships in *Letters*, 175. Between 1742 and 1775 the population of slaves on St. Croix grew from 1,906 to 23,834, and it continued growing the rest of the century; see Loftin, "The Abolition," 12 and 17.

45. Per Hernæs has the following definition of *panyar* (from the Portuguese *penhorar*, "to arrest"): "To 'penyar' (penjare) was a customary method of debt collecting. The creditor had the right to capture the debtor whose debts were overdue"; see "Fort Slaves," 26.

46. This incident is described in more detail in Hernæs, "A Sombre," 215–23. Enslavement is always an act of violence, and during the era of the Atlantic slave trade many people were directly or indirectly killed by the slave trade. For an introduction to historical literature on the question of how the slave trade impacted West African coastal societies, see Lovejoy, "The Impact." Joseph Miller has estimated that deaths in Africa related to capture and enslavement roughly equaled the number of slaves exported; see *Way of Death*, 153.

47. Bosman is cited in Kea, "Firearms," 194. For estimates on the number of weapons imported, see Inikori, "The Import"; and Richards, "The Import." There has been a substantial debate about the number and the impact of weapons brought to West Africa during the slave trade. In "A Microcosm," 383, George Metcalf claimed that "the sickening cycle where slave traders sold slaves to get guns to get more slaves has been discarded as simplistic" and argued that textiles were more important than firearms in the 1770s on the Gold Coast. In *Slaves*, 384, Per Hernæs argued that there was no direct correlation between the number of guns imported to the Gold Coast and the number of slaves exported, and that it was finally time to stop looking for this correlation. Instead we should focus on "the role that this new weapon technology in West African economic, political and social transformations during the slave trade." I agree, and for the purpose of the present book it is enough to conclude that many weapons were imported and that they contributed to warfare and violent conflicts. For a recent clear articulation that firearms led to more slave trading, conflict, and warfare, see Inikori, "Changing." For an introduction to the debate among Africanist historians about the numbers of imported firearms and, more generally, the Atlantic slave trade's impact on Africa, see also Lovejoy, "The Impact."

48. Monrad, *A Description*, 88.

49. Ibid., 216.

50. For a famous exception to this rule, see Randy J. Sparks's story of two sons of a slave trader in Old Calabar, who succeeded in returning to Africa after being sold into Atlantic slavery, in *The Two Princes*.

51. Barbot, *Barbot on Guinea*, 2:550; Rask, *A Brief*, 51. Considering that some slave ship captains hung dead bodies on lines behind their ships to attract sharks and create terror on board the ship, it is not so surprising that Africans would think that Europeans were using African slaves as bait; see Rediker, *The Slave Ship*, 39; Rømer, *A Reliable*, 182; Isert, *Letters*, 175; Monrad, *A Description*, 220; about the social climate that such rumors must have produced on the coast, see V. Brown, *The Reaper's*, chapter 1; for literature on African beliefs of European cannibalism, see Thornton, "Cannibals"; Shaw, *Memories*; Law, *Ouidah*, 151; Smallwood, *Saltwater*; Nwokeji, *The Slave*; Law, "West Africa's."

52. Cited in Chapter 1, p. 24 and n. 12.

53. Rømer, *A Reliable*, 212. How the Danes were going to find three hundred Africans to "man" the Danish fort if the Africans were indeed "united" is an open question.

54. The Danes kept account books with lists of Africans with growing debts to the fort; see examples of long lists of Africans in debt to the company in RtK. Antegnelser til, decisioner og kvittancer på de af bogholderen på forterne Christiansborg og Fredensborg samt logen Ada førte bøger og negotieregnskaber, 1755–61, box 2249–65. For examples of pawns listed in the debt books, see Justesen, *Danish Sources*, 384–85 and 501–4. In *Slaves*, 119, Hernæs describes a case from the palaver books were Noythe, Cuma, and Assiapa accused Governor Resch of having sold their children. The children had been pawned to the governor, and when the family had not paid the debt in time, they had been sold to the West Indies. See Chapter 1 for more on the difference between pawns and slaves in Gold Coast society, and Chapter 3 for the case about the free woman from Krobo where a person of free status was sold. See other references to people being sold who were not considered slaves in Africa in Hernæs, *Slaves*, 26; and Lovejoy and Richardson, "The Business," 70.

55. Monrad, *A Description*, 85.

56. Monrad, for example, wrote about being sentenced to "death or sale" in *A Description*, 96. On p. 86 he also described how no African traveling alone in Africa could be sure that "he will not be panyarred before he reaches home." Here it is perhaps in order to remind the reader that Monrad was highly critical of the slave trade. About pawns being sold to European ships, see Lovejoy and Richardson, "Trust," 336. See two cases of Africans wanting to use sale as a punishment in disputes in Justesen, *Danish Sources*, 656 and 681. Though many enslaved people sold to Europeans still had the status of slaves in West Africa later in the century the number of free people exported had grown; see Lovejoy, *Transformations*, 84–85; and Shumway, *Fante*, 56. See also Sparks, "Gold Coast," and *Where*.

57. About the importance of human pawning as a credit system in the trade, see

Lovejoy and Richardson, "The Business," 69; see Lovejoy and Richardson, "Trust," about pawning on a time schedule, 350; and Kea, *Settlements*, 238.

58. See Rattray, *Ashanti*, 48, quoted and discussed in Grier, "Pawns," 312. About Oku pawning his family, see Justesen, *Danish Sources*, 675. Kea, *Settlements*, 240, mentions that debt lists of the trading companies on the Gold Coast from the seventeenth century already indicate that debtors usually were of high social status. This pattern continued in the eighteenth century. Here I therefore disagree with John Thornton that this should lead us to conclude that the people who were "making the decisions about participation" in the Atlantic slave trade were not also "adversely affected" by the trade; see Thornton, *Africa*, 74.

59. Justesen, *Danish Sources*, 675.

60. Rømer, *A Reliable*, 178. Rømer called him Kurentsi Corrantryn—he was also known as John Currantee.

61. Ibid.

62. See Rømer's conflict with Bojesen in Justesen, *Danish Sources*, 803. In "The Last Resort," 83, Sylviane A. Diouf mentions another Gold Coast incident of using the threat of sale to put pressure on debtors: slave trader "Fat Sam" sent kidnapped people on board slave ships without actually selling them—hoping that this would make their families redeem them.

63. This and the other quotes in this paragraph from Isert, *Letters*, 141–42.

64. Monrad, *A Description*, 36, 42. On p. 233 Monrad further described Kiøge as a "unusual, noble and cultivated man," who was opposed to the slave trade. Why Kiøge chose to make a living as governor of a slave-trading post is then a bit mysterious.

65. See Monrad's critique of the slave trade in ibid. on pp. 61, 102, 209, 289, 290, 292, 293. Monrad's account contains many horrific stories from the slave trade and would have been very useful in the abolition movement had its publication occurred in the eighteenth century and not 1822. Anne C. Bailey describes the stress and fear caused by living with the slave trade in Ghanaian coastal communities in *African Voices*.

66. The concept of Euro-African "insiders" taking on European cultural markers is used by Lovejoy and Richardson in "Anglo-Efik," where the authors discuss to what extent establishing oneself as "insider" in the slave trade in Old Calabar could be a protective measure against enslavement. In that same study (p. 114), Lovejoy and Richardson have also noted that few people were "totally secure" in the slave-trading community once human pawning became common. In *"Portuguese,"* 28, Peter Mark has likewise noted a direct link between European heritage and protection against enslavement: "To be white was to be non-slave, recalling that their ancestors had been slave traders."

67. About Lene Kühberg's daughter Anna Barbara, her grandson Henrich, and her son-in-law Johan Emanuel Richter, see Ole Justesen, "Henrich Richter."

68. In other words, Lene Kühberg helped move the "gender frontier," as Kathleen Brown has called it in "Brave New," 313.

Chapter 5. Familiar Circles

1. This description is based on Wulff Joseph Wulff's letters home to his parents and his brother-in-law printed in Wulff, *A Danish*, 61, 169–72. Frederiksminde is still occupied by the Wulff family. When the plaque finally did arrive from Denmark the Danish king's name was spelled the German way, "Frederich Minde, 1840, W. I. Wulff," ibid., plate 5.

2. Sara's father could have been any one of a number of Malms working at the fort in the nineteenth century. Abraham Malm was listed as Corporal Abraham Malm in 1815, and in May 1816 he paid 8 rdl. for "cassaring" to the "Mulatte Kasse." In 1794 three soldiers by the name of Malm (Cornelius, Jonas, and Peter) were mentioned in a case dated January 8; see KGG2. Justitsprotokol, 1794–1813, box (kasse) 6. On "gagerulle" from 1786 Andreas, Jonas Christian, Peder, and Hans Malm are listed. Sara was "approximately" forty in 1852 according to Sill, *Encounters*, 171. Wulff and Sara met in 1836 or 1837, their first son Theodor Ulysses was born in 1837, then Wilhelmina about 1840.

3. In his letters home Wulff Joseph Wulff mentioned his bad health and his homesickness quite a lot. For his transition from homesickness to never wanting to leave the coast, see especially pp. 95 and 158 in Wulff, *A Danish*. It was typical to bury people in their houses; see Parker, "Cultural Politics," 209; Isert, *Letters*, 132.

4. See description of Wulff's death and E. Carstensen finding Wulff's wil three days later in Wulff, *A Danish*, 205. See Sill, *Encounters*, 181–87, for a description of Sara Wulff's life after Wulff Joseph Wulff died. The quote about Sara Malm's respectability from the Basel missionaries is from ibid., 168. Wulff's will is translated and printed in *A Danish*, 205–7.

5. Edward Carstensen is quoted in the Introduction (source in note 11 there). Severine's father, Niels Brock, for example, was presumably a good trading ally. He was the storekeeper at Christiansborg and had the very best access to European trading goods. It is hard to imagine that his cassare marriage to Caroline Truelsen, whose father, H. C. Truelsen, had made his living as a slave trader, was not also a trading alliance.

6. The expression "merchant class elite" is borrowed from Buah, *A History*, 16; "Christiansborg Mulattos" is from Parker, "Mankraloi," 34.

7. The British colonization of the Gold Coast did not happen overnight. It was preceded by a series of wars during the nineteenth century, primarily between the Asante and the British, but also involving the Ga, the Danes, the Akwamu, the Fante, and other groups on the coast. I have adopted the idea of describing the community in Osu in the nineteenth century as "protocolonial" from Ole Justesen in a personal interview.

8. As mentioned in Chapter 1, private trading was mostly not allowed at the Danish slave-trading forts, with the exception of a ten-year period, 1755–65, when the trade had been opened to private slave traders after the king's administration dissolved the West India and Guinea Company; see Justesen, "Vestafrika," 373–78. Employees working at the fort were the only ones who were still not allowed to trade in slaves, which they complained about, and from 1795 all Danish employees on the coast were given permission to

trade in slaves on their own; see ibid., 413–14. About the private traders and their attention to their Ga families in Osu, see Justesen, "Danish Settlements," 26. For references to high prices on slaves in different areas of the Atlantic in the 1790s, see Getz, "Mechanisms, 81–82; Miller, "Slave Prices," 43. I have borrowed "Many Tender Ties" from the title of Sylvia Van Kirk's book from 1980 about the Canadian fur trade. The population of enslaved Africans in the Danish West Indies did not reproduce itself, but by bringing in as many slaves as possible—especially women—the hope was that this would change; see Hopkins, "Peter Thonning," 781. See the royal edict that announced the abolition of the Danish slave trade from 1803 in Monrad, *A Description*, 276–78.

9. GtK2. Guineisk Journal, 1776–1893, box 985–86, no. 501. Dated September 29, 1804.

10. GtK2. Guineisk Journal, 1776–1893, box 985–86, no. 502. Dated May 2, 1804. Received in Copenhagen September 21, 1804.

11. Ibid.

12. GtK2. Guineisk Journal, 1776–1893, box 985–86, no. 501. Dated September 29, 1804.

13. GtK2. Guineisk Journal, 1776–1893, box 987–88, no. 706. Dated August 5, 1805.

14. About dropping slave prices in West Africa immediately following abolition (but not until after 1820 in West Central Africa), see Lovejoy and Richardson, "British Abolition." Manning, "Contours," 853, also argues that prices of slaves fell in nineteenth-century Africa, which allowed people in Africa to buy more slaves.

15. The Danish wording for recognizing kith and kin is to "lyse i kuld og køn." KGG2. Rådsprotokol, 1806–15, box 50–54. Dated January 2, 1808. It may also have added to the men's sense of insecurity that their home city, Copenhagen, had been massively bombed in 1807 by the English during the Napoleonic Wars, an event that historians have seen as marking the end of the "florrisante" trading period of the eighteenth century.

16. Ibid. Richter's is dated October 20, 1807; Ramus's is dated January 7, 1812.

17. For a few references to English and Dutch traders' wills that mention their African families, see Priestley, *West African*, 108. Trader Brew mentioned his two christened daughters and his wife, Effua Ansah, in his will. For important wills from nineteenth century Elmina, see Yarak, "West African," 46. One interesting exception to the rule about Danish traders not writing their African families into their wills in the earlier eighteenth century is the case about the estate of Governor Enevold Boris that came up in Copenhagen in 1742. The company directors found that Boris's estate had been settled incorrectly in Africa and went through the case in detail. The documents from the case show that Governor Boris had left 500 rdl. (a large sum) to his "slegfred" (illegitimate) son Jacob Andreas in Africa, but this does not seem to have been the primary reason why the directors were trying the case in Copenhagen. See VgK. Direktionen. Skiftedok.m.m., 1680–1754. Guvernør Boris's arvesag, box 244, point 5, pp. 3–4.

18. KGG2. Letter book, 1806–15, box 50–54, book (bog) 54, p. 60.

19. This large sum of money in trust with a merchant in Denmark might explain why Niels Holm's son Christian traveled to Denmark after his father's death to claim his

inheritance. Besides the wills by Danish merchants and administrators on the coast already mentioned in this chapter, see also Niels Brock's (Severine's father) will of May 30, 1836, in GtK2. Sager til guineisk journal, 1839–40, box 1023, where Severine's mother, Caroline Truelsen, inherited her house in Osu, a plantation in the Akwapim mountains, and a large number of slaves. There is a big folder of interesting sources on "Holm's estate-case" detailing how Euro-African Christian Holm and his nephew, Peter Svane Steffens (son of Christian's sister Caroline), claimed their inheritance from their father/grandfather on behalf of their families in Osu, while in Copenhagen in the early 1840s. The governor's wage is listed in KGG2. Gagebog ved hovedfortet Christiansborg, 1815–17, box 66.

20. KGG2. Rådsprotokol, 1806–15, box 50–54, book 50, p. 345.

21. GtK. Skiftebreve indsendt af det kgl. Guvernement på Guineakysten, 1793–99, box 1051. Mandix died November 16, 1799.

22. For patriarchal language, see merchant Truelsen's plea, January 17, 1811, that if he did not get help he would not be able to "provide for [his] wife and five kids," in KGG2. Justitsprotokol, box 61.

23. Larsen, *Guvernører*, 47, has Biørn born around 1748, which means he would have been around thirteen when he came to Africa. In the decades from the dissolution of the West India and Guinea Company in 1753 until the trade was "given free to all nations" in 1792, a series of private trading companies tried to run the Danish slave trade without great continuity. In 1787 the "Østersøisk-guineisk" Company was handed over to a consortium of merchants in Copenhagen under the name of the Guinean Entrepreneurs. Justesen, "Vestafrika," 400–401. The "Overleveringsforretning" when the new company took over in 1789, where the two Biørn's are listed as creditors, is on pp. 69–70; see GtK. Guineiske uafgjorte journalsager, 1775–1803, box 1037.

24. Biørn, *Tanker*.

25. GtK2. Sager til guineisk journal, 1797–98, box 995, dated November 3, 1796, and January 25, 1798.

26. GtK2. Sager til guineisk journal, 1794–93, box 995; the Secret Council comment and resolution is dated January 31, 1798. Schiønning suggested that the Secret Council wait until further notice from the Chamber of Customs before acting. Jørgen Mandix agreed and added that he thought it would be irresponsible to let the Euro-African soldiers go, since it might lead to a revolt among the fort slaves. J. D. Ahnholm thought that the fort slaves would most certainly revolt, particularly those at Prindsensteen, since they had their old enemy the Keta "negroes" nearby and would therefore be in danger if they stayed at the fort without the Euro-African soldiers to "protect" them.

27. GtK2. Guineisk kopibog, 1816–27, box 976 , no. 71, December 17, 1816.

28. Richter in GtK2. Guineisk kopibog, 1804–27, book, 987, no. 1599, June 25, 1817.

29. Three of the four remaining Danish forts were closed down in 1817; see Hopkins, "Peter Thonning," 789.

30. GtK2. Guineisk journal, 1804–27, box 987–88, no. 34, June 28, 1821.

31. Ibid. No. 52, August 4, 1821. It is not surprising that the king had grown to believe

that Africans on the Gold Coast were under his "dominion," since Danes with colonial interests had made it a point to stress how much control the king already had over the area; see Peter Thonning's letter to the king quoted in Hopkins, *Peter Thonning*, 444.

32. Isert, *Letters*, 156–57.

33. Ibid., 157.

34. In her commentary on Ludewig Rømer's account, Selena Winsnes doubts that the African women who married Danish men were considered wives in Osu in the same way as women who were wives of Africans. The Ga and Akan families' acceptance of the unions to men at Christiansborg, and their protests when expectations about the marriages were not met, are, to me, the clearest indications that they regarded the cassare marriages as an official union. But I agree with Selena Winsnes that Ga families may have ascribed other meanings and practices to marriages to European men than for marriages to African men; see *A Reliable*, xxvii n. 57.

35. Schimmelmann, who had been on a commission that considered the consequences of abolishing the slave trade, was also one of the largest and wealthiest plantation owners in the Danish West Indies, and he had much experience with sugar plantations. About Schimmelmann, see Hopkins, "The Danish" and Hopkins, *Peter Thonning*. Ideas about the possibilities of an agricultural colony on the Gold Coast circulated among Danes with knowledge about the coast earlier as well. Rømer, for instance, suggested building cotton and coffee plantations at the River Volta; see *A Reliable*, 230.

36. Selena Winsnes has translated several documents regarding the plans to establish a plantation colony in Africa and appended them to her translation of Isert's account; for the mentioned points, see *Letters*, 232–35. In her translation of Isert's documents (232) Winsnes has rendered the text a little differently than I do here. She translates "Hvorvidt og under hvilke betingelser " as "To what extent and under what conditions," which takes it for granted that free Africans would be allowed to settle in the colony. I do not think that the Danish *hvorvidt* (if) allows for such a reading. Isert's Danish text was published in "Isert's beretning" in Frederick Thaarup, *Archiv for Statistik* (Copenhagen, 1795–98), 256. About Isert's expedition in 1788, see also Hopkins, *Peter Thonning*, chapter 1.

37. Schimmelmann and Brandt, "Instruction for hr. P. E. Isert," in Frederick Thaarup, *Archiv for Statistik* (Copenhagen, 1795–98), 233–40. Translated in Selena Winsnes, in ibid., 237.

38. For a place to start in the literature on the Enlightenment and racial ideology, see Fredrickson, *Racism*, chapter 2; Todorov, "Race."

39. Isert, *Letters*, 157.

40. According to the former governor J. A. Kiøge, who wrote an obituary for Isert, the Enlightenment doctor and colonist was both "ridiculed and mocked" by many, and it is easy to see how Isert's abolitionist leanings could have provoked tension at Christiansborg and Osu in the 1780s. See obituary in *Letters*, 246. In Denmark he was not alone with his critique of the slave trade, though the movement to abolish the export of

slaves from Africa gathered more political momentum in the 1780s and 1790s; see Hopkins, "Danish," 370.

41. KGG2. Justitsprotokol, 1794–1813, box 61, quote from p. 139. Mathias Thonning was the brother of Peter Thonning; see Hopkins, *Peter Thonning*, 262.

42. KGG2. Justitsprotokol, 1794–1813, box 61, quote from p. 139. Cathrine Sonne was probably a granddaughter of assistant Jørgen Andreas Sonne and his cassaret wife, who was the daughter of the important Osu broker Soya. The Sonne family appear to have been closely associated with the Danish fort; they show up on school and wage lists in the late eighteenth century and are mentioned in trading documents. See Johan Peter Sonne, Carl Sonne, Jørgen Sonne, and Knud Sonne on Christian Protten's school list in his letter to Copenhagen of March 29, 1765, in GtK. Indkomne guineiske breve, box 70; and reference to the Euro-African soldier Carl Sonne at Christiansborg in KGG2. Justitsprotokol, 1794–1813, box 61, pp. 20-23. For the practice of making announcements with a drum, Monrad, *A Description*, 70, mentions a man going around town with a basin announcing cassarings and lost articles.

43. See Selena Winsnes's chronology of Isert's life in Isert, *Letters*, 218. Monrad described the different Danish private and company initiatives to establish plantations on the Gold Coast in Monrad, *A Description*, 229-52; see also Jeppesen, "Danske"; Bredwa-Mensah, "Landscapes," "Archaeology," and "Slavery."

44. About Kings High Road, see Bredwa-Mensah, "Landscapes," 151, where he also says that "the Danish planters' landscape was created to infuse a new order into a "barbaric," natural Gold Coast countryside." About Peter Thonning, see Hopkins, "Danish," 369–418, and *Peter Thonning*.

45. Hopkins, *Peter Thonning*, 788–89.

46. About a hardening cultural/racial frontier in Accra in the nineteenth century, see Parker, *Making*, 35, and, "Mankraloi," 37. For studies describing similar developments of shrinking "middle grounds" in Atlantic cultural encounters, see R. White, *The Middle* (where he also coined the term "middle ground," repeated so often since); Merrell, *Into*; and Barr, *Peace*.

47. The documents in the case alternate between calling her Cathrine Schalz and Cathrine Holthe.

48. The case is described in documents dated June 25, 1808, in KGG2. Rådsprotokol, 1806–15, box 50-54. I thank Per Hernæs for help finding the documents for this case.

49. Ibid.

50. KGG2. Brevkopibog ført på Christiansborg, 1807–12, box 57–58, April 7, 1808. Esau Quist claimed that Cathrine had bribed commandant Flindt to bribe the Accra priest to deprive Esau of his right to address his wife's "indecency," which explains why they could not settle the conflict in Accra but had to travel to Ada.

51. See Commandant Holm's note about the case on April 7, 1808, in ibid. Esau Quist had worked in the service of the fort for years and might have gone to school at the fort too. There was a Jacob and a Johan Albrecht Quist on the school list from 1763 (March 27); see SSB.

52. June 25, 1808, p. 112, in KGG2. Rådsprotokol, 1806–15, box 50–54.

53. I acknowledge my debt to Everts, "A Motley," 56, where she explicitly makes this point.

54. GtK2. Guineisk kopibog, 1816–27, no. 122 (July 29, 1817) and no. 343 (May 18, 1820). Justesen, "Henrich," 98. Richter was not the first European governor to hire his own son on the Gold Coast. In 1754 a Dutch Euro-African son of a director general was governor at Crevecour in Accra for a while, though as soon as his father died in Elmina, the son was dismissed from his position. Doortmont, "The Dutch," 104–5. Euro-African James Bannerman was also governor at Cape Coast a short time, from 1850 to 1851; see Parker, "Cultural," 212, and "Mankraloi," 36.

55. Justesen, "Henrich," 104–5; Justesen mentions that Henrich Richter attended the school at Christiansborg on 99.

56. Some Euro-Africans in Elmina clearly aspired to the same status as Europeans in the early nineteenth century and indeed even thought of themselves as "white"; see Yarak, "West African," 47.

57. GtK2. Sager til Guineisk Journal, 1839–40, box 1023, April 20, 1840. See also Justesen, "Henrich," 179–80.

58. "The Christiansborg Mulattos" is from Parker, "Mankraloi," 34, who also refers to this group as "the large, self-conscious Euro-African community of nineteenth century Osu." One of the more famous Euro-Africans from this group was Carl Reindorf, who wrote what has been described as the first historical account of the Gold Coast. About Richter's influence in the 1820s, see Balthazar Christensen's description of Richter's position in Osu, quoted in Hopkins, *Peter Thonning*, 386. Kwame Arhin makes a distinction between a "modern" and a "traditional" elite in "Rank," 15. See also Haenger, *Slaves*, chapter 3. F. K. Buah has called these nineteenth-century merchants "the new merchant class elite"; see *A History*, 16.

59. In Elmina, with about fifteen to twenty thousand inhabitants, up to three thousand people were of Euro-African descent; see Yarak, "West African," 44–47 and n. 5 on 46; and Yarak explicitly expresses the opinion that Euro-Africans in Elmina considered themselves a distinct class on p. 57 n. 7.

60. About Governor Schiønning's reference to the Euro-African asafo, see Justesen, "Political," n. 17. About a "Christian asafo" in Osu after 1850, see J. Osei-Tutu, *The Asafoi*, 95–97. About Osu being divided into distinct quarters in the early nineteenth century, see Monrad, *A Description*, 77; Parker, *Making*, 14–15. In "Mankraloi," 34–35, John Parker mentions four town quarters in Osu: Kinkawe, Asante Blohum, Alata, and Aneho. At that point, Parker notes, most of the Euro-Africans of Osu were concentrated in the Asante Blohum akutso. See Evert, "A Motley," 53–69, about the Euro-African asafo company in Elmina.

61. See Evert's discussion of the position of Euro-Africans in Elmina in "A Motley." About African kin attending Euro-African funerals, see Monrad, *A Description*, 39–40; on p. 37 Monrad also notes that the Danes could place greater trust in "the so-called Inventory-Negroes, or royal slaves, than in the free mulatto soldiers, who have a family

relationship to the Negroes living in the environs"; about the importance of asafo companies in Osu, see p. 75.

62. About the social prestige attached to education and Christianity, see Greene, *Sacred*, 136. For education and Christianity's link to the Euro-African elites in Gold Coast towns, see Parker, *Making*, 159; and Priestley, *West African*, xv; see also Sill, *Encounters*. About Euro-African heritage being associated with wealth and power, see Monrad, *A Description*, 271; Parker, "Mankraloi," 35. On power in Akan states being linked to wealth and "accumulation and conspicuous consumption," see Akyeampong, "C. C. Reindorf," 109.

63. Monrad, *A Description*, 189.

64. Quoted from Winsnes's introduction to her English translation of Wulff's letters in Wulff, *A Danish*, 29.

65. About Euro-Africans in Cape Coast being proud of their European heritage, see Reese, "Sheep," 362. At a different point in his account Monrad also spoke directly to such feelings in Osu: "Mulatto men and women are much more proud of the European blood that flows in their veins than are the Europeans themselves"; see *A Description*, 62–63. Historians have noted such remarks later in the nineteenth century too; see Parker quoting (from Reindorf) a group of farmers from La calling Euro-Africans "slaves to Europeans" in 1872, in "Mankraloi," 35; on that same page Parker also describes how "intimate association with European power was a double-edged sword. It offered not only the prospect of material wealth and status, but could also generate suspicion and hostility." In his preface to Winsnes's translation of Wulff's letters, Per Hernæs also refers to Euro-Africans being in between, or rather "straddling two worlds and being 'sealed off' from the top echelons of the European establishment on the Coast."

66. Monrad, *A Description*, 183.

67. The English translation occurs in Wulff, *A Danish*, plate 9. I have added the parenthesis with Mulatresses, which Winsnes had not translated. About the importance of dress in expressing Christian Euro-African womanhood in nineteenth century Accra, see Sill, *Encounters*, 311–12. As Ulrike Sill has noted, European apparel did not necessarily indicate the Christian faith of its wearer. "It rather indicated an association with or aspiration to contacts with the transatlantic world, that is mainly with Europeans," 312, to which I would add the long history of Euro-African intermarriage on the coast. Sill, 313–14, also has an image of a girl from 1883–88 wearing a bustle (the high bump on the dress in the water color of Sara Malm). She quotes a German text about dress and custom of particularly Euro-African women of wearing such bustles (in Ga, *atofo/atufu*): "a part of a woman's dress which was designed to enhance the hips and back."

68. Carstensen, *Noter*, in EC, 34.

69. Wulff, *A Danish*, 172. About not being able to live anywhere else, see 108 and 158.

70. Ibid., 75.

71. Ibid., 89.

72. Ibid., 157, 160, 161, 181.

73. Ibid., 161.

74. Sill, *Encounters*, 168. See also 168–71.

75. About Sara Wulff renting pawns to serve as soldiers at the fort, see Justesen, "Slaveri," 149–50. Sara Wulff rented two pawns, Badu Pam and Menza Wulff, according to the list of dismissed soldiers by interim governor Schmidt, December 18, 1849, GtK2. Sager til Guineisk Journal, 1849–50, no. 43, box 1169.

76. Sill, *Encounters*, 182.

77. This summary of the incident is based on ibid., 182–84.

78. Ibid., 185–86.

79. About the decline in interracial marriage, concubinage, and, more generally, social interactions between black and white in the nineteenth century, see Parker, "Mankraloi," 37. Official marriages were the first to go, since they posed a more direct threat to colonial order than unofficial relationships. About this development, see Ray, "Policing." About Gold Coasters' and English administrators' responses to interracial intimacy in the early twentieth-century Gold Coast colony, see Ray, "Decrying." See also Stoler's introduction to *Carnal Knowledge* for literature on colonial legislation and inter-racial intimacy.

80. Quoted in A. Jones, "Female," 103. About such petitions from Euro-African women in Cape Coast, see also Akurang-Parry, "Aspects"; and Adu-Boahen, "A Worth-while." In Osu, Anna Ludderodt was another Euro-African woman with many slaves who comes up in the missionary sources; see Haenger, *Slaves*, 71; Parker, *Making*, 62. Like other important Euro-Africans in Osu and in other towns on the Gold Coast, Sara Malm had a large part of her wealth invested in slaves and pawns; she inherited a number from Wulff Joseph Wulff and, given that prices on slaves had gone down on the Gold Coast since the abolition of the Atlantic slave trade, she could therefore presumably have expanded her household over the years. Africanists have argued that the number of slaves in West Africa grew in the nineteenth century. Richard Rathbone, "The Gold Coast," 56. In 1862 Carl Christian Reindorf estimated that a large part of the Ga population were of "unfree" origin; quoted in Parker, *Making*, 32. About Euro-African women who were wealthy slave owners in the nineteenth century, see Jones, "Female Slave-Owners"; Yarak, "West African."

81. Haenger, *Slaves*, 61, 104–11.

82. Chaplain Hagerup to bishop, June 1, 1765, in SSB.

83. About missionaries admiring Euro-African women's business skills, see Sill, *Encounters*, 174 n. 74; and on 175, see a missionary's quote about a wife of another missionary trading and hosting "Accra-dances [Ga-dances], drumming and brandy drinking." About establishing a separate school for boys and girls in 1843, see ibid., 152. The missionary reasoning behind establishing a boarding school sounds similar to the earlier chaplains; see ibid., 181; the girls should live with the mission to be "protected" and educated in the right Christian norms and values.

84. For an entry into the literature on women's diminishing opportunities in nine-teenth-century Gold Coast, see Grier, "Pawns." See also Akyeampong and Hippolyte, "The Contribution," 15. About missionaries on the Gold Coast having ideals for

"Christian womanhood" that conflicted with Euro-African women's lifestyles as traders, see Sill, *Encounters*.

85. Carl Ulysses Wulff's 1893 letter to the postmaster general in Copenhagen is mentioned in Wulff, *A Danish*, 207.

Epilogue

1. Translated from French by Lady Mary Loyd; see Joinville, 276–77.

2. Ibid., 260–63.

3. Heertz, *De Frifarvede*.

4. Bang, "Løse Indtryk," 151.

5. Ibid.

6. "Genealogical Register and Historical Notes," compiled by William Godwin Sohne, 2–6 (copy obtained by the author at expedition to Keta with an official delegation headed by the Danish ambassador to Ghana in 2006).

7. Unsworth, *Sacred*, 353; also quoted in Rediker, *The Slave Ship*, 12.

8. The Quist's family motto is mentioned in "Genealogical Register and Historical Notes," compiled by William Godwin Sohne, 2.

9. See more about Alex Frank Larsen's series on http://www.slaver.dk/. About the politics and recent history of remembering the Atlantic slave trade and more broadly Danish colonial history, see Ipsen and Für, "Introduction"; Vuorela, "Colonial"; Brichet, "Generating."

10. Bailey, *African Voices*. The literature on the politics and complications of public and family remembrance of the slave trade in Ghana is helpful and growing; see Holsey, *Routes*; Schramm, "The Transatlantic"; B. Osei-Tutu, "The African"; Bailyn, "Introduction"; Opoku-Agyemang et al., *Africa*, esp. chapters by Ella Keren and Robin Law about the representation of the Atlantic slave trade in West African history.

11. Cited in Aidt, "Afrikanere," 41.

Note on Sources

1. In this project I have chosen not to use oral accounts. Given the politics of remembering slavery and the slave trade in both Denmark and Ghana (see Epilogue), writing a history based on oral accounts would have been a very different project.

2. From 1680 to 1814 the conglomerate state under the king of Denmark consisted of present-day Norway, Iceland, and the Faroe Islands, and a part of northern Germany, besides the kingdom of Denmark. See Map 1.

3. The travel accounts I cite were printed in the Netherlands, Germany, and England, as well as in Denmark. However, wherever they came from in northern Europe, the printed texts were quickly circulated and translated in other European countries. About the Danish state leaving highly detailed archives, see Nakken, *Sentraladministrationen*; Gøbel, *De styrede*, 16 and 31. Luckily for the wider reading public, as well as for

the historian who is trying to cover long periods of time, Ole Justesen has published a collection of a thousand pages of transcribed and translated trading documents from Christiansborg (*Danish Sources*). Justesen's work has been a tremendous help for my project, as my many notes referring to his books and articles show. For colonial ideology's structuring of colonial archives, see Stoler, *Along*.

4. For a treatment of perceptions of West African women in European travel accounts, see J. Morgan, "Some Could." For an introduction to the field of historical travel writing, see Mancall, *Travel*; Hulme and Youngs, *The Cambridge*.

5. As Gerard Chouin has noted in a discussion of the travel accounts from precolonial West Africa, the otherwise methodologically meticulous treatments of the accounts have not always paid as much attention to "the discursive structure of travel accounts"; see "Seed," 67. About uncritical citations of travel accounts from precolonial West Africa, see Jones, "Drink," 354.

6. The question of the relationship between European discourse and European and indigenous historical contexts in European travel writing is fascinating and important. A good place to start is Neil Whitehead's explanation of why indigenous historical contexts are just as important to consider as European ones; see Introduction, 37. Whitehead was responding to Stephen Greenblatt's rather nonchalant dismissal of indigenous influences on Columbus's early writing from Hispaniola in *Marvelous*, 6–7. For the argument that European (colonial) sources from Africa should be used to "engage, challenge, and refashion" African colonial history, see Cooper, "Africa," 308.

7. A few of the articles that directly treat problems in editing and translating travel accounts from precolonial West Africa are Jones, "Double"; Jones, "Decompiling"; Hair, "Barbot"; Hair, "On Editing"; Hair, "Portuguese"; Dantzig, "English." Selena A. Winsnes's work on the Danish travel accounts has allowed non-Danish readers access to great sources to the precolonial Gold Coast (see Isert, Monrad, Rask, Rømer, and Wulff in the bibliography). Adam Jones has done an equally breathtaking amount of work in his many translations and editing of German and Dutch accounts. Other scholars who deserve mention are Albert van Dantzig and Robin Law, in addition to the already cited P. E. H. Hair.

8. Spivak, "Can," 287.

9. Ghosh, *Sex and the Family*, 252.

10. If we expected the sources to hand us a full description of the historical subjects we are studying, or refused to write histories of historical subjects who cannot speak to us directly, very few women or men would enter history. As Gunvor Simonsen has recently argued in her work about the representation of slaves' testimonies in the colonial court in the Danish West Indies, histories of people who are mis- or underrepresented in written historical sources "should not stop short when faced with the silences constituted by specific sets of sources"; see "Slave Stories," 22.

11. Among many others I want to note, see Allman, Geiger, and Musisi, eds., *Women*, as a starting place for the study of African women's history in the colonial era. Strobel, "African," discusses the development of the field of African women's history in the 1970s.

For reviews of the more recent literature, see Geiger, "Women," and some historical essays in Cornwall, *Readings*, and Oyewùmí, *African Gender*. Robertson, *Sharing*, has been particularly useful for my understanding of Ga women's roles in families and trade. The main exception to the pattern of West Africanist women's historians working on the colonial period is Sandra Greene, whose work on gender and ethnicity among the Anlo-Ewe east of Accra has been important to me in phrasing my questions.

12. In 1999 Iris Berger and Frances E. White also mentioned that the "the simple notion that women were only victims of the slave trade has to be put aside," in *Women*, 72. The limited historiography of the Danish trading posts on the Gold Coast started out with a strong tendency to romanticize what was conceived as an all-male "bachelor" community of employees at Christiansborg, where young men could sow their wild oats, drink, and relax, free from the socially restraining home environment. Not surprisingly there was also very little focus on the importance of African women in the lives of young European men on the coast in these bachelor narratives. Kay Larsen wrote a series of more or less popular accounts of Danish men in Africa and the West Indies, one of which is listed in the bibliography. Georg Nørregaard's account of the Gold Coast was first published in the series *Vore gamle Tropekolonier* (Copenhagen: Westermanns Forlag, 1952) and later reprinted several times and translated to English in 1966. More surprisingly, even historians who have consciously moved away from traditional "colonial" histories to write more Africa-centered interpretations of the slave-trading era have paid very little attention to the cassare marriages. An exception to this general tendency is Per Hernæs's article about Cornelius Petersen from Bergen, describing the impact that the Euro-African woman Anna Sophia had on Cornelius Petersen's life on the coast. See Hernæs, "Den balstyrige." Thorkild Hansen's popular account of the Danish trade on the Gold Coast has been translated into English as *Coast of Slaves*.

13. As Durba Ghosh has noted, without a name, the archival trail goes cold; see "Decoding," 315.

Daughters of the Trade is based mainly on three groups of sources: letters and documents from the Danish administration at Fort Christiansborg to the trading companies and to the king of Denmark in Copenhagen; documents and letters from the chaplains at the fort to the bishop of Zealand in Copenhagen and to the Danish companies trading in Africa; and finally, northern European travel accounts about West Africa.[1]

In the era of absolute monarchy in the Danish conglomerate state,[2] from 1660 to 1814, the Danish state administration became a great archival organizer. The Danish West India and Guinea Company and chaplains' letter and documents in the archives in Copenhagen are extensive and orderly. The trading and administrative documents from Christiansborg are the main sources for the daily trade and contacts between Europeans and Africans on the coast. Unlike colonial archives, which are usually structured and organized by a colonial ideology that made indigenous or non-European presence and agency a threat, the trading archives from Christiansborg were produced by a trade that depended on—and hence recorded—interaction with their African trading partners. In practice this means that Africans (particularly but not exclusively as trading partners) are frequently present in the Danish sources from Christiansborg, which also means that West African women are commonly referred to in the sources, since they, just as in West Africa today, did most of the day-to-day market trading in eighteenth-century Osu.[3]

The chaplains' letters differ from the trading documents in their often longer descriptions of life at the fort, the running of the fort school, problems with the congregation, and so on. Unlike for the other employees at

Christiansborg, the chaplains' work on the coast was ideological, and some of the chaplains appear to have taken their mission very seriously. They reported in detail about life at the fort and what they found to be the "ungodly" behavior of the company employees. Their letters are therefore important sources for the nature and extent of the cassare, or interracial, marriages in Danish Guinea, and, more generally, the social worlds in which they took place. It is clear the letters are shaped by the chaplains' intentions to regulate the social life of their congregation, and by their need to report to their employer, the bishop, about these intentions. Read on their own, the letters can give the impression that the chaplains had a much larger impact on the social world of Christiansborg and Osu than they actually did, yet it is fortunate for this history that the chaplains were so interested in the social life of their congregation.

Printed West African travel accounts are easily accessible. Travel writing was a popular genre in early modern Europe, and there are a great number of printed travel accounts from the Gold Coast. Like pamphlets about witches or murderers on trial, early modern travel accounts owed much of their popularity to their shock and excitement value, but at the same time travel accounts were crucially important for European trading and colonial expansion. Investors, captains, and merchants needed precise and trustworthy information to follow the development of the trade and plan future expeditions, and trading companies served their interests by supporting both the writing and printing of travel accounts, which also helps explain the genre's explosive growth in the early modern era. The two very different interests shaping the travel accounts meant that trade facts and exotic tales often were placed side by side in the texts. Some subjects were more likely to play the part of exotic and exciting sales elements than others, though, and West African women and interracial intimacy seem to have been almost as marketable as "heathen" religion, witchcraft, and cannibals.[4]

The printed European travel accounts from the Gold Coast in the precolonial era therefore all contain shorter or longer descriptions of African women and interracial sexual relations, as well as descriptions of life and society on the Gold Coast and social life among the European men stationed in Africa. They are irreplaceable sources to this history, but they must be read with constant attention to their origin in the minds of European men with the purpose of both entertaining and informing other Europeans—mostly men—about worlds very foreign to them.[5] However, even though early modern European travel writers and observers often misunderstood what they saw and heard in encounters with foreign cultures, their texts contain both the European contexts of their authors and the contexts of the worlds they were describing, and, as ethnohistorians have long recognized, we cannot ignore indigenous contexts any more than European ones.[6] In the case of West Africa, historians who want to use early modern travel accounts as sources to a history grounded in Africa benefit tremendously from the growing and vibrant field of research on African history, which has produced a host of monographs, as well as accessible and annotated travel accounts and archival documents.[7]

All three groups of sources share the problem that they were written by European men. If this were a history about Europeans' perceptions of their encounters with and marriages to African women, this commonality would not be as troubling, but a central premise of this history of Euro-African marriages is that they were two-sided cultural encounters. This makes for some methodological challenges. European sources from the Gold Coast constantly shift attention away from African women and back to European men. The absence of African women's voices is in part a classic historical problem, since most historical subjects produced few or no written sources to document their existence. But in the case of historical cultural encounters, the European sources were recording the presence of historical subjects who were almost completely foreign to them. Such representation is not only inherently impure but at times impossible.

In 1988 Gayatri Chakravorty Spivak famously asked, "Can the Subaltern Speak?" She concluded that indigenous voices were so distorted in historical sources that we cannot hear them. Women's voices were particularly muffled within European texts; "the subaltern as female is even more deeply in shadow."[8] It is true that African women are very poorly represented in European sources, and that we seldom can hear them. But they are not absent. As Durba Ghosh has pointed out in her work on Indian women married to English men, we need to expand our range of methodologies to work with sources that constantly under- or misrepresent the women we are interested in.[9] One strategy, as we insist on the importance of women in the Euro-African encounters on the Gold Coast, is to be aware of which questions the sources do allow us to ask. Most important, the sources will not allow us to get closer to African women than to their actions and to the contexts they lived in. Many of the questions that would be interesting to ask are impossible to get at: Did the women have more personal interests or hesitations in marrying Danish men? What did they think of their Euro-African mothers and European fathers? About the slave trade? Questions about specific women's subjective perceptions would at best lead to an interesting methodological discussion but would not produce a coherent historical narrative.[10]

It is not only limited and difficult historical sources that have assigned West African women to the margins of history; lack of historiographical attention and interest has been an at least as important an obstacle. Or to put it differently, very few historians have looked for African women in Danish or other European sources from the slave trade. Not until the emergence of African women's history in the 1970s did scholars pay more systematic attention to the presence or absence of women in the European sources, but even this field has in general been focused on women's experiences during the later colonial period of West African history rather than during the period of the slave trade.[11] The few women who have entered the general narrative of the Atlantic slave trade have, almost exclusively, been enslaved victims of the trade. Yet, as *Daughters of the Trade* has shown, women in West Africa—both enslaved and free—were in fact important historical agents in both the West African and Atlantic slave trades.[12]

Finally, a disclaimer: The women in this history are by no means representative of the majority of women in Osu. Rather, they were among the few who were considered important enough by European men to be mentioned by name in the sources. Their families were often extraordinarily well connected and powerful, and because they were out of the ordinary and because they and their families were active traders, they are mentioned more often in the sources than most women living in Osu during the slave trade. Even among the important traders, though, many Ga women in the Danish sources are not referred to by name, but as "negresses" or "mulatresses," which makes it difficult to follow them over the years. Often I have deduced cassare marriages from the names of children at the school and of soldiers working at the fort. A few women actually do have names in the Danish sources, which allowed me to follow them more closely.[13]

BIBLIOGRAPHY

Archives in Rigsarkivet in Copenhagen

All archival sources used are registered online at Statens Arkiver: www.sa.dk.

Governor Edward Carstensen's private archive Erindringer og dagbøger 1842–75

Det Guineiske Kompagni, 1765–90

Generaltoldkammeret, Vestindisk-Guineisk Renteskriverkontor, 1760–1816

Generaltoldkammer- og Kommercekollegiet, Indisk Kontor, 1816–41

KGG1 Det Kongelige Guvernement på Guineakysten, 1755–66

Det Kongelige Guvernement på Guineakysten, 1778–1850

Rentekammeret Danske Afdeling, Vestindisk-Guineisk Renteskriverkontor, 1754–60

Sjællands Stifts Bispeembede, Indkomne Sager fra korrespondenter uden for stiftet, 1710–1820

Vestindisk-Guineisk Kompagni, 1671–1755

Printed Sources

Aarestrup, Biørn, Kjøge, Gjønge, and Rasmussen. "Nogle Bidrag til Kundskab om den danske Strækning paa Guinea Kysten." In *Archiv for Statistik*, edited by Frederick Thaarup, 169–90. Copenhagen, 1795–98.

Atkins, John. *A Voyage to Guinea, Brasil and the Westindies*. London, 1735.

Bang, Herman. "Løse Indtryk fra Læsningen af l'Estangere og dens Fortale (1880)." In *Vekslende Themaer, 1.*, 144–52. Copenhagen: C. A. Reitzels Forlag, 2006.

Barbot, Jean. *Barbot on Guinea: The Writings of Jean Barbot on West Africa 1678–1712*. Translated and edited by P. E. H. Hair, Adam Jones, and Robin Law. London: Hakluyt Society, 1992.

Biørn, Andreas Riegelsen. "Beretning 1788 om de Danske Forter og Negerier." In *Archiv for statistik* vol. 4, edited by Friderick Thaarup, 193–230. Copenhagen, 1795–98.

———. *Tanker om Slavehandelen: Resultater efter Iagttagelser og mangeaarige Erfaringer*. Copenhagen, 1806.

Bosman, William. *A New and Accurate Description of the Coast of Guinea*. London: Frank Cass, 1967.

Brun, Samuel. "Voyages of 1611–20." In *German Sources for West African History 1599–1669*. Translated and edited by Adam Jones. Wiesbaden: Franz Steiner Verlag, 1983.

Carstensen, Edward. *Closing the Books: Governor Edward Carstensen on Danish Guinea 1842–1850*. Translated by Tove Storsveen. Accra: Sub-Saharan Publishers, 2010. [Danish original: *Guvernør Edward Carstensens Indberetninger fra Guinea 1842–1850*. Edited by Georg Nørregård. Copenhagen: G. E. C. Gad, 1964.]

Christensen, Balthazar Matthias. "Correspondents-Efterretninger." *Valkyrien—et maanedskrift for dannede læsere*, edited by Ove Thomsen, 172–77. Copenhagen, 1831–33.

Christian V, king of Denmark, *Des Aller-Durchlauchtigsten, Großmächtigsten Königs und Herrn, Herrn Christian des Fünften von Gottes Gnaden Königs zu Dännemarck, Norwegen etc. Articuls-Brief und Kriegs-Gerichts-Instruction Belangende den Krieg zu Lande*. Copenhagen, 1683. (King Christian's "war articles." Danish: krigsartikler).

de Marees, Pieter. *Pieter de Marees: Description and Historical Account of the Gold Kingdom of Guinea 1602*. Translated and edited by Albert van Dantzig and Adam Jones. Oxford: Oxford University Press, 1987.

Fortegnelse paa afg. Frue Geheime-Raadinde Harboes Stervboe tilhørende Gods og Bøger, som ved offentlig Auktion . . . den 5te Martii førstkomende om formiddagen ved 8te Slet og efterfølgende Dage udi bemeldte Salige Frues fradøde Gaard i Storm-Gaden beliggende. Copenhagen, 1736.

Fortegnelse paa Endeel meget gode og velconditionerede historiske Bøger og Reyse-Beskriveser, som mandage den 10. mart. førstkommense, om Formiddagen kl. 9 Sletved Auktion skal bortselges hos Viinhandler, Sr. Petersen paa hjørnet af Klædeboderne og Gammel-Torv. Copenhagen, 1760.

Hertz, Henrik. *De Frifarvede*. Copenhagen: Dansk Vestindisk Selskab og Poul Kristensens Forlag, 1998. [Original: Copenhagen, 1836.]

Isert, Paul. *Letters on West Africa and the Slave Trade: Paul Erdmann Isert's Journey to Guinea and the Caribbean Islands in Columbia 1788*. Translated and edited by Selena Winsnes. Oxford: Oxford University Press, 1992. [Original German: *Reise nach Guinea und den Caribaischen Inseln in Columbien, in Briefen an seine Freunde beschrieben*. Copenhagen, 1788.]

Justesen, Ole, ed. *Danish Sources for the History of Ghana, 1657–1754*. Vol. 1–2. Copenhagen: Royal Danish Academy of Sciences and Letters, 2005.

Law, Robin, ed. *Correspondence of the Royal African Company's Chief Merchants at Cabo Corso Castle with William's Fort, Whydah, and the Little Popo Factory 1727–1728*. Madison: African Studies Program, University of Wisconsin, 1991.

———, ed. *The English in West Africa 1681–1683: The Local Correspondence of the Royal African Company of England 1681–1699*. Oxford: Oxford University Press, 1997.

Joinville, prince of. *Memoirs (Vieux Souvenirs) of the Prince de Joinville*. Translated and edited by Lady Mary Loyd. New York: Macmillan, 1895.

Monrad, H. C. *A Description of the Guinea Coast and its Inhabitants*. Translated by Selena Winsnes. Accra: Sub-Saharan Publishers, 2008. [Danish original: *Bidrag til en skildring af Guineakysten og dens Indbyggere, og til en Beskrivelse over de danske Colonier paa denne Kyst, samlede under mit ophold i Afrika i Aarene 1805 til 1809.* Copenhagen, 1822.]

Müller, Wilhelm Johann. "Description of the Fetu Country, 1662–9." In *German Sources for West African History 1599–1669.* Translated and edited by Adam Jones, 134–259. Wiesbaden: Franz Steiner Verlag, 1983.

Protten, Christian. *En nyttig grammaticalsk Indledelse til tvende hidindtil gandske ubekiendte Sprog, Fanteisk og Acraisk paa Guldküsten udi Guinea, efter den danske Pronunciation og Udtale.* Copenhagen, 1764.

Rask, Johannes. *A Brief and Truthful Description of a Journey to and from Guinea.* Translated and edited by Selena Winsnes. Accra: Sub-Saharan Publishers, 2008. [Danish original: *En kort og sandferdig Rejsebeskrivelse til og fra Guinea.* Tronheim, 1754.]

Rømer, Ludewig Ferdinand. *A Reliable Account of the Coast of Guinea (1760).* Translated and edited by Selena Winsnes. Oxford: Oxford University Press, 2000. [Danish original: *Tilforladelig Efterretning om Kysten Guinea.* Copenhagen, 1760.]

Smith, William. *A New Voyage to Guinea.* London, 1744.

Tilleman, Erick. *A Short and Simple Account of the Country Guinea and Its Nature.* Translated and edited by Selena Axelrod Winsnes. Madison: University of Wisconsin Press, 1994.

Wulff, Wulff Joseph. *A Danish Jew in West Africa: Wulff Joseph Wulff Biography and Letters 1836–1842.* Translated and edited by Selena Axelrod Winsnes. Trondheim: Norwegian University of Science and Technology, Department of History, 2004.

Secondary Sources

Adu-Boahen, Kwabena. "A Worthwhile Possession: A Reading of Women's Valuation of Slaveholding in the 1875 Gold Coast Ladies' Anti-Abolition Petition." *Itinerario* 33.3 (2009): 95–112.

Aidt, Mik. "Afrikanere med dansk blod." *Kontakt* 6 (1995/96): 41.

Akurang-Parry, Kwabena O. "Aspects of Elite Women's Activism in the Gold Coast, 1874–1890." *International Journal of African Historical Studies* 37.3 (2004): 463–82.

Akyeampong, Emmanuel. "C. C. Reindorf on the Cultural Articulation of Power in Precolonial Ghana: Observations of a Social Historian." In *The Recovery of the West African Past*, edited by P. Jenkins, 103–13. Basel: Basler Afrika Bibliographien, 1998.

———. *Drink, Power, and Cultural Change: A Social History of Alcohol in Ghana, c. 1800 to Recent Times.* Portsmouth, N.H.: Heinemann, 1996.

———. "Sexuality and Prostitution Among the Akan of the Gold Coast c. 1650–1950." *Past and Present* 156 (1977): 144–73.

Akyeampong, Emmanuel, and Fofack Hippolyte. "The Contribution of African Women to Economic Growth and Development: Historical Perspectives and Policy Implications. Part 1: The Pre-Colonial and Colonial Periods." Policy Research Working Paper 6051. Washington, D.C.: World Bank, 2012.

Allman, Jean, Susan Geiger, and Nakanyike Musisi, eds. *Women in African Colonial Histories*. Bloomington: Indiana University Press, 2002.

Alpern, Stanley B. "What Africans Got for Their Slaves: A Master List of European Trade Goods." *History in Africa* 22 (1995): 5–43.

Andersen, Niels Knud, and Banning, Knud, eds. *Kirkehistoriske Samlinger* 7:4. Copenhagen: G. E. C. Gads Forlag, 1960–62.

Arhin, Kwame. "Rank and Class Among the Asante and Fante in the Nineteenth Century." *Africa: Journal of International African Studies* 53.1 (1983): 2–22.

Austin, Gareth. "Human Pawning in Asante, 1800–1950: Markets and Coercion, Gender and Cocoa." In *Pawnship in Africa: Debt Bondage in Historical Perspective*, edited by Toyin Falola and Paul E. Lovejoy, 119–59. Boulder: Westview Press, 1994.

Azu, Diana Gladys. *The Ga Family and Social Change*. Leiden: Afrika-Studiecentrum, 1974.

Bhabha, Homi K. "Signs Taken for Wonders: Questions of Ambivalence and Authority Under a Tree Outside Delhi, May 1817." In *The Location of Culture*, 145–74. London: Routledge, 1994.

Bailey, Anne C. *African Voices of the Atlantic Slave Trade: Beyond the Silence and the Shame*. Boston: Beacon Press, 2005.

Bailyn, Bernard. *Atlantic History: Concept and Contours*. Cambridge, Mass.: Harvard University Press, 2005.

———. Introduction to "Considering the Slave Trade: History and Memory." Special issue of *William and Mary Quarterly* 58.1 (2001): 245–52.

Ballhachet, Kenneth. *Race, Sex and Class Under the Raj: Imperial Attitudes and Politics, 1793–1905*. New York: St. Martin's Press, 1980.

Bardaglio, Peter W. "'Shamefull Matches': The Regulation of Interracial Sex and Marriage in the South Before 1900." In *Race, Love, Sex: Crossing Boundaries in North American History*, edited by Martha Hodes, 112–40. New York: New York University Press, 1999.

Barr, Juliana. "A Diplomacy of Gender: Rituals of First Contact in the 'Land of the Tejas.'" *William and Mary Quarterly* 61.3 (2004): 393–434.

———. *Peace Came in the Form of a Woman: Indians and Spaniards in the Texas Borderlands*. Chapel Hill: University of North Carolina Press, 2007.

Barrera, Giulia. "Colonial Affairs: Italian Men, Eritrean Women and the Construction of Racial Hierarchies in Colonial Eritrea 1885–1941." Ph.D. diss., Northwestern University, 2002.

Bech, Niels. "Christiansborg i Ghana 1800–1850: Det tropiske hus af europæisk oprindelse." *Architectura* 11 (1989): 67–111.

Bech, Sv. Cedergreen. *Storhandelens by: København s historie*, vol. 3, 1728–1830. Viborg: Gyldendal, 1981.

Bellhouse, Mary L. "Candide Shoots the Monkey Lovers: Representing Black Men in Eighteenth-Century French Visual Culture." *Political Theory* 34.6 (2006): 741–84.

Berger, Iris, and Frances White. *Women in Sub-Saharan Africa: Restoring Women to History*. Bloomington: Indiana University Press, 1999.

Berlin, Ira. "From Creole to African: Atlantic Creoles and the Origins of African-American Society in Mainland North America." *William and Mary Quarterly* 53.2 (1996): 251–88.

———. *Many Thousands Gone: The First Two Centuries of Slavery in North America.* Cambridge, Mass.: Harvard University Press, 1998.

Beswick, Stephanie, and Jay Spaulding, eds. *African Systems of Slavery.* Trenton, N.J.: Africa World Press, 2010.

Blier, Suzanne Preston. *African Vodun: Art Psychology, and Power.* Chicago: University of Chicago Press, 1995.

Blussé, Leonard. *Bitter Bonds: A Colonial Divorce Drama of the Seventeenth Century.* Princeton, N. J.: Markus Weiner, 1997.

Bourdieu, Pierre. *The Logic of Practice.* Translated by Richard Nice. Stanford, Calif.: Stanford University Press, 1990.

———. *Distinction: A Social Critique of the Judgement of Taste.* Translated by Richard Nice. Cambridge, Mass.: Harvard University Press, 1984.

Boydston, Jeanne. "Gender as a Question of Historical Analysis." *Gender and History* 20.3 (2008): 558–83.

Bredwa-Mensah, Yaw. "Archaeology of Slavery in West Africa." *Transactions of the Historical Society of Ghana* 3 (1999): 27–45.

———. "Landscapes of Slavery: The Danish Plantation Complex in the Akuapem Mountains, Southeastern Gold Coast (Ghana)." In *The Transatlantic Slave Trade: Landmarks, Legacies, Expectations*, edited by James Kwesi Anquandah, 148–63. Accra: Sub-Saharan Publishers, 2007.

———. "Slavery and Resistance on Nineteenth Century Danish Plantations in Southeastern Gold Coast Ghana." *African Study Monographs* 29.3 (2008): 133–45.

Brichet, Nathalia Sofie. "Generating Common Heritage: Explorations into the Reconstruction of a Former Danish Plantation in Ghana." PhD diss., Copenhagen University, 2012.

Brooks, George. *Eurafricans in Western Africa: Commerce, Social Status, Gender, and Religious Observance from the Sixteenth to the Eighteenth Century.* Athens: Ohio University Press, 2003.

———. *Landlords and Strangers: Ecology, Society, and Trade in Western Africa, 1000–1630.* Boulder, Colo.: Westview Press, 1993.

———. "A Nhara of the Guinea-Bissau Region: Mae Aurélia Correia." In *Women and Slavery in Africa*, edited by Claire Robertson and Martin Klein, 295–319. Madison: University of Wisconsin Press, 1983.

Brown, Kathleen M. "Brave New Worlds: Women's and Gender History." *William and Mary Quarterly* 50.2 (1993): 311–28.

———. *Good Wives, Nasty Wenches and Anxious Patriarchs: Gender, Race and Power in Colonial Virginia.* Chapel Hill: University of North Carolina Press, 1996.

Brown, Vincent. *The Reapers' Garden: Death and Power in the World of Atlantic Slavery.* Cambridge, Mass.: Harvard University Press, 2008.

Buah, F. K. *A History of Ghana*. Revised and updated. London: Macmillan Education, 1998.

Candido, Mariana P. "Marriage, Concubinage, and Slavery in Benguela, ca. 1750–1850." In *Slavery in Africa and the Caribbean: A History of Enslavement and Identity Since the Eighteenth Century*, edited by Nadine Hunt and Olatunji Ojo, 65–83. London: I. B. Tauris, 2012.

Canny, Nicholas. "Writing Atlantic History; or, Refiguring the History of Colonial British America." *Journal of American History* 86.4 (1999): 1093–1114.

Chatterjee, Indrani. "Testing the Local Against the Colonial Archive." *History Workshop Journal* 44 (1997): 215–24.

Chouin, Gerard. "Seed, Said, or Deduced? Travel Accounts, Historical Criticism, and Discourse Theory: Towards an 'Archeology' of Dialogue in Seventeenth-Century Guinea." *History in Africa* 28 (2001): 53–70.

Christaller, J. G. *A Dictionary of the Asante and Fante Language Called Tshi Chweem Twi*. Basel: Evangelical Missionary Society, 1881.

Christopher, Emma. *Slave Ship Sailors and Their Captive Cargoes, 1730–1807*. Cambridge: Cambridge University Press, 2006.

Clancy-Smith, Julia, and Gouda, Frances, eds. *Domesticating the Empire: Race, Gender and Family Life in French and Dutch Colonialism*. Charlottesville: University Press of Virginia, 1998.

Clark, Emily. *The Strange History of the American Quadroon: Free Women of Color in the Revolutionary Atlantic World*. Chapel Hill: the University of North Carolina Press, 2013.

Clark, Gracia. *Onions Are My Husband: Survival and Accumulation by West African Market Women*. Chicago: University of Chicago Press, 1994.

Cooper, Frederick. "Africa and the World Economy." *African Studies Review* 24.2/3 (1981): 1–86.

———. "Africa's Past and Africa's Historians." *Canadian Journal of African Studies* 34.2 (2000): 298–336.

Cornwall, Andrea, ed. *Readings in Gender in Africa*. Bloomington: Indiana University Press, 2005.

Curtin, Philip D. "The Atlantic Slave Trade 1600–1800." In *History of West Africa*, vol. 1, edited by J. F. A. Ajayi and Michael Crowder, 302–30. New York: Columbia University Press, 1976.

———. *Economic Change in Precolonial Africa: Senegambia in the Era of the Slave Trade*. Madison: University of Wisconsin Press, 1975.

Daaku, Kwame Yeboa. *Trade and Politics on the Gold Coast, 1600–1720: A Study of the African Reaction to European Trade*. Oxford: Clarendon Press, 1970.

Dakubu, M. E. Kropp. *Korle Meets the Sea: A Sociolinguistic History of Accra*. New York: Oxford University Press, 1997.

Dalrymple, William. *White Mughals: Love and Betrayal in Eighteenth-Century India*. London: Penguin, 2002.

Dantzig, Albert van. "English Bosman and Dutch Bosman: A Comparison of Texts: VIII." *History in Africa* 11 (1984): 307–29.

Davies, K. G. "The Living and the Dead: White Mortality in West Africa, 1684–1732." In *Race and Slavery in the Western Hemisphere: Quantitative Studies*, edited by Stanley L. Engerman and Eugene D. Genovese, 83–98. Princeton, N.J.: Princeton University Press, 1975.

Davis, David Brion. *Inhuman Bondage: The Rise and Fall of Slavery in the New World*. Oxford: Oxford University Press, 2006.

Debrunner, Hans. "Friedrich Pedersen Svane, 1710–1789." *Evangelisches Missions-Magazin* 101 (1957): 24–35.

———. *A History of Christianity in Ghana*. Accra: Waterville, 1967.

———. "Pioneers of Church and Education in Ghana: Danish Chaplains to Guinea, 1661–1850." In *Kirkehistoriske Samlinger* 7:4, edited by Niels Knud Andersen and Knud Banning, 373–425. Copenhagen: G. E. C. Gads Forlag, 1960–62.

———. *Presence and Prestige: Africans in Europe: A History of Africans in Europe Before 1918*. Basel: Basler Afrika Bibliographien, 1979.

Denzer, LaRay. "Yoruba Women: A Historigraphical Study." *International Journal of African Historical Studies* 27.1 (1994): 1–39.

Diouf, Sylviane A., ed. *Fighting the Slave Trade: West African Strategies*. Athens: Ohio University Press, 2003.

———. "The Last Resort: Redeeming Family and Friends." In *Fighting the Slave Trade: West African Strategies*, edited by Sylviane A. Diouf, 81–100. Athens: Ohio University Press, 2003.

Doortmont, Michel R. "The Dutch Atlantic Slave Trade as Family Business." In *The Transatlantic Slave Trade: Landmarks, Legacies, Expectations*, edited by James Kwesi Anquandah, 92–137. Accra: Sub-Saharan Publishers, 2007.

Dresser, Madge. *Slavery Obscured: The Social History of the Slave Trade in an English Provincial Port*. London: Continuum, 2001.

Dübeck, Inger. *Kvinder, familie og formue: Studier i dansk og europæisk retshistorie*. Copenhagen: Museum Tusculanums Forlag, 2003.

Dumett, Raymond E. "The Work of Slaves in the Akan and Adangme Regions of Ghana in the Nineteenth Century." In *African Systems of Slavery*, edited by Jay Spaulding and Stephanie Beswick, 67–104. Trenton, N.J.: Africa World Press, 2010.

Earle, T. F., and K. J. P. Lowe, eds. *Black Africans in Renaissance Europe*. Cambridge: Cambridge University Press, 2005.

Eltis, David, and Stanley L. Engerman. "Fluctuations in Sex and Age Ratios in the Transatlantic Slave Trade, 1663–1864." *Economic History Review* 46.2 (1993): 308–23.

Erickson, Amy Louise. "The Marital Economy in Comparative Perspective." In *The Marital Economy in Scandinavia and Britain 1400–1900*, edited by Maria Ågren and Amy Louise Erickson, 3–22. Aldershot, Hants.: Ashgate, 2005.

Eriksholm, A. J. "En Degn I Havrebjerg. Frideric Petri Svane Africanus." In *Fra Holdbæk*

Amt: Historiske Aarbøger udgivet af Historisk Samfund for Holbæk Amt, 32–49. Copenhagen: Lehmann and Stage, 1907.

Everaert, J., and J. Parmentier, eds. *International Conference on Shipping, Factories and Colonization*. Brussels: Royal Academy of Overseas Sciences, 1996.

Everts, Natalie. "'Brought Up Well According to European Standards': Helena van der Burgh and Wilhelmina van Naarssen: Two Christian Women from Elmina." In *Merchants, Missionaries and Migrants: 300 Years of Dutch-Ghanian Relations*, edited by I. Van Kessel, 101–10. Amsterdam: Sub-Saharan Publishers, 2002.

———. "Cherchez la Femme: Gender-Related Issues in Eighteenth-Century Elmina." *Itinerario* 20.1 (1996): 45–57.

———. "A Motley Company: Differing Identities Among Euro-Africans in Eighteenth-Century Elmina." *Brokers of Change: Atlantic Commerce and Cultures in Precolonial Western Africa*. Proceedings of the British Academy 178. London: British Academy, 2012: 53–69.

Fage, J. D. "African Societies and the Atlantic Slave Trade." *Past and Present* 125 (1989): 97–115.

———. "Slaves and Society in Western Africa, c. 1445–c.1700." *Journal of African History* 21.3 (1980): 289–310.

Falola, Toyin, and Paul E. Lovejoy. Introduction to *Pawnship in Africa: Debt Bondage in Historical Perspective*, 15–21. Boulder, Colo.: Westview Press, 1994.

Feldbæk, Ole. "Den lange fred, 1700–1800." In *Gyldendal og Politikens Danmarkshistorie* vol. 9. Copenhagen: Nordisk Forlag, 1990.

Feldbæk, Ole, and Ole Justesen. *Kolonierne i Asien og Afrika*. Copenhagen: Politikens Forlag, 1980.

Field, M. J. *Religion and Medicine of the Ga People*. London: Oxford University Press, 1937.

———. *Social Organization of the Ga People*. London: Crown Agents for the Colonies, 1940.

Feinberg, H. M. "Africans and Europeans in West Africa: Elminans and Dutchmen on the Gold Coast During the Eighteenth Century." *Transactions of the American Philosophical Society* 79.7 (1989): 1–186.

Fredrickson, George M. *Racism: A Short History*. Princeton, N.J.: Princeton University Press, 2002.

Foucault, Michel. *The History of Sexuality*. Vol. 1. New York: Random House, 1978.

Für, Gunlög. "The Struggle for Civilized Marriages in Early Modern Sweden and Colonial North America." In *Collisions of Cultures and Identities: Settlers and Indigenous Peoples*, edited by Patricia Grimshaw and Russell McGregor, 59–86. Melbourne: University of Melbourne, 2006.

Gamrath, Helge. *Residens og hovedstad: Københavns historie*, vol. 2, 1600–1728. Viborg: Gyldendal, 1980.

Geiger, Susan. "Women and Gender in African Studies." *African Studies Review* 42.3 (1999): 21–33.

Getz, Trevor R. "Mechanisms of Slave Acquisition and Exchange in Late Eighteenth Century Anomabu: Reconsidering a Cross-Section of the Atlantic Slave Trade." *African Economic History* 31 (2003): 75–89.

Ghosh, Durba. "Decoding the Nameless: Gender, Subjectivity, and Historical Methodologies in Reading the Archives of Colonial India." In *A New Imperial History*, edited by Kathleen Wilson, 297–316. Cambridge: Cambridge University Press, 2004.

———. *Sex and the Family in Colonial India.* Cambridge: Cambridge University Press, 2006.

Glassman, Jonathan. "Slower Than a Massacre: The Multiple Sources of Racial Thought in Colonial Africa." *American Historical Review* 109.3 (2004): 720–54.

———. *War of Words, War of Stones: Racial Thought and Violence in Colonial Zanzibar.* Bloomington: Indiana University Press, 2011.

Godbeer, Richard. "Eroticizing the Middle Ground: Anglo-Indian Sexual Relations Along the Eighteenth-Century Frontier." In *Race, Love, Sex: Crossing Boundaries in North American History*, edited by Matha Hodes, 91–111. New York: New York University Press, 1999.

Green, Tobias. "Building Creole Identity in the African Atlantic: Boundaries of Race and Religion in Seventeenth-Century Cabo Verde." *History in Africa* 36 (2009): 103–25.

Greenblatt, Stephen. *Marvelous Possessions: The Wonder of the New World.* Chicago: Chicago University Press, 1992.

Greene, Sandra. "Crossing Boundaries/Changing Identities: Female Slaves, Male Strangers, and Their Descendants in Nineteenth- and Twentieth-Century Anlo." In *Gendered Encounters: Challenging Cultural Boundaries and Social Hierarchies in Africa*, edited by Maria Grosz-Ngate and Omari H. Kolole, 23–42. New York: Routledge, 1997.

———. "Family Concerns: Gender and Ethnicity in Pre-Colonial West Africa." In *Complicating Categories: Gender, Class, Race and Ethnicity: International Review of Social History Supplements* 44.7, edited by Eileen Boris and Angélique Janssens, 15–32. Amsterdam: The Internationaal Instituut Voor Sociale Geschiedenis, Cambridge University Press, 1999.

———. *Gender, Ethnicity, and Social Change on the Upper Slave Coast: A History of the Anlo-Ewe.* Portsmouth: James Currey, 1996.

———. *Sacred Sites and the Colonial Encounter: A History of Meaning and Memory in Ghana.* Bloomington: Indiana University Press, 2002.

Green-Pedersen, Sv. E. "Danmarks ophævelse af negerslavehandelen: Omkring tilblivelsen af forordningen af 16. Marts 1792." In *Arkiv: Tidsskrift for Arkivforskning* 3 (1970–71): 19–37.

———. "Negro Slavery and Christianity (On Erik Pontoppidan's Preface to L. F. Roemer, Tilforladelige Efterretning om Kysten Guinea), 1760." *Transactions of the Historical Society of Ghana* 15.1 (1974): 85–103.

———. "The Scope and Structure of the Danish Negro Slave Trade." *Scandinavian Economic History Review* 19.1–2 (1971): 149–97.

Grier, Beverly. "Pawns, Porters, and Petty Traders: Women in the Transition to Cash Crop Agriculture in Colonial Ghana." *Signs* 17.2 (1992): 304–28.

Gøbel, Erik. "Den danske besejling af Vestindien og Guinea 1671–1838." In *Handels- og Søfartsmuseet på Kronborgs Årbog*, edited by Hans Jeppesen et al. Helsingør: Selskabet Handels- og Søfartsmuseets Venner, 1991.

———. *A Guide to the Sources of the Danish West Indies U.S. Virgin Islands, 1671–1917.* Odense: University of Southern Denmark Press, 2002.

———. *De styrede rigerne: Embedsmændene i den Dansk-Norske civile central-administration 1660–1814.* Odense: Odense Universitetsforlag, 2000.

Haenger, Peter. *Slaves and Slave Holders on the Gold Coast: Towards an Understanding of Social Bondage in West Africa.* Edited by J. J. Shaffer and Paul E. Lovejoy. Basel: P. Schlettwein, 2000.

Hair, P. E. H. "Barbot, Dapper, Davity: A Critique of Sources on Sierra Leone and Cape Mount." *History in Africa* 1 (1974): 25–54.

———. "On Editing Barbot." *History in Africa* 20 (1993): 53–59.

———. "Portuguese Documents on Africa and Some Problems of Translation." *History in Africa* 27 (2000): 91–97.

Hall, Bruce S. *A History of Race in Muslim West Africa, 1600–1960.* Cambridge: Cambridge University Press, 2011.

Hall, Kim F. *Things of Darkness: Economies of Race and Gender in Early Modern England.* Ithaca, N.Y.: Cornell University Press, 1995.

Hansen, Thorkild. *Coast of Slaves.* Translated by Kari Dako. Accra, 2002. [Danish original: Slavernes Kyst.]

Harms, Robert. *The Diligent: A Voyage Through the Worlds of the Slave Trade.* New York: Basic Books, 2002.

Havik, Philip J. "Gendering the Black Atlantic: Women's Agency in Coastal Trade Settlements in the Guinea Bissau Region. In *Women in Port: Gendering Communities, Economies, and Social Networks in Atlantic Port Cities, 1500–1800*, edited by Douglas Catterall and Jodi Campbell, 315–56. Leiden: Brill, 2012.

———. *Silences and Soundbytes: The Gendered Dynamics of Trade and Brokarage in the Pre-Colonial Guinea Bissau Region.* Leiden: LIT Verlag, 2004.

Hawthorne, Walter. *Planting Rice, Harvesting Slaves: Transformations Along the Guinea-Bissau Coast, 1400–1900.* Portsmouth, N.H.: Heinemann, 2003.

Henige, David. "John Kabes of Komenda: An Early African Entrepreneur and State Builder." *Journal of African History* 18.1 (1977): 1–19.

Herbstein, Manu. *Ama: A Story of the Atlantic Slave Trade.* Johannesburg: Picador Africa, 2000.

Hernæs, Per. "African Power Struggle and European Opportunity: Danish Expansion on the Early Eighteenth Century Gold Coast." *Transactions of the Historical Society of Ghana* 7 (2003): 1–92.

———. "Den balstyrige bergenser på Gullkysten." In *Nordmenn i Afrika—afrikanere i*

Norge, edited by Kirsten Alsaker Kjerland and Anne K. Bang, 17–25. Bergen: Vigmostad and Bjørke, 2002.

———. "European Fort Communities on the Gold Coast in the Era of the Slave trade." In *International Conference on Shipping, Factories and Colonization*, edited by J. Everaert and J. Parmentier, 167–80. Brussels: Royal Academy of Overseas Sciences, 1996.

———. "'Fort Slaves' at Christiansborg on the Gold Coast: Wage Labour in the Making?" In *Slavery Across Time and Space: Studies in Slavery in Medieval Europe and Africa*, edited by Per Hernæs and Tore Iversen, 197–229. Trondheim: Norwegian University of Science and Technology, Department of History, 2002.

———. Introduction to "Asafo History: An Introduction." *Transactions of the Historical Society of Ghana* 2 (1998): 1–5.

———. *Slaves, Danes, and African Coast Society: The Danish Slave Trade from West Africa and Afro-Danish Relations on the Eighteenth-Century Gold Coast*. Trondheim: Norwegian University of Science and Technology, Department of History, 1996.

———. "'A Sombre Affair': The History of a Slave Ship Mutiny and the Destiny of the Mutineers upon Their Return to Africa." *Transactions of the Historical Society of Ghana* 10 (2006–7): 215–23.

Heywood, Linda, and John K. Thornton. *Central Africans, Atlantic Creoles, and the Foundation of the Americas, 1585–1660*. Cambridge: Cambridge University Press, 2007.

Hodes, Martha. *White Women, Black Men: Illicit Sex in the Nineteenth-Century South*. New Haven, Conn.: Yale University Press, 1997.

Holsey, Bayo. *Routes of Remembrance: Refashioning the Slave Trade in Ghana*. Chicago: Chicago University Press, 2008.

Hopkins, Daniel P. "The Danish Ban on the Atlantic Slave Trade and Denmark's African Colonial Ambitions, 1787–1807." *Itinerario* 25.3–4 (2001): 154–84.

———. "Danish Natural History and African Colonialism at the Close of the Eighteenth Century: Peter Thonning's 'Scientific Journey' to the Guinea Coast, 1799–1803." *Archives of Natural History* 26.3 (1999): 369–418.

———. *Peter Thonning and Denmark's Guinea Commission: A Study in Nineteenth-Century African Colonial Geography*. Leiden: Brill, 2013.

———. "Peter Thonning and the Guinea Commission, and Denmark's Postabolition African Colonial Policy, 1803–50." *William and Mary Quarterly* 65.4 (2009): 781–808.

Horta, José da Silva. "Evidence for a Luso-African Identity in 'Portuguese' Accounts on 'Guinea of Cape Verde.'" *History in Africa* 27 (2000): 99–130.

House-Midamba, Bessie, and Felix K. Ekechi, eds. *African Market Women and Economic Power: The Role of Women in African Economic Development*. Westport: Greenwood Press, 1995.

Hulme, Peter, and Tim Youngs, eds. *The Cambridge Companion to Travel Writing*. Cambridge: Cambridge University Press, 2002.

Hunt, Lynn, and Victoria E. Bonnell, eds. *Beyond the Cultural Turn*. Berkeley: University of California Press, 1999.

————, eds. *The New Cultural History*. Berkeley: University of California Press, 1989.

Hyam, Ronald. *Empire and Sexuality: The British Experience*. Manchester: Manchester University Press, 1990.

Inikori, Joseph E. "Changing Commodity Composition of Imports into West Africa, 1650–1850: A Window into the Impact of the Transatlantic Slave Trade on African Societies." In *The Transatlantic Slave Trade: Landmarks, Legacies, Expectations*, edited by James Kwesi Anquandah, 57–80. Accra: Sub-Saharan Publishers, 2007.

————. "The Import of Firearms into West Africa 1750–1807: A Quantitative Analysis." *Journal of African History* 18.3 (1977): 349–51.

Inikori, Joseph E., and Stanley Engerman, eds. *The Atlantic Slave Trade: Effects on Economies, Societies, and Peoples in Africa, the Americas, and Europe*. Durham, N.C.: Duke University Press, 1992.

Ipsen, Pernille. "'The Christened Mulatresses': Euro-African Families in a Slave-Trading Town." *William and Mary Quarterly* 70.2 (2013): 371–98.

————. "Kolonisering." In *Fokus—Kernestof i Historie*, vol. 2: *Fra oplysningstid til imperialisme*, 9–33. Copenhagen: Gyldendal, 2007.

Ipsen, Pernille, and Gunlög Für. Introduction to "Scandinavian Colonialism." Special issue of *Itinerario* 2 (2009): 7–16.

Jensen, Anette. "Staten, kirken og stridbare ægtefolk: Et nyt syn på ægteskabet i første halvdel af 1800-tallet." *Den jyske Historiker* 98–99 (2002): 109–28.

Jeppesen, Henrik. "Danske plantageanlæg på Guldkysten 1788–1850." *Geografisk Tidsskrift* 65.1 (1966): 50–72.

Johansen, Hans Chr. "Danmark i tal." In *Gyldendal og Politikens Danmarks Historie*, vol. 16. Copenhagen: Nordisk Forlag, 1991.

Johnson, Susan. "'A Memory Sweet to Soldiers': The Significance of Gender in the History of the 'American West.'" *Western Historical Quarterly* 24.4 (1993): 495–517.

Johnson, Walter. "On Agency." *Journal of Social History* 37.1 (2003): 113–24.

Jones, Adam. "Decompiling Dapper: A Preliminary Search for Evidence." *History in Africa* 17 (1990): 171–209.

————. "Double Dutch? A Survey of Seventeenth-Century German Sources for West African History." *History in Africa* 9 (1982): 141–53.

————. "Drink Deep, or Taste Not: Thoughts on the Use of Early European Records in the Study of African Material Culture." *History in Africa* 21 (1994): 348–70.

————. "Female Slave-Owners on the Gold Coast: Just a Matter of Money?" In *Slave Cultures and the Cultures of Slavery*, edited by Stephan Palmie, 100–111. Knoxville: University of Tennessee Press, 1995.

————. "Prostitution, Polyandrie oder Vergewaltigung? Zur Mehtdugtigkeit europäischer Quellen über die Küste Westafrikas zwischen 1660 und 1860." In *Außereuropäische Frauengeschicte: Probleme der Forschung*, edited by Adam Jones, 123–58. Pfaffenweiler: Centaurus, 1990.

————. "Schwarze Frauen, weibe Beobachter: Die Frauen der Goldküste in den Augen der europäischen Männer, 1600–1900." *Zeitschrift für Historische Forschung: Beiheft* 7 (1989): 153–68.

Jones, Hilary. "From Marriage à la Mode to Weddings at Town Hall: Marriage, Colonialism, and Mixed-Race Society in Nineteenth-Century Senegal." *International Journal of African Historical Studies* 38.1 (2005): 27–37.

———. *The Metis of Senegal: Urban Life and Politics in French West Africa*. Bloomington: Indiana University Press, 2012.

Justesen, Ole. "Danish Settlements on the Gold Coast in the Nineteenth Century." *Scandinavian Journal of History* 4.1 (1979): 4–33.

———. "Henrich Richter 1785–1849: Trader and Politician in the Danish Settlements on the Gold Coast." *Transactions of the Historical Society of Ghana* 7 (2003): 93–192.

———. "Political Relations Between Osu and Christiansborg 1803–1826." Unpublished paper at "The Shadows of Empire: Study of European Colonial Forts and Castles." International Workshop at Trondheim University, 2011.

———. "Slaveri og emancipation på Guldkysten 1830–1850." In *Fra Slaveri til Frihed: Det dansk vestindiske slavesamfund 1672–1848*, edited by Per Nielsen, 136–53. Copenhagen: Nationalmuseet, 2001.

———. "Vestafrika og det transatlantiske handelssystem." In *Kolonierne i Asien og Afrika*, edited by Ole Feldbæk and Ole Justesen, 289–461. Copenhagen: Politikens Forlag, 1980.

Kea, Ray A. "'But I Know What I Shall Do': Agency, Belief and Social Imaginary in Eighteenth-Century Gold Coast Towns." In *Africa's Urban Past*, edited by David M. Anderson and Richard Rathbone, 163–88. Oxford: James Currey, 2000.

———. "Firearms and Warfare on the Gold and Slave Coasts from the Sixteenth to the Nineteenth Centuries." *Journal of African History* 12 (1971): 185–213.

———. *Settlements, Trade, and Politics in the Seventeenth-century Gold Coast*. Baltimore: Johns Hopkins University Press, 1982.

Kilson, Marion. *African Urban Kinsmen: The Ga of Central Accra*. London: C. Hurst, 1974.

Klein, Martin A. "Women in Slavery in the Western Sudan." In *Women and Slavery in Africa*, edited by Claire C. Robertson and Martin A. Klein, 67–92. Madison: University of Wisconsin Press, 1983.

Koefoed, Nina Javette. *Besovede kvindfolk og ukærlige barnefædre: Køn, ret og sædelighed i 1700-tallets Danmark*. Copenhagen: Museum Tusculanum, 2008.

———. "Synd og forsørgelse: Seksualitet udenfor ægteskab i Danmark 1700–1850." *Den jyske Historiker* 98–99 (2002): 45–46.

Larsen, Kay. *Guvernører, residenter, kommandanter og chefer samt enkelte andre fremtrædende personer i de tidligere danske tropekolonier*. Copenhagen: Arthur Jensens forlag, 1940.

Law, Robin. "'Here Is No Resisting the Country': The Realities of Power in Afro-European Relations on the West African 'Slave Coast.'" *Itinerario* 18.2 (1994): 50–64.

———. "On Pawning and Enslavement for Debt in the Pre-Colonial Slave Coast." In *Pawnship in Africa: Debt Bondage in Historical Perspective*, edited by Toyin Falola and Paul E. Lovejoy, 55–69. Westview Press: Boulder, Colo., 1994.

———. *Ouidah: The Social History of a West African Slaving "Port" 1727–1892*. Athens: Ohio University Press, 2004.

———. "Slave-Raiders and Middlemen, Monopolists and Free-Traders: The Supply of Slaves for the Atlantic Trade in Dahomey c. 1715–1850." *Journal of African History* 30.1 (1989): 45–68.

———. "West Africa's Discovery of the Atlantic." *International Journal of African Historical Studies* 44.1 (2011): 1–27.

Law, Robin, and Kristin Mann. "West Africa in the Atlantic Community: The Case of the Slave Coast." *William and Mary Quarterly* 56.2 (1999): 307–35.

Lawrence, A. W. *Trade Castles and Forts of West Africa*. Stanford, Calif.: Stanford University Press, 1964.

Lever, J. T. "Mulatto Influence on the Gold Coast in the Early Nineteenth Century: Jan Nieser of Elmina." *African Historical Studies* 3.2 (1970): 253–61.

Lévi-Strauss, Claude. *The Elementary Structures of Kinship*. 1949. Translated and edited by James Harle Bell, John Richard von Sturmer, and Rodney Needham. London: Eyre and Spottiswoode, 1969.

Livesay, Daniel Alan. "Children of Uncertain Fortune: Mixed-Race Migration from the West Indies to Britain, 1750–1820." Ph.D. diss., University of Michigan, 2010.

———. "Extended Families: Mixed-Race Children and Scottish Experience, 1770–1820." *Journal of Scottish Literature* (2008): 1–17.

Loftin, Joseph Evans. "The Abolition of the Danish Atlantic Slave Trade." Ph.D. diss., Louisiana State University, 1977.

Lovejoy, Paul E. "An Atlantic Odyssey from Old Calabar." Review of *The Two Princes of Calabar: An Eighteenth-Century Atlantic Odyssey*, by Randy Sparks. *Journal of African History* 46.2 (2005): 347–48.

———. "The Impact of the Atlantic Slave Trade on Africa: A Review of the Literature." *Journal of African History* 30.3 (1989): 365–94.

———. *Transformations in Slavery: A History of Slavery in Africa*. Cambridge: Cambridge University Press, 1983.

Lovejoy, Paul E., and David Richardson. "Anglo-Efik Relations and Protection Against Illegal Enslavement at Old Calabar, 1740–1807." In *Fighting the Slave Trade: West African Strategies*, edited by Sylviane A. Diouf, 101–20. Athens: Ohio University Press, 2003.

———. "British Abolition and Its Impact on Slave Prices Along the Atlantic Coast of Africa, 1783–1850." *Journal of Economic History* 55.1 (1995): 98–119.

———. "The Business of Slaving: Pawnship in Western Africa, c. 1600–1810." *Journal of African History* 42.1 (2001): 67–89.

———. "Trust, Pawnship, and Atlantic History: The Institutional Foundations of the Old Calabar Slave Trade." *American Historical Review* 104.2 (1999): 333–55.

Mancall, Peter C., ed. *Travel Narratives from the Age of Discovery: An Anthology*. Oxford: Oxford University Press, 2006.

Manning, Patrick. "Contours of Slavery and Social Change in Africa." *American Historical Review* 88.4 (1983): 835–57.

———. "Frontiers of Family Life: Early Modern Atlantic and Indian Ocean Worlds." *Modern Asian Studies* 43.1 (2009): 315–33.

Mark, Peter. "The Evolution of 'Portuguese' Identity: Luso-Africans on the Upper Guinea Coast from the Sixteenth to the Early Nineteenth Century." *Journal of African History* 40.2 (1999): 173–91.

———. *"Portuguese" Style and Luso-African Identity: Precolonial Senegambia, Sixteenth–Nineteenth Centuries*. Bloomington: Indiana University Press, 2002.

McCarthy, Mary. *Social Change and the Growth of British Power in the Gold Coast*. New York: Lanham, 1983.

McClintock, Anne. *Imperial Leather: Race, Gender and Sexuality in the Colonial Contest*. Routledge: New York, 1995.

Metcalf, George. "A Microcosm of Why Africans Sold Slaves: Akan Consumption Patterns in the 1770s." *Journal of African History* 28.3 (1987): 377–94.

Merrell, James H. " 'The Customes of Our Countrey': Indians and Colonists in Early America." In *Strangers Within the Realm: Cultural Margins of the First British Empire*, edited by Bernard Bailyn and Philip D. Morgan, 117–56. Chapel Hill: University of North Carolina Press, 1991.

———. *Into the American Woods: Negotiations on the Pennsylvania Frontier*. New York: Norton, 1999.

Miller, Joseph C. "Slave Prices in the Portuguese Southern Atlantic, 1600–1830." In *Africans in Bondage: Studies in Slavery and the Slave Trade: Essays in Honor of Philip D. Curtin of the Occasion of the Twenty-Fifth Anniversary of African Studies at the University of Wisconsin*, edited by Paul E. Lovejoy, 43–78. Madison: University of Wisconsin Press, 1986.

———. *Way of Death: Merchant Capitalism and the Angolan Slave Trade, 1730–1830*. Madison: University of Wisconsin Press, 1988.

Morgan, Edmund S. *American Slavery, American Freedom: The Ordeal of Colonial Virginia*. New York: W. W. Norton, 1975.

Morgan, Jennifer L. *Laboring Women: Reproduction and Gender in New World Slavery*. Philadelphia: University of Pennsylvania Press, 2004.

———. " 'Some Could Suckle over Their Shoulder': Male Travelers, Female Bodies, and the Gendering of Racial Ideology, 1500–1770." *William and Mary Quarterly* 54.1 (1997): 167–92.

Nakken, Alfhild Nakken. *Sentraladministrasjonen i København og sentralorganer i Norge 1660–1814*. Copenhagen: Rigsarkivet, 2000.

Nedergaard, Paul. "Den Sorte Degn i Havrebjerg: Et Moment af Dansk Missions Historie paa Guineakysten." *Kirketidende* (1917): 372–79.

Neylan, Susan. *The Heavens Are Changing: Nineteenth-Century Protestant Missions and Tsimshian Christianity*. Montreal: McGill-Queen's University Press, 2003.

Nielsen, Pia Dudman. *Udviklingen af magtstrukturen i Vestindisk-guineisk Kompani i perioden for dets handel og transport med slaver.* M.A. thesis, University of Copenhagen, 2002.

Nukunya, G. K. *Tradition and Change in Ghana: An Introduction to Sociology.* Accra: Ghana University Press, 2003.

Nwokeji, Ugo. *The Slave Trade and Culture in the Bight of Biafra: An African Society in the Atlantic World.* New York: Cambridge University Press, 2010.

Nørregaard, Georg. *Danish Settlements in West Africa, 1658–1850.* Boston: Boston University Press, 1966.

Odotei, Irene. "External Influences on Ga Society and Culture." *Institute of African Studies Research Review* 7.1–2 (1991): 61–71.

——. "Gender and Traditional Authority in the Artisanal Marine Fishing Industry in Ghana." *Institute of African Studies Research Review* 15.1 (1999): 15–38.

——. "Pre-Colonial Economic Activities of Ga." *Institute of African Studies Research Review* 11.1–2 (1995): 60–74.

——. "What Is in a Name? The Social and Historical Significance of Ga Names." *Institute of African Studies Research Review* 5.2 (1989): 34–51.

Opoku-Agyemang, Naana, Paul E. Lovejoy, and David V. Trotman, eds. *Africa and Trans-Atlantic Memories: Literary and Aesthetic Manifestations of Diaspora and History.* Trenton, N. J.: Africa World Press, 2008.

Osei-Tutu, Brempong. "The African American Factor in the Commodification of Ghana's Slave Castles." *Transactions of the Historical Society of Ghana* 6 (2002): 115–33.

Osei-Tutu, John Kwadwo. *The Asafoi (Socio-Military Groups) in the History and Politics of Accra (Ghana) from the 17th to the Mid 20th Century.* Trondheim: Norwegian University of Science and Technology, Department of History, 2000.

Owusu-Ansah, David. *Historical Dictionary of Ghana.* Lanham: Scarecrow Press, 2005.

Oyewùmí, Oyèrónké. "De-Confounding Gender: Feminist Theorizing and Western Culture, a Comment on Hawkesworth's 'Confounding Gender.'" *Signs* 23.4 (1998): 1049–62.

——, ed. *African Gender Studies: A Reader.* New York: Palgrave Macmillan, 2005.

Pagden, Anthony. *European Encounters with the New World.* Cambridge: Cambridge University Press, 1991.

Parker, John. "Cultural Politics of Death and Burial in Early Colonial Accra." In *Africa's Urban Past*, edited by David M. Anderson and Richard Rathbone, 205–21. Oxford: James Currey, 2000.

——. *Making the Town: Ga State and Society in Early Colonial Accra.* Portsmouth, N.H.: Heinemann, 2000.

——. "Mankraloi, Merchants and Mulattos—Carl Reindorf and the Politics of 'Race' in Early Colonial Accra." In *The Recovery of the West African Past*, edited by P. Jenkins, 31–47. Basel: Basler Afrika Bibliographien, 2000.

Pearsall, Sarah M. S. "Gender." In *The British Atlantic World, 1500–1800*, edited by David Armitage and Michael J. Braddick, 133–51. London: Palgrave Macmillan, 2009.

Perbi, Akusua Adoma. *A History of Indigenous Slavery in Ghana: From the 15th to the 19th Century*. Accra: Sub-Saharan Publishers, 2004.

Premo, Bianca, Julie Hardwick, and Karin Wulf. "Cluster: Rethinking Gender, Family, and Sexuality in the Early Modern Atlantic World." *History Compass* 8.3 (2010): 223–57.

Priestley, Margaret. *West African Trade and Coast Society: A Family Study*. London: Oxford University Press, 1969.

Quaye [Odotei], Irene. "The Ga and Their Neighbours 1600–1742." Ph.D. diss., University of Ghana, 1972.

Rathbone, Richard. "The Gold Coast, the Closing of the Atlantic Slave Trade, and Africans of the Diaspora." In *Slave Cultures and the Cultures of Slavery*, edited by Stephan Palmie, 55–66. Knoxville: University of Tennessee Press, 1995.

Rattray, R. S. *Ashanti Law and Constitution*. Oxford: Clarendon Press, 1929.

Ray, Carina E. "Decrying White Peril: Interracial Sex and the Rise of Anticolonial Nationalism in the Gold Coast." *American Historical Review* 199.1 (2014): 78–110.

———. "Policing Sexual Boundaries: The Politics of Race in Colonial Ghana." Ph.D. diss., Cornell University, 2007.

Rediker, Marcus. *Between the Devil and the Deep Blue Sea*. Cambridge: Cambridge University Press, 1987.

———. *The Slave Ship: A Human History*. New York: Viking, 2007.

Reese, Ty. "'Eating' Luxury: Fante Middlemen, British Goods, and Changing Dependencies on the Gold Coast, 1750–1821." *William and Mary Quarterly* 66.4 (2009): 853–72.

———. "'Sheep in the Jaws of So Many Ravenous Wolves': The Slave Trade and Anglican Missionary Activity at Cape Coast Castle, 1752–1816." *Journal of Religion in Africa* 34.3 (2004): 348–72.

———. "Wives, Brokers, and Laborers: Women at Cape Coast, 1750–1807." In *Women in Port: Gendering Communities, Economies, and Social Networks in Atlantic Port Cities, 1500–1800*, edited by Douglas Catterall and Jodi Campbell, 291–314. Leiden: Brill, 2012.

Reindorf, Carl Christian. *The History of the Gold Coast and Asante*. Basel: Basel Mission Book Depot, 1951. [Original 1889.]

Richards, W. A. "The Import of Firearms into West Africa in the Eighteenth Century." *Journal of African History* 21.1 (1980): 43–59.

Richardson, David. "The Slave Trade, Sugar, and British Economic Growth, 1748–1776." *Journal of Interdisciplinary History* 17.4 (1987): 739–69.

Robertson, Claire C. "Developing Economic Awareness: Changing Perspectives in Studies of African Women, 1976–1985." *Feminist Studies* 13.1 (1987): 97–135.

———. "Ga Women and Socioeconomic Change in Accra, Ghana." In *Women in Africa: Studies in Social and Economic Change*, edited by Nancy J. Hafkin and Edna G. Bay, 111–33. Stanford, Calif.: Stanford University Press, 1976.

———. "Post-Emancipation Slavery in Accra: A Female Affair?" In *Women and Slavery in Africa*, 220–45. Madison: University of Wisconsin Press, 1983.

———. *Sharing the Same Bowl: A Socioeconomic History of Women and Class in Accra, Ghana*. Bloomington: Indiana University Press, 1984.

Robertson, Claire C., and Martin Klein. Introduction to *Women and Slavery in Africa*, edited by Claire C. Robertson and Martin Klein, 3–25. Madison: University of Wisconsin Press, 1983.

Rodney, Walter. *A History of the Upper Guinea Coast, 1545–1800*. Oxford: Clarendon Press, 1970.

Rostgaard, Marianne, and Lotte Schou. *Kulturmøder i dansk kolonihistorie*. Copenhagen: Gyldendal, 2010.

Rothman, Joshua D. *Notorious in the Neighborhood: Sex and Families Across the Color Line in Virginia, 1787–1861*. Chapel Hill: University of North Carolina Press, 2003.

Schlegel, Alice. "Marriage Transactions: Labor, Property, Status." *American Anthropologist* 90.2 (1988): 291–309.

Schramm, Katharina. "The Transatlantic Slave Trade: Contemporary Topographies of Memory in Ghana and the USA." *Transactions of the Historical Society of Ghana* 9 (2005): 125–40.

Sensbach, Jon F. *Rebecca's Revival: Creating Black Christianity in the Atlantic World*. Cambridge, Mass.: Harvard University Press, 2005.

Sewell, William H. "The Concept(s) of Culture." In *Beyond the Cultural Turn*, edited by Lynn Hunt and Victoria E. Bonnell, 35–61. Berkeley: University of California Press, 1999.

Shaw, Rosalind. *Memories of the Slave Trade: Ritual and the Historical Imagination of Sierra Leone*. Chicago: University of Chicago Press, 2002.

Sheperd, Verene A., and Glen L. Richards. Introduction to *Questioning Creole: Creolisation Discourses in Caribbean Culture*, ix–xxvi. Oxford: James Currey, 2002.

Shumway, Rebecca. *The Fante and the Transatlantic Slave Trade*. New York: University of Rochester Press, 2011.

Sill, Ulrike. *Encounters in Quest of Christian Womanhood*. Leiden: Brill, 2010.

Simonsen, Gunvor. "Skin Colour as a Tool of Regulation and Power in the Danish West Indies in the Eighteenth Century." *Journal of Caribbean History* 37.2 (2003): 256–76.

———. "Slave Stories: Gender, Representation, and the Court in the Danish West Indies, 1780–1820." Ph.D. diss., European University Institute, Florence, 2007.

Sleeper-Smith, Susan. *Indian Women and French Men: Rethinking the Cultural Encounter in the Western Great Lakes*. Amherst: University of Massachusetts Press, 2001.

———. "'An Unpleasant Transaction on This Frontier': Challenging Female Autonomy and Authority at Michilimackinac." *Journal of the Early Republic* 25.3 (2005): 417–43.

Smallwood, Stephanie. *Saltwater Slavery: A Middle Passage from Africa to American Diaspora*. Cambridge, Mass.: Harvard University Press, 2007.

Smits, David D. "Abominable Mixture: Towards the Repudiation of Anglo-Indian

Intermarriage in Seventeenth-Century Virginia." *Virginia Magazine of History and Biography* 95.2 (1987): 157–92.

Solow, Barbara L., ed. *Slavery and the Rise of the Atlantic System*. Cambridge: Cambridge University Press, 1991.

Sparks, Randy. "Gold Coast Merchant Families, Pawning, and the Eighteenth-Century British Slave Trade." *William and Mary Quarterly* 70.2 (2013): 317–40.

——. *The Two Princes of Calabar: An Eighteenth-Century Atlantic Odyssey*. Cambridge, Mass.: Harvard University Press, 2004.

——. *Where the Negroes Are Masters: An African Port in the Era of the Slave Trade*. Cambridge, Mass.: Harvard University Press, 2014.

Spear, Jennifer M. "Colonial Intimacies: Legislating Sex in French Louisiana." *William and Mary Quarterly* 60.1 (2003): 75–98.

——. *Race, Sex, and Social Order in Early New Orleans*. Baltimore: Johns Hopkins University Press, 2009.

——. "They Need Wives: Méstissage and the Regulation of Sexuality in French Louisiana, 1699–1730." In *Sex, Love, Race: Crossing Boundaries in North American History*, edited by Martha Hodes, 35–60. New York: New York University Press, 1999.

Spivak, Gayatri Chakravorty. "Can the Subaltern Speak?" In *Marxism and the Interpretation of Culture*, edited by Cary Nelson and Lawrence Grossberg, 271–316. London: Macmillan, 1988.

Stoler, Ann Laura. *Along the Archival Grain: Epistemic Anxieties and Colonial Common Sense*. Princeton, N.J.: Princeton University Press, 2009.

——. *Carnal Knowledge and Imperial Power: Race and the Intimate in Colonial Rule*. Berkeley: University of California Press, 2002.

Strobel, Margaret. "African Women." *Signs* 8.1 (1982): 109–31.

Svalesen, Leif. *The Slave Ship Fredensborg*. Translated by Pat Shaw and Selena Winsnes. Bloomington: Indiana University Press, 2000.

Sveistrup, P. P. and Rich. Willerslev. *Den danske sukkerhandels og sukkerproduktions historie*. Copenhagen: Gyldendalske Boghandel, 1945.

Sweet, James H. *Domingos Alvares, African Healing, and the Intellectual History of the Atlantic World*. Chapel Hill: University of North Carolina Press, 2011.

——. "The Iberian Roots of American Racist Thought." *William and Mary Quarterly* 54.1 (1997): 143–66.

——. *Recreating Africa: Culture, Kinship, and Religion in the African-Portuguese World, 1441–1770*. Chapel Hill: University of North Carolina Press, 2003.

Tashjian, Victoria B., and Jean Allman. "Marrying and Marriage on a Shifting Terrain: Reconfigurations of Power and Authority in Early Colonial Asante." In *Women in African Colonial Histories*, edited by Jean Allman et al., 237–59. Bloomington: Indiana University Press, 2002.

Thomsen, Asbjørn Romvig. "Hor: Om ægteskabsbruddets udbredelse og baggrund i 1700- og 1800-tallets landbosamfund." *Den jyske Historiker* 98–99 (2002): 87–108.

Thornton, John. *Africa and Africans in the Making of the Atlantic World, 1400–1800*. Cambridge: Cambridge University Press, 1998.

———. "Cannibals, Witches, and Slave Traders in the Atlantic World." *William and Mary Quarterly* 60.2 (2003): 273–94.

———. *Warfare in Atlantic Africa 1500–1800*. London: UCL Press, 1999.

Todorov, Tzvetan. "Race and Racism." In *Theories of Race and Racism*, edited by Les Back and John Solomos. New York: Routledge, 2000.

Unsworth, Barry. *Sacred Hunger*. New York: Norton, 1992.

Van Kirk, Sylvia. "From 'Marrying-In' to 'Marrying-Out': Changing Patterns of Aboriginal/Non-Aboriginal Marriage in Colonial Canada." *Frontiers: A Journal of Women's Studies* 23.3 (2002): 1–11.

———. *Many Tender Ties: Women in Fur-Trade Society, 1670–1870*. Norman: University of Oklahoma Press, 1980.

Vuorela, Ulla. "Colonial Complicity: The "Postcolonial" in a Nordic Context." In *Complying with Colonialism: Gender, Race and Ethnicity in the Nordic Region*, edited by Suvi Keskinen, Salla Tuori, Sari Irni, and Diana Mulinari, 19–34. Farnham, Surrey: Ashgate, 2009.

Ward, Colleen, Stephen Bochner, and Adrian Furnham. *The Psychology of Culture Shock*. Philadelphia: Routledge, 2001.

Wheeler, Roxann. *The Complexion of Race: Categories of Difference in Eighteenth-Century British Culture*. Philadelphia: University of Pennsylvania Press, 2000.

White, Richard. *The Middle Ground: Indians, Empires, and Republics in the Great Lakes Region, 1650–1815*. Cambridge: Cambridge University Press, 1991.

White, Sophie. *Wild Frenchmen and Frenchified Indians: Material Culture and Race in Colonial Louisiana*. Philadelphia: University of Pennsylvania Press, 2012.

Whitehead, Neil L. Introduction to *The Discoverie of the Large, Rich and Bewtiful Empyre of Guiana by Sir Walter Ralegh*, 3–116. Norman: University of Oklahoma Press, 1997.

Wilks, Ivor. *Akwamu 1640–1750: A Study of the Rise and Fall of a West African Empire*. Trondheim: Norwegian University of Science and Technology, Department of History, 2001.

———. "The Danes in Guinea." Review of *Danish Settlements in West Africa, 1658–1850*, by Georg Nørregaard. *Journal of African History* 9.1 (1968): 162–64.

Williams, Eric. *Capitalism and Slavery*. Chapel Hill: University of North Carolina Press, 1994. [Original 1944.]

Yarak, Larry. *Asante and the Dutch: A Case Study in the History of Asante Administration 1744–1873*. Oxford: Oxford University Press, 1990.

———. "West African Coastal Slavery in the Nineteenth Century: The Case of the Afro-European Slaveowners of Elmina." *Ethnohistory* 36.1 (1989): 44–60.

INDEX

ACKNOWLEDGMENTS

When I presented my first paper on this project at the African Studies Association in Washington, D.C., in 2005 a fellow panelist told me that he had once been interested in something very different than the slave trade (something having to do with photography, I believe), but before he knew it, ten years had gone by. Naive as I was, I thought my own book couldn't possibly take that long. Now, a decade later, I am certain that this book could not have been written without the sustained and enormous support my project and I have received from friends, mentors, colleagues, and family.

At Copenhagen University I had all the help I could have hoped for. I am grateful to Jan Pedersen for convincing me that a career as a professional historian was really what I needed, and then mentoring and reading for years. Ole Justesen shared from his lifelong research on Danes in precolonial Ghana. It has been such a privilege following in his footsteps and finding his notes in the archives, and in Ghana, where I also drew on his friendships, particularly with Irene Odotei and his contacts at the Institute for African Studies at Legon. In Copenhagen I also learned from and shared with Christina Folke Ax, Helle Bjerg, Natalia Brichet, Juliane Engelhardt, Gunlög Für, Anne Katrine Gjerløff, Erik Gøbel, Brian Hamilton, Michael Harbsmeier, Anne Folke Henningsen, Per Hernæs, Birgitte Holten, Sanne Ipsen, Niklas Thode Jensen, Anne Mette Jørgensen, Mette Lindberg, Anne Løkke, Birgitte Munch, Henrikke Terp Møllevang, Elsemarie Gert Nielsen, Marie Louise Nosch, Birgitte Lind Petersen, Bente Rosenbeck, Bjarke Rosenbeck, Louise Sebro, Dorthe Gert Simonsen, Pernille Sonne, Niels Steensgaard, Marianne Tjur, Tue Tjur, Karen Vallgårda, Vibeke Vasbo, Iben Wyff, and many others. Mange tak. I thank them warmly for their continued support across the ocean! Also a special thanks to the staff at Rigsarkivet in Copenhagen. One of my favorite parts of working on this history was spending time at that wonderful archive with the most helpful archivists one could wish for.

In Wisconsin many people went far out of their way to welcome me and help me make a new home—both intellectually and in other ways. Perhaps it was a sign of just how friendly everyone would be in the United States when Jennifer Morgan flew from New York to Copenhagen just to read my work! Or when Birgit Brander Rasmussen was right here in the neighborhood when I needed it the most. For continued support and friendship—from those early years until today—also many thanks to Julie Allen, Ned Blackhawk, Jeanne Boydston, Chuck Cohen, Emily Callaci, Suzanne Desan, Shanee Ellison, Nan Enstad, Christina Ewig, Barbara Forrest, Christina Greene, Will Jones, Neil Kodesh, Florencia Mallon, David McDonald, Perri Morgan, Seth Pollak, Jennifer Ratner-Rosenhagen, Ulli Rosenhagen, Jenny Saffran, Tom Spear, Steve Stern, Jim Sweet, Margaret Sweet, Tim Tyson, Peggy Vergeront, Mike Weiden, Ethelene Whitmire, and Sue Zaeske. In addition to their support, Lou Roberts, Jane Collins, Finn Enke, and Maria Lepowsky also provided excellent mentoring and advice. In the Department of Gender and Women's Studies, my wonderful colleagues have helped me create an intellectual space of my own. Particular thanks to my cohort Eunjung Kim, Keisha Lindsay, and Ellen Samuels, but also to Araceli Alonso, Nina Valeo Cooke, Julie D'Acci, Judy Houck, Su Ann Rose, Aili Tripp, and Diane Walton.

Randy Sparks has been an enormous help—believing in my project from the very beginning and generously supporting it all the way. Also thanks to the Center for Historical Research at the University of Texas at Austin and the Omohundro Institute for organizing the conference "Centering Families in Atlantic Worlds, 1500–1800." The conference and the work on the subsequent special issue of *William and Mary Quarterly* were really helpful. Thanks to Sarah Pearsall for encouragement and interesting conversations, and to Chris Grasso and Meg Musselwhite at *WMQ* for helpful suggestions. A semester at the Institute for Research in the Humanities here at the University of Wisconsin was exactly what it took to finish the book—time off from teaching, along with the focus and resolve that followed from an inspiring and intellectually stimulating weekly seminar. A special thanks to Henry Drewal, Susan Friedman, and Craig Werner at the institute.

At the University of Pennsylvania Press, Robert Lockhart and Peter Mancall have been the best editors I can imagine. Their excitement and encouraging words about the project made it come alive for me again after its few years on the back burner, while I cared for children and focused on teaching. I have been fortunate in enjoying every minute of this editing process. Also many thanks to Emily Clark and to the anonymous reader, as well as to Noreen O'Connor-Abel and the rest of the staff at the press, for helping me go the last few steps of the long way with this text.

A few other people have been particularly involved in this project: Karin Thomsen worked with me in the archives, first transcribing, and then later finding invaluable little phrases, thought to be lost, to send across the Atlantic. Gunvor Simonsen and Natalie Everts have been amazing readers and intellectual partners through all the years. What a gift to have such kind and generous friends! Also a special thanks to Cynthia Milton in Montreal, Selena Winsnes in Bergen, and Dan Hopkins in Texas.

Finally, I cannot say that this book has taken detrimental amounts of attention away from my children. There were a few weeks when I did forget the names of day-care teachers or had trouble focusing on conversations with Elliot, who has been alive almost exactly as long as this project, but nearly all of the time Elliot and Sophie could not help but remain my highest priority. Unlike the world of the Atlantic slave trade, my kids, friends, and family are alive and wonderful to be around, and I am so grateful for them—including for their patience and tolerance when I have spent a little too much time in that other world. My partner, Steve Kantrowitz, has felt the book a bit more. Not so much because we didn't get to spend time together, but because many of those hours together were spent on the book. *Tak* is but a small word. It would have been enough that he is such a wonderful and supportive human being, but in addition he is the most amazingly devoted assistant a historian could dream of. Thank you.